© David Kumin

HEATHER HARPHAM's fiction, essays, and reviews have appeared in *Slate*, *The Guardian*, *Parents*, *American Theater*, the *Water~Stone Review*, and *Red* magazine in the United Kingdom. Her writing for the stage includes six solo plays. Harpham's work has been recognized with the Brenda Ueland Prose Prize, a Marin Arts Council Independent Artist Grant, support from the Barbara Deming Memorial Fund for Women, and a New York Innovative Theater Award nomination. She has taught as a guest artist at colleges and universities throughout the United States, as well as Estonia and Nepal. Originally from Northern California, she now lives in New York, near the Hudson River, with her family and other animals.

Additional Praise for *Happiness*

"*Happiness* is Heather Harpham's utterly gorgeous (heartbreaking, staggering, genius) story of life with a seriously sick child . . . told in riveting, plot-twisting fashion . . . with care and courage and humor, and it will deepen your understanding of not just life with a sick child, but life."
—*Chicago Tribune*

"Harpham . . . has a gift for comedy that glints through this . . . heartfelt exploration of mortality and life . . . [in which she] explores the complex pulls and pushes of human relationships, and the deep debt we owe to family, friends, and modern medicine. At heart, it is a sobering meditation on the lasting impermanence of its titular emotion, happiness."
—*NPR Book Reviews*

"There are so many kinds of love stories, and Heather Harpham's affecting new memoir, *Happiness: The Crooked Little Road to Semi-Ever After*, tells two: her maternal love for her daughter born with a chronic, debilitating blood disease; and her romantic, scattershot, passionate love for the man who fathered the girl—but didn't want to be a father. An at times achingly painful, ultimately feel-good book for those who cringe at mawkish sentimentality." —*Elle*

"Harpham's writing is tender and frank. . . . A compelling story about life and death, illness and health, and, above all, family." —*Minneapolis Star Tribune*

"In this moving memoir . . . [Harpham] describes with warmth, fearless honesty, and humor the harrowing saga of what happened after she gave birth. . . . Harpham has written a heartfelt exploration of familial bonds and the sometimes incredibly bumpy journey one must take to get to contentment." —*Publishers Weekly*

"[*Happiness* is] wrought with deft storytelling ability, tight, poetic language, entertaining anecdotes, and startling insight. . . . Harpham's keen observations about society, and her tendency toward biting self-deprecation—as well as her quick-witted linguistic style—elevate musings on consumerism, beauty, and celebrity to universal truths." —*HuffPost*

"Although a personal story, Harpham's memoir provides a larger, universal picture of unconditional love toward a child and the push-pull of an adult relationship and all its inherent highs and lows. A frank and often affecting memoir from a mother determined to do whatever it takes for her child." —*Kirkus Reviews*

"*Happiness* is an incredibly moving account of survival and love that will inspire readers to hold on tight to what's truly important." —*Booklist*

"Harpham's ability to capture an audience's emotions takes center stage as a memoirist. Her deeply personal yet witty narrative style makes the reader feel instantly connected, as if Harpham is a close friend. . . . Within the first few pages of *Happiness*, Harpham immediately grabs for the heart, juxtaposing the roller-coaster reality of caring for a critically ill newborn alongside her exhilarating, romantic courtship." —*Shelf Awareness*

"Harpham's memoir about the birth of a child with a life-threatening condition contains flashes of brilliance.... [She] has a keen eye and a quirky turn of phrase.... Ultimately, the happiness this couple realize is anything but trite. Harrowed by loss, their state of 'dazed grace' is all the more precious for having been so precarious."

—*Sunday Herald* (Scotland)

"This memoir is gorgeous. Harpham writes about giving birth alone with an ambivalent-at-best boyfriend—and then how their love evolves and changes as they find out their newborn daughter is very sick. The writing is just exquisite, and will make you feel lucky that she put pen to page and let you into her life."

—*Kveller*

"Harpham tells a heartrending story of young love, getting pregnant, her partner's lack of interest in having children, and ... a crooked little road to follow toward some kind of radiant happiness."

—*Library Journal*

"A book about one of the healthiest romances I've ever seen committed to paper, about neighborly grace, about balancing one child's needs against another's. It is a book, most of all, about the value of that most commonplace and staggering of miracles: 'the spontaneous eruption of an individual consciousness out of nothingness.'"

—*The Millions*

"*Happiness* absolutely thrums with energy and is infused with such emotion, it's hard to set it down. The writing is genuine and engaging.... This is one memoir that I won't be forgetting about anytime soon."

—alwayswithabook.blogspot.com

"I can think of very few novels that have encompassed the emotional complexity of marriage as well as this memoir, and even fewer that portray marriages between two such well-intentioned people."

—*The Daily Blague*

"Reads almost like a suspenseful novel at times, with the unexpected turns readers expect to find in fiction ... A sensitive portrayal of Harpham's sometimes painfully fraught relationship . . . A tender look at female friendship and a stirring chronicle of a mother's devotion. [*Happiness*] is filled with both pain and beauty, and shares a clear-eyed view of messy relationships and the journey toward something that resembles joy."

—*BookPage*

"Well-written and poignantly narrated, this is a book that will make you bawl, while at the same time make you feel warmth in your chest. This is truly an extraordinary memoir written by a compassionate mother and author."

—*Vagabomb*

"Recently, memoirs by such dazzling writers as Ann Patchett and Dani Shapiro have explored and illuminated happiness: what it means, how we find it, and how hard-won it can sometimes be. Now add Heather Harpham to this stellar company. With intelligence and lyricism and compassion, Harpham gives us her story of the rocky road that sometimes leads right where you want it to."

—Ann Hood, bestselling author of *The Knitting Circle*

"At first glance, *Happiness* is a wry, honest, captivating story about parenting a sick child, and that would be enough. But it turns out that Harpham is up to something even more interesting here, exploring the complexities of love. Told with abundant charm and insight, this book is a beautifully drawn portrait of one family—its comforts, disappointments, and, on the very best days, moments of grace."

—Cynthia D'Aprix Sweeney, bestselling author of *The Nest*

"An extraordinary and bewitching book, *Happiness* has staked a claim among the most beautiful and moving portraits of parenthood and partnership."

—Susan Cheever, bestselling author of *Treetops:
A Memoir* and *Home Before Dark*

"*Happiness* touches on nearly every emotion—fear, passion, appreciation—and we wouldn't be surprised if you finish the entire memoir in one sitting."

—*Departures*

HAPPINESS

The Crooked
Little Road
to Semi–Ever After

A MEMOIR

∽

Heather Harpham

PICADOR
HENRY HOLT AND COMPANY
NEW YORK

HAPPINESS. Copyright © 2017 by Heather Harpham. All rights reserved. Printed in the United States of America. For information, address Picador, 175 Fifth Avenue, New York, N.Y. 10010.

picadorusa.com • instagram.com/picador
twitter.com/picadorusa • facebook.com/picadorusa

Picador® is a U.S. registered trademark and is used by Macmillan Publishing Group, LLC, under license from Pan Books Limited.

For book club information, please visit facebook.com/picadorbookclub or email marketing@picadorusa.com.

Designed by Meryl Sussman Levavi

The Library of Congress has cataloged the Henry Holt edition as follows:

Names: Harpham, Heather Elise, 1967– author.
Title: Happiness: the crooked little road to semi–ever after : a memoir / Heather Harpham.
Description: First edition. | New York : Henry Holt and Company, 2017.
Identifiers: LCCN 2016040488 | ISBN 9781250131560 (hardcover) | ISBN 9781250131577 (ebook)
Subjects: LCSH: Harpham, Heather Elise, 1967– —Health. | Newborn Infants—Diseases—United States—Biography. | Blood diseases in pregnancy—United States. | Blood—Transfusion. | Parent and child—Biography.
Classification: LCC RJ255 .H36 2017 | DDC 618.3'6130092 [B]—dc23
LC record available at https://lccn.loc.gov/2016040488

Picador Paperback ISBN 978-1-250-30114-7

Our books may be purchased in bulk for promotional, educational, or business use. Please contact your local bookseller or the Macmillan Corporate and Premium Sales Department at 1-800-221-7945, extension 5442, or by email at MacmillanSpecialMarkets@macmillan.com.

First published by Henry Holt and Company, LLC

First Picador Edition: November 2018

10 9 8 7 6 5 4 3

For my mother,
Jessica Flynn, artist of loving kindness

HAPPINESS

PROLOGUE

MY BEST FRIEND FROM COLLEGE, SUZI, HAS ACCUSED ME FOR years of not remembering well, or enough. Parties we went to, men we kissed. Girls we gossiped about. A trip we took to Southeast Asia. I know we were in Southeast Asia for ten months, and that on a boat between Sumatra and Bali a fist-sized flying cockroach landed near Suzi's ear. I know I was unable to say anything except "big bug, Suzi, big bug." I know we went to parties where we kissed men and gossiped about the girls. (We didn't have the foresight or sophistication to kiss the girls and gossip about the men.) But most of the details are blurry or nonexistent.

It's not that I'm a drunk, I barely drink. And it's not that I don't want to remember, I mostly do. It's that my brain is wired for the present. By vocation, I'm an improviser. A person trained to pay attention to the here and now. I know exactly what's happening as I write this. I am with a group of friends in New Mexico, on our annual retreat. Two of them are writing by the light of a single yellow bulb, out on the porch. Between them is a green vase holding four chrysanthemum blossoms. One friend is using a gleaming gold fountain pen. She's European, she's rich. Everything she owns gleams, and she's often trying to give it to you. The other friend is writing with the stub of a pencil; it has bite marks and most of the yellow paint has flaked off. That friend is American and brilliant and has no money. Against the sound of their instruments moving across the page, crickets are constructing a multirhythmic evensong. Next week, if you ask me to describe this moment, I *might* retain the crickets. The rest—the gold pen, the stubbed pencil, even the diffuse feeling of contentment that comes from being close by, but quiet, with good friends—will recede.

My memory captures the shiny, pretty, easy things and lets the rest drop away. It's finicky. For instance, I remember the night I met Suzi. My college boyfriend and I were driving the thin, snaking road to our campus on a Northern California hilltop. Suzi, striding the middle line, was a slim silhouette beneath a billowing nimbus of hair. We pulled over to offer her a ride; this girl I kept hearing about was suddenly real, in the backseat of my car. I turned to say hello. Her face was lit intermittently by the streetlamps, flash, high cheekbones, flash, rosy Irish skin, flash, kind eyes. Big eyes. Kind eyes.

I don't remember every Indonesian island we visited together in 1991, but I know exactly what Suzi looked like on one night, in the fall of 1987.

Memory is stubborn, revisionist, and fickle. Everything I'm about to tell you is subject to persuasion, bias, and desire, as much as any history is. It is singularly one-sided. Time molds things retroactively, usually into what we wanted them to be. I've tried to remember everything that mattered, even those things I didn't want to remember. I've read and reread the notes I took along the way, which reflect point of view as much as recorded fact. Most of all, I've tried to figure out how to tell a story that is not strictly mine.

TWO COASTS

I

MY FIRST CHILD, MY GIRL, WAS BORN JUST BEFORE SEVEN ON A
spring night, perfect. She was compact and fully formed, a little over
five pounds. She smelled like sliced apple and salted pretzels, like the
innocent recent arrival from a saline world that she was.

But the midwife was worried. "She's small for gestational age," she
kept saying. "Any problems or issues during pregnancy?"

I wanted to ask her if heartbreak counted. If sharing a bed with a
good-hearted dog, rather than the baby's father, might do it.

"Also," the midwife said, "she looks a little jaundiced."

"That's just the Greek side," my mom cut in, "we're all yellow."

The midwife finally handed her over, a waxy, pinched little thing.
Gory and unkempt. Not serenely smiling like the dolls of my youth. But
a real baby, mine.

When I breathed her in, a straight, bright synaptic path lit up the
center of my brain. Every neuron said to its neighbor, yes, yes, yes, yes,
this is the one, yes. This reaction is hardwired. Animals identify their
offspring by scent. But to me, it felt like magic. Smelling her elicited
euphoria akin, I imagined, to the unadulterated delight of smoking crack
cocaine for the first time. After a few hours of life outside the womb, she
began to smell less like apples and more like an element, tin or iron.

Something practical, a garden tool or an old coin, sprung from dark soil and delivered into the palm of my hand.

After months of waiting to see who this child would be, after fending off the broad hints of a sonographer who was dying to give away the mystery of her gender, after sleeping alone in a thicket of unhappiness, after praying to skip over incubation to active motherhood—here she was. A little football of a person, tucked into the oval between my arm and torso, breathing on her own, making minor noises. Preoccupied with the job of being alive. Under a fringe of downy hair, at the base of her still soft skull, I found a pale pink birthmark, strawberry shaped.

For the next ten hours I lay awake, breathing her in, stunned to find a small human body nestled against mine. I couldn't figure out where on earth she came from. The biology I understood; I knew about the genome, the dim lights, the Richard Buckner music, the curved helix of DNA. But none of that could account for her. Her birth was both an utterly quotidian event (245 new children are born into every minute) and a jaw-dropping miracle to rival loaves and fishes. There was no one. And then, poof—her.

I didn't sleep. I couldn't sleep; I didn't want to miss anything. What if she sighed or pursed her lips or splayed her fingers or jerked her arms upward?

I was still awake, a little before 3 a.m., when a gentle-faced nurse came in. He didn't seem surprised to find me up, smelling the baby. Typical new-parent behavior. He said, casually, that they'd like to take her to the nursery for a few tests. The oddity of routine tests at three in the morning didn't register. It was obvious that my child was totally healthy; what harm could tests do?

Healthy babies were all I knew. The array of placid baby dolls I'd spent hours clucking over as a girl had smelled faintly of vanilla. They had coy smiles and carefully molded plastic hair. I tucked them in. I burped them. I crooned into their plastic ears. None of them ever ran a fever or broke out in hives. Even baby Jesus (the biggest celebrity baby of all time) was a robust little soul. *Holy infant so tender and mild.*

The nurse promised to bring her right back. Without her, I was at a loss. I motored the bed up and down, edgy, unfocused, waiting for my fix. An hour later the nurse came back empty-handed. "Where's my baby?" I said, sounding, even to myself, absurdly panicked.

He gave me a pointed look, half sympathy, half crowd control, and said, "We'd like to run a few more tests." At the door he added, "The doctor will be in to talk with you in a few minutes." I didn't know anything about hospitals yet; I didn't know enough to be terrified that an actual doctor would appear bedside before daybreak.

When I had imagined threats to my future children, they'd been external. Strangers hovering at the edge of playgrounds in loose, gray sweatshirts; rotting rope swings fraying over jagged rocks; cars, everywhere, callous, steely-eyed killer-cars. These were possibilities I could conceive of. Illness had never slunk across the screen of my anxieties, with its curved spine and sallow cheeks. I probably wouldn't have recognized it even if it did. Serious illness, life-threatening illness, was outside the realm of my imagination. If pushed to consider the question, I might have responded that I was protected from the possibility by the mere fact that it had never occurred to me. I might have said, "If I can't imagine it, how can it happen?"

* * *

On my first date with the father of this five-pound girl we went to an intimate place on the corner of Jane Street in Greenwich Village. The kind of place where, to reach your table, you're obliged to wedge sideways and apologize to strangers whom you've brushed with your hips. Seated, we leaned over the small table to breathe the same air and figure each other out. He said he'd read recently that everyone has a personal "happiness quotient," that your happiness in life is essentially set, regardless of circumstances. He reckoned his was low, and guessed mine was high.

I'd never heard of a happiness quotient. I'd never stopped to consider happiness as anything other than an assumed default state, a place to return to after the occasional thick fog. If, as a kid, I had been asked to state the one thing I believed to be true about my future, I'd have said, "I'll have a happy life."

Not that I'd had a blindingly happy childhood. I hadn't. I'd had a childhood of being profoundly loved amid serial chaos. I grew up as the only child of a warmhearted, fleet-footed single mom who was always exploring her options, in men, jobs, lifestyles. It was California in the 1970s. For a while I attended school in a geodesic dome on a hilltop. A herd of goats grazed on long, golden grass outside the open door. Sometimes we ran among them without shirts, boys and girls alike. One of the male teachers enjoyed watching, too much. Everything in my world moved fast, and my job was to hang on. Still, I'd emerged with the idea that my own adult life would be happy and essentially free of adversity. The optimism of youth, which I'd somehow hung on to until thirty, thirty-one even.

A happy life, at the time of that Jane Street first date, did not include, from my point of view, being the mother of a child who required extensive neonatal medical care. Or spending a pregnancy alone, heartsick. Those possibilities weren't visible from the corner of Jane Street; all I saw was the man before me in a pressed blue dress shirt, delivering literary jokes with a shy, sly humor. The amused look in his eye when I chirped with surprise at the arrival of our salads. "Do you always greet your food so enthusiastically?" he asked. "Not always," I said. "Only sometimes." Only now.

* * *

The 4 a.m. doctor was short and bespectacled with a round, soft face. A pleasant-looking bearer of bad news; he seemed personally pained by what he was about to say. He started by explaining the baby had high levels of something I didn't catch, emphasizing the need to transfer "the patient" to a larger hospital. "Right," I said, trying to muster a little dignity in my flapping nightshirt. "But what is actually wrong with her?"

"Your baby is at risk of brain damage or"—he paused and glanced around the room as though looking for something he'd mislaid—"death."

I felt embarrassed for him; clearly he was in the wrong room. He'd confused my baby with another baby. I tried to break it gently, "This is the baby born at seven p.m., the five-pound, five-ounce girl, with a strawberry on the back of her neck."

"Yes," he said. "I know."

Still, I refused to apply these words—*death* or *brain damage*—to my swaddled and fabulous-smelling daughter. Death was ludicrous. And brain damage was out of the question. Way, way, way out of the question. In fact, the question and brain damage didn't even know each other. The question was: when can I take her home? Still, the doctor was in earnest. I decided to play along. "OK," I said. "OK, right. OK. Then what do we do?"

He explained that her red cells lacked stability and were breaking apart in the bloodstream. The iron inside each cell was spilling into the blood and floating freely throughout her body, at risk of lodging into the soft tissue of her brain. "So you are saying what, exactly?" I said. "She's at risk for rust head?" He looked at me, appraising. A long silent moment went by. "That's humor," he said finally, "common coping mechanism."

At the door he added, "We need to clean her blood immediately. We're transferring you to UCSF Med Center. The ambulance is waiting." University of California San Francisco Medical Center, the place I'd elected not to give birth. The big-city hospital. The tall, silver fortress on top of the hill, across the Golden Gate. The last place on earth a brand-new baby wants to go.

* * *

On our second date, we ate at a bright, loud diner along Seventh Avenue. If harshly lit Formica can feel romantic, I told myself, then this is foreordained. He asked me to list my "diner worries," those anxieties so slight they could be jotted onto the waxy parchment of a placemat. I have no idea what I said. I likely made things up, things to make me seem Frenchly philosophical or politically courageous or, failing all this, mysterious. I was young, I owned an apartment in New York City, had a good university job, and was on the cusp of what might be a relationship with a serious, kind man. Diner worries were in short supply.

But I loved that he asked, that he wanted to etch a record of my preoccupations onto a placemat. Later I would learn that he often took notes about things his students said, their goals, their literary heroes—to keep them straight, to accumulate an understanding of what they hoped for. At first this seemed excessive. But later it struck me as intrinsic to his way of being. He wanted to know, understand, remember who people were. *How* they were. And the best, truest way he knew to burrow toward the truth was to write things down. On the page he could add up a girl's diner worries and see what they amounted to.

* * *

The ambulance driver told me to ride up front.

"What about the baby?" I asked.

"She'll ride in back, with the paramedics," he said.

"The paramedics are great," I said, "but they don't really know her."

"We're just going over the bridge," the driver said, "she'll be fine."

At this point I became what was probably noted in the trip log as *combative mom*. Logically, I knew the driver was not responsible for my girl's precipitous need to be transferred, at less than twenty hours old, to a neonatal intensive care unit—but neither did he grasp how my entire world was encased in the plastic box that was her incubator. My job was to stick with the plastic box, no matter what.

"Actually, I'm going to ride with her," I said, trying to make it sound as if, after weighing his various options, I'd settled on this. Somehow, that worked.

In the back of the ambulance were four people: two paramedics, me, and her. It was just beginning to get light as we crossed the Golden Gate, leaving Marin County and entering San Francisco. In between the black mass of the bay and a gray bank of clouds, a pale, thin line of pink wavered. Daylight. I relaxed a little. Surely nothing catastrophic could happen during business hours.

My mother's car was trailing the ambulance. I knew she was filled with worry. Worry was undeniably called for given the situation: ambulance, dawn, newborn, bad blood. But the baby sleeping peacefully under my hand defied worry. She had a rosebud mouth and delicately veined eyelids. She didn't stir, not even when the driver turned on the siren to speed through red lights. I stroked her forehead and tried to get my mind around our situation. Inside this tiny person, microscopic red blood cells were falling apart. She was a stressed creature, straining to deliver sufficient oxygen to the outposts of her body. How could she appear so serene?

The repertoire of reptilian brain function—fight, flight, denial, play dead—is great for emergencies. It wedges space between the event and the self. I had been swinging between denial and fight (my two personal favorites) from the moment the round-faced doctor said *ambulance*. Now, sitting with the baby, I felt the unwelcome return of higher reasoning. I began to pump the paramedics for information: What would happen when we arrived at the hospital? Would I be allowed to stay with the baby? How long would it take to clean her blood? What were the odds for babies in this situation?

One of them explained that the method for cleaning her blood was called an *exchange transfusion*. An exchange transfusion works, she said, by removing all the blood from the body, passing it through a device that extracts excess iron, warming the blood back up, and returning it to circulation.

Are you insane? I wanted to ask. Bloodletting? So cliché. So over. So Middle Ages. Consider your reputation, if not the baby.

I sat there in silence, trying to visualize what a blood cleaning/warming machine might look like and how they would attach it to her. It dawned on me that the next few hours mattered, really mattered, and that even babies who smelled just right might drift off.

I looked down at my girl, sleeping, gathering air, converting it into oxygen.

"All the blood? Out of her body? At the same time? " I asked. "Is that prudent?"

The paramedic touched my shoulder and said, "She'll be OK. They're much stronger than they look."

Through the small window at back of the ambulance, I could see a steady streak of green. My mom's Volvo sedan, behind us. I had the sense that she would follow us anywhere, no matter how fast, no matter how far. When I had called my mom, only an hour ago, she'd been asleep. "What do you mean rusty blood?" she'd said. "Is this about *the baby*?"

"Drive here," I'd said. "We need you."

She'd arrived in time to catch the ambulance's wake. For her, I was the girl, and this whole ambulance was the plastic box.

* * *

After our third date, we went back to his apartment. He was a studio dweller on the Upper West Side, twenty-sixth floor, a view of the George Washington Bridge, which he revered. A wall of windows and little else. He had a single pot and stacks of books. Against the barrenness, he'd waged the smallest possible stand—a decorative postage stamp. Joe Louis.

That is how I began to fall in love with Brian, all that emptiness, and then, suddenly, a black-and-white postcard of Paris or Beckett; the hidden trapdoor to something more.

The art in my apartment was as big as I could afford it to be, giant posters from foreign museums, hand-carried on the plane ride home, trying always not to dent them, destined for cheap oversized Ikea frames. My favorite was by the Mexican painter Rufino Tamayo; it showed a figure, sitting facedown at a table, the circumference of his head dominating the space in pinks, yellows, violets. *Man Radiating Happiness*.

In contrast to Brian's, my daily life was erratic, unorganized, and subject to an appetite for salty snacks, phone chats, trashy magazines, generalized rose-sniffing. My mornings were spent teaching drama in public schools with kids all over the city as an "actor-teacher" with the Creative Arts Team at NYU. Afternoons, when I should have been doing my own schoolwork (I was a grad student) or rehearsing a new solo piece, I would instead lollygag about town. If I did rush home, it was to watch *General Hospital* and eat ice cream. If a friend called to say let's go to Battery Park and check out the river, I was game. Even if I had a pile of more pressing things. Around 11 p.m., when the hourly studio rates fell, I would go rehearse. If I had a performance coming, I'd focus. Otherwise, I was a creative malingerer.

But Brian knew how to work. His life was ordered, boundaried to the extreme. A man who, by his own admission, ate broccoli with brown rice and garlic sauce every night for dinner. A man who pruned back the trivial decisions, who wore French Blue dress shirts and black pants every day of the week, for consistency's sake. A man with an embedded internal clock, which told him to sit and write at the same hour, day after day. A man with a gift, and the dense garden of habit grown around it for protection.

We were a study in opposites; hopelessly attracted. We floated about from dinners to concerts to parties with friends. Holding hands, touching each other's clothes. When we walked through the Village, along Sixth Avenue, shoulder to shoulder, I had a liquid sense of well-being. We were in the throes of infatuation, soft-minded and easily persuaded of our rightness for each other by sexual thrill. But there was a bedrock quality beneath the giddiness, something I hadn't felt before. Being with him gave me the unfamiliar feeling of being what I was—a grown woman.

* * *

Within minutes of arriving at UCSF Medical Center we were hustled upstairs to the Neonatal Intensive Care Unit (NICU, pronounced *nick-u*). I stood beside the baby's incubator; it had two portals you could slip your hands through, to touch your person. This was the extent of what you could do for your baby in the NICU—stand beside the box stroking a finger or toe or tiny elbow beneath the blanket. I stroked my girl's knee.

A petite doctor with a blond bun crossed the room.

"Listen," she said, nodding in the baby's direction, "she needs a central line placed into her umbilicus, immediately, for the exchange transfusion." The doctor projected the air of an overachieving-homecoming-queen-valedictorian-tennis-champ. Probably played Rachmaninoff's harder pieces for fun and relaxation. "Please sign this release. It's just a procedure, not surgery. The umbilicus is numb, so she won't feel a thing." Beneath her lab coat, visible at the collar and cuffs, was a heavy silk blouse, cream colored. She was too young, too pretty, too sure of herself to be a decent doctor. But she was who we had. I tried to parse what she'd said: *just a procedure, not surgery.* She wanted to attach a tube to the baby. That much I got.

I wanted to talk to the nice doctor with the soft boyish face and glasses, from Marin General. But he had sent us to *her*. The blond doctor was waiting for my answer; would I allow her to attach the tube or not? She held out the form and a pen.

Would a plastic part really improve the baby per se?

What would Brian do? I tried to summon some of his steadiness, his ability to lever rationality into crisis. I signed. She exhaled, her shoulders dropped. Astonishing! This woman was as nervous about my judgments and decisions as I was about hers. A nurse scooped up the baby and left the room.

2

Everyone in the world should have the chance to fall in love in a New York City spring, at least once. Spring, in New York, is like a new epoch in history. The sludge recedes; the trees return as green civilizers of the streets. Your beloved finally takes off all those obfuscating layers, and you can see skin. The Josh Ritter song goes something like, "This trip has been done a hundred thousand times before, but this one is *mine*."

On a Saturday, three or four months into our courtship, I found myself staring down from Brian's twenty-sixth-floor window, watching the Upper West Side swish below. I wanted to go to a gallery, a café, Riverside Park, bike riding along the Hudson. I wanted to take the train downtown to Magnolia Bakery for a lemon-frosted cupcake. Anything, just out into the tides of the town. But Brian was at his desk, happy in his misery. Wringing something more out of the imagination by sheer attendance. Showing up. Seeking. Day by day. He had his hands on the keyboard and his eyes closed, tunneling in, burrowing down. This was something he did occasionally, write blind. He was deep in conversation with his unconscious, his imagination, his genie. Whatever the hell it was that wrote his books, he was chatting with it. Just the two of them, tête-à-tête.

He didn't seem to need a lemon cupcake.

I knew we'd go out later. I watched the sun drop into the river, pressed my cheek against the cool glass, and waited. The world was out there, true, but it was also in here.

When we left, to meet friends for dinner, it was still warm out. The sidewalks felt almost pliable underfoot, willing to bear us in any direction. We linked arms and headed downtown. My sweet hermetic boyfriend, out in the world. Traipsing around. I tucked one hand into his jacket pocket. The payoff for this simple gesture was absurdly inflated. I wanted to see a scan of my brain, to know exactly which synapses electrified, a bright web of lightning, when Brian put his hand in my pocket too.

* * *

I was not allowed to watch the procedure in which they inserted the tube into the baby, but I heard crying from down the hall. Was it my girl? Impossible to know. Even more impossible to know what she might be feeling, thinking, or understanding about the world—alone in a room of white coats.

My mom brought me a tea; I sipped it, queasy. I wanted the baby back. We should be at home together. I should be in a flannel nightgown, snuggling her, emitting the primary message: you are loved.

When I could no longer stand listening to the cries of a baby who might or might not be mine, I stepped into the pay phone booth in the waiting room. I shut the door. Silence. At last, a small private space in which to feel something.

My mom tapped on the glass of the booth, holding out the tea. "Don't let it get cold." I opened the glass door and took the tea, annoyed. If, years from now, my own daughter was in this same situation, I would, undoubtedly, hover. Peddle tea. But it was still annoying. I considered calling Brian. I wanted his support but not enough to make the baby's illness real by telling him about it. Instead, I dialed my health insurance company. When a representative answered, I told her my name, my group ID number, and said, "My daughter is sick. We've been transferred to UC Med." It was the first time I'd said *my daughter.*

My voice broke, and the woman paused. "It'll be OK, dear," she said.

She could be empathizing from Ohio, Singapore, or a block away. She could be anywhere. So how the hell did she know how it would go?

When I returned to the waiting area, I picked up an old issue of the *New Yorker*. On the cover, beleaguered cartoon figures marched through eddies of gray sludge and snow, huddled beneath a banner that read "Misery Day Parade." February. I held it up for my mom to see, pointing to the banner of hand-printed letters, *Misery Day Parade*. "Oh, sweetie," she said. "I know." And she did know. She was a professional understander, a therapist. The rare kind, with a heart of true compassion. Maybe because she'd suffered so much as a kid, maybe because she was born that way. She never dealt in pity, only empathy. But at the exact moment I needed it most, I didn't want it.

Every gesture of comfort she offered only underlined the obvious: she was my mom and, therefore, not Brian.

* * *

I loved, for one, his books. Not just the books he'd written but also the books he read. They were everywhere, on every surface: the lip of the bathroom sink, the windowsill, stacked in unstable towers on the DVD player, in doorways, and, endlessly, on the bed.

He'd climb into bed with his intellectual posse: Chekhov, G. K. Chesterson, George Scialabba, Irving Howe, Raymond Williams, but also Robert B. Parker and Roger Angell. In terms of heroes, he had a take-all-comers approach; he'd once written an essay on his affection for the TV show *The Equalizer*. Books on antiquated English grammar by patrician midcentury taskmasters, on efficiency in the workplace, labor histories, lurid crime novels—all would flop over the pillows, work their way under our feet. Reading the ideas of others wasn't just what he did, it was what forged him into who he was, word by word.

He was not a person who called himself a writer but was actually an architect or a pastry chef. He was a writer, who wrote. Reading and writing were his air and water. Every day. For hours. A novelist. A published, award-winning novelist. A self-doubting, slow-working, often frustrated novelist, but a serious artist. Writing was at the core of his existence, and everything else fell into place around that central fact.

Even when he wasn't writing, he was writing, inventing, trying things out. Once, when I asked him to tell me the story of his name, he reported that instead of Brian his parents almost named him Barrel after a Hungarian relative, a glue maker and war hero, who died by falling, face-first and drunk, into a barrel of glue. He told me this very solemnly, and I was relieved that he had not been named Barrel. It might have changed the course of his life. Would we have met? When I asked his mother about her cousin Barrel who had tragically, ironically, drowned in a barrel, she laughed and laughed. "For such an honest guy," she said, "Brian is the world's biggest liar."

He had his books, his Joe Louis postage stamp, his habits, his broccoli, his blue shirts, his cabal of imaginary friends, his never-ending mental arguments with Noam Chomsky. He had his uninterrupted days and nights at the keyboard. He had *solitary writer* written all over him. And, as much as he enjoyed being with me, he obviously didn't want kids or a family. Writing was the sun around which the rest of his life orbited, including me. So how long could this last?

If we went on, if he allowed me into the inner courtyard, then what? I was afraid I'd have the perverse urge to blow things up, disturb and disrupt, the way you want to toss your hat from the top level of the Guggenheim into the tiny reflecting pool below.

* * *

The first few weeks of my pregnancy, oblivious to my condition, I dashed into every Starbucks I saw. I couldn't understand this sudden compulsion—I'd never been a coffee person. Not even close. In fact, I'd once presented myself to the NYU medical center with heart palpitations after eating a bag of chocolate-covered espresso beans. The doctor asked, "Have you had a lot of coffee today?" I was indignant: "I don't drink coffee." Then I remembered, but didn't confess. Just slunk away in shame, the only woman in New York City who couldn't hold her caffeine.

I ordered lattes, macchiatos, cappuccinos, any foamed formula with espresso. I was puzzled but compliant, caffeine's willing handmaiden. The more sophisticated drinks lent me, I hoped, a certain chic. I loved their

Italian names, the long vowels. Holding a perfectly frothed macchiato was tantamount, in my book, to wearing a blue cashmere wrap. And then I began to wonder; a little seed of doubt presented itself. Why was I craving coffee? Why was I craving milk? Why was I *craving*?

I happened to be in California, visiting my family. Our local drugstore was a ten-minute tromp through a wooded park, a trek I'd taken a thousand times for candy, makeup, or magazines. I went straight to the feminine hygiene aisle, a place I was once loath to be seen loitering, and bought four pregnancy kits of various brands, all promising speed and accuracy.

You are supposed to pee on the stick at a certain time of day, under particular conditions. (Reading the directions, I kept hearing the slogan from a radio show I'd liked as a kid, "It's Science!") But I couldn't wait for science. I just pulled out a stick and tried not to pee on my hand. I put the plastic cap back on and waited. One minute, two. A faint line began to appear, just the dimmest purple dash across one display window, and then another line, crossing the first, forming a lavender plus sign. Plus one. Oh God. Oh God's God.

I ripped open another package and forced myself to pee on that. And another and then the last. They all had dashes and checks or hazy blue lines. I couldn't believe these little sticks. They were unanimous, unwilling to negotiate.

I found my running shoes, laced them up. I'd walk up the hill. By the time I got back, maybe the pregnancy would have run its course.

Next to my shoes was one of Brian's, a black Converse sneaker. He'd just spent two weeks with me in California, meeting my family, laughing with my college friends. We'd driven up the coast together, along Highway 1, traveling from LA to Marin County, passing through Big Sur, the most beautiful place on the planet, where we'd pulled the car off the road onto a secluded apron of land above the ocean, just to kiss. We'd spent the whole two weeks in a bubble of our own invention.

I'd taken the fact that he left a sneaker behind as a good omen, his tangible wish to still be here. I picked it up on my way out. I puffed up the hill toward the fire trails, assimilating the news, clutching his sneaker. At the top of the hill was a long narrow ridge lined by giant eucalyptus trees, with an animate presence. Two sentinel rows of stolid, immovable elders who had offered me sanctuary since I was ten. The trees had delicate scythe-shaped leaves and trunks with silvery outer layers that peeled away from a pink undercoat. As a kid, I liked to rub my check against the silky inner bark, or crush the leaves in my palm; the smell cleared my head, straightened my gait. Not now.

What on God's green earth was I going to do? Or *we*. Since it takes two people to set a baby in motion, it seemed fair that those same two should have a say in whether or not the baby comes to fruition. But I didn't have that capacity for democracy. I'd told Brian all along: *if I get pregnant, I will have the baby*. I was willing to stand in the rain with a dripping placard for the right of women to choose (though I'd never done anything remotely so noble), but I didn't experience it as a choice. I wanted to be a mother and he was a man I loved. He might opt out, fairly or unfairly, I might hate him for that, fairly or unfairly, but the baby was a foregone conclusion.

As I walked home, the hills soaked up the dusk, turning blue-black. Then, slowly, they lit up, house by house, like a night sky. Each pinprick of light was a family. Was I technically now a family too? I housed a cluster of cells, dividing at a breakneck pace. I was, at the very least, a party of two.

I walked home swinging Brian's sneaker by its laces. A few feet shy of our driveway, I must have loosened my grip. Brian's shoe flew up and away from me, in a high arc, and landed in a bramble of blackberry. I forced my arm into the dense thicket; inside the soil was moist and yielding under my fingertips as I traced methodical, concentric circles where the shoe should be. But I found only a velvety scattering of decayed berries and something spherical and slick, maybe a dog toy. I started to push in deeper, then stopped and drew my arm back. I was suddenly afraid of being bitten by a creature whose solitary home I'd invaded.

* * *

After what felt like hours, the blond doctor arrived back in the room, upbeat, followed by a nurse carrying my baby. She was awake. When I took her into my arms, her eyes moved slowly from my face, to the nurse's face, back to mine. "Good news," the doctor said. "She's out of immediate danger. We've avoided the exchange transfusion for now. However, we may still need to transfuse her with red cells. We're admitting you."

Which part of this was the good news?

"What about the tube?" I asked. "Did you attach it to her?"

"Yes," the doctor said. "We inserted the central line, in case she needs blood or meds. It's the easiest way in."

I dipped my nose to the baby's head; she still smelled like herself. At least I was getting back the same girl I'd given them.

I was afraid to look at her stomach. I pictured something Frankensteinish, a rusted bolt or a spare bike part holding the central line in place. But it was just as the doctor had described, a soft rubber tube, extending from her stomach.

"OK," my mom said. "We can live with that."

"So," I said, "the iron isn't getting into her brain?"

"Iron is not crossing the blood/brain barrier at this time," the doctor said.

I should have felt relief, the doctor looked relieved, but I was confused and bizarrely disappointed. They'd said she needed her blood cleaned only a short time ago, so wouldn't cleaning it still be a good idea?

"If you aren't going to clean her blood, why does she have a rubber hose in her torso?"

"Sweetie," my mom said. She laid a hand on my arm and gave me a look. *Be grateful. Don't go looking for trouble.*

* * *

When I'd finally accepted that I was pregnant and was not going to magically become less pregnant, I called Brian. The phone was an inadequate tool, but it was the only immediate way to bridge a continent. As I dialed, my teeth chattered in intermittent bursts. This is new, I thought, psychosomatic teeth. Calm down, I told myself. Don't be melodramatic. People get pregnant. But I couldn't calm down. I couldn't even think of how to break the news. "I'm pregnant" sounded so unoriginal, so teenager-in-the-heartland and—here was the real rub—too much like something happening exclusively to me. When I finally managed to say it, he melted.

"My darling," Brian said. "My sweetheart." And then he went silent. He was silent for a long time, and when he spoke again his voice sounded clotted with pain, half-aspirated, as though he literally could not swallow this knowledge.

Having kids—what kids do to an adult life already in motion, what they do to romance, to your couch, your car, your time, your money, most of all your art—had been the constant bass line thrumming through our conversations in the months before I got pregnant. It was the issue that sent us, oddly early, into therapy together. It was the gun in the room. If he wanted to have kids with anyone, Brian kept saying, it would be with me. *If.*

But *if* is a wisp of a word. You could hardly hang your hat on that. Or build a life. Plus Brian already had a life, as a writer, a semi-happy bachelor of the Upper West Side, as a diffident, sexy Jewish intellectual. As the editor of a left-leaning magazine, a jazz detester, TV lover, kind friend, and surprising gossip. But first of all, last of all, most of all—as a writer. His entire adult existence had been organized around writing. If he had a creed, it would have been Nietzsche: "The essential thing in heaven and in earth . . . is a long obedience in the same direction."

His obedience was to life at the desk, life as it shimmered onto the page. The unruly emissaries of real life—food and flowers, snow, slush, the Vermont night sky, sex, the Grand Canyon, the East Village, twisted ankles, soured wine, the Hudson River at close range—all these were fine, but were interlopers on his essential mission: animating a humane vision of the world.

Fine, OK, be a writer. Life of the mind, live for your art and all that. I could respect his calling, his need. But, then, what the hell had he been doing swinging around town with me? I'd never kept my wish to have kids secret, quite the opposite. I'd said emphatically, many times over, that I could not, would not, contemplate a life without children. Impossible. And he'd made his wish to avoid kids just as obvious. So, then, what the hell was I doing swinging around town with him?

After that initial declaration, *My darling, my sweetheart*, Brian remained shattered and unhappy on the phone, but I kept believing we'd work this out. If we could just see each other face to face, all the pieces would find a place: life, art, baby, love, writing—wasn't there room for everyone on the couch? Pluralism, isn't that what he believed in?

I'd remind him that we were the same two people who'd been made delirious by walking hip to hip; that he had been an eager partner in the (knowingly unprotected) act that produced this very dilemma.

Knowingly unprotected: Brian, by the age of forty-five, had never gotten a girlfriend pregnant; I, by the age of thirty-two, had never been pregnant. Luck or best practices, hard to say, but with each other we were bizarrely laissez-faire. Like naive dolts worldwide, we thought that since it had never happened before it couldn't happen now. We'd been enacting a fantasy that turned into a vertigo-inducing reality.

Over the years, two different doctors told Brian he might encounter trouble conceiving; he'd chosen to believe them. He had room, he thought, to flirt with a possibility that a very submerged part of him wanted. When we'd made love without protection, I was discounting the things Brian said to me in therapy every week about not wanting kids. I was believing in some version of him that didn't exist except in bed. But I was acting in alignment with my own deepest wishes.

I'd hoped he was too—that his willingness to be so cavalier about birth control was an unconscious wish to have the issue decided for him. For us. This interpretation now looked to be somewhere between wildly self-delusional and outright self-destructive.

* * *

The baby's bird-sized rib cage rose and fell in a steady rhythm under the sunlight lamps. I sat beside her, in a rocking chair, watching her sleep. She had, I noticed, a preferred sleep pose, with her head tossed back, one ear angled upward as though waiting for the answer to a question. Occasionally, she emitted a high-pitched squeak, like a small wind instrument.

Once we were officially admitted and assigned a spot in the NICU, the nurses encouraged me to treat the baby like any newborn. "She's not a china cup; she won't shatter on ya," a young Irish nurse said. She was my immediate favorite; she had a face of wide-spaced, pale freckles and red hair cut in a thick, exuberant bob. "Listen," she told me, "the thing the babies like best is to be tucked into your clothes, naked. Skin-to-skin contact."

"Won't she get cold?" I asked.

"Not so long as you're not dead," the Irish nurse said, and winked.

In the wee hours of our first night there, with the baby tucked inside my shirt against my skin, I relaxed enough to notice the NICU rhythms. Someone had tried to soften the blow of this place with kitten posters and rocking chairs, to pretend it wasn't a giant room of plastic boxes with very sick babies inside.

Sometime after midnight, the young mother of a baby boy beside us called home to Mexico. She told her own mother, in Spanish, a language I don't speak but somehow understood, that she was scared. She suspected her son's heart lacked confidence.

Beside this boy was an infant girl whose teenage parents had come by earlier in stained sweatshirts and stricken faces. They'd peered at their creation and quickly left. The little name card above the girl's head remained blank. In her sleep, she held two fingers in the palm of her other hand, already practicing the art of self-comfort. My girl's name card was also blank. In countries with high infant mortality rates people often delay naming their children. In Nepal it is customary to wait until "Janku," or first rice, when the baby is about six months old. It had only been two days, but already my family and friends were pushing.

"Just decide," Suzi said. "This is starting to get weird."

3

ON THE FINAL APPROACH TO JFK, NOT YET VISIBLY PREGNANT,
I tried to cry discreetly, so as not to alarm my fellow passengers. I was
flying toward Brian, without any assurance that he wanted a future with
me or the baby. I wasn't even sure if he would be at the airport to pick me
up. Outside the clouds were puffed into a layered, edible meringue of
lilac and indigo. I knew I should be stunned by this much beauty; I should
stop crying and say thank you. But I didn't. Everyone in California, most
especially Suzi, told me to stop crying, "You're flooding the baby with
stress hormones." *Sorry, baby.*

At JFK, I trudged through the crowd, sticky, pudgy, sick at heart,
looking for Brian's blue shirt. He was there, amid the throngs, a cool spot
of color, of calm. I wanted to run to him, but I stood still and waited for
him to notice me.

We decided we'd drive straight out to the Hamptons to meet with
our chic French therapist, who was at her summer house but willing to
see us anyway.

She opened the door before we knocked. "*Bon,* you found us," she said
in the accent that made everything sound vaguely philosophical. "After
such a long drive, you'd like a glass of wine?"

On the one hand, how very European and unuptight of her, red wine for the baby! Or maybe she did not acknowledge the existence of a baby at all, at such an early stage.

In her office she listened to us sum up our positions. Brian wanted to be with me but did not want to be a father. He felt fatherhood wasn't something that should be forced onto another person. He wasn't asking me to terminate the pregnancy, but he was clear that he would not, or could not, be the partner I hoped for. As much as I wanted to be with Brian, I was incredibly hurt that he would reject something (someone) he'd tacitly helped create. The therapist sat quietly for a while and then turned to me: "Heather, you are living in an illusion. You must wake up from your dream. Brian does not want what you want." What I wanted most, at that moment, was to smash one of her tasteful ceramic objets d'art over her sleek French head.

I stood up. "Time to go," I said. "Time's up!" I wanted to add, *Fuck off and go back to France. This is the land of opportunity! The land of figure-it-out!*

Brian and the chic French therapist stared at me. Neither stood. I stayed standing. Finally, Brian wrote a check; maybe I did too? We were splitting everything. We made it out onto her groomed gravel driveway and into the car.

We drove to the ocean, sat together on a log.

"Do you think this is an illusion?" I said.

"I think we've both seen what we wanted to," Brian said, and pulled me down onto his lap.

Between us, inside me, was an apple seed of differentiating cells. It was amazing how someone so small could cause such colossal disruption.

"What should we do?" I said.

"I love you," he said. "That is as much as I know."

He began to cry. I had this shock; he felt as abandoned as I did. My choice was making it impossible, from his point of view, for us to continue to be together.

His choice, from my point of view, was the worst choice of all time. I understood his dilemma on a cognitive level, sort of, but on a gut level I just kept thinking, *If two people are in love, and one of them is pregnant, show me the problem! Point to it! There is no problem.*

We drove back to Manhattan in silence, each of us leaning into our wound. All the way up the West Side Highway, the river ran beside us, an unperturbed ribbon of greenish silver. The tension in the car was so thick I wanted to jump out and swim uptown. In Brian's neighborhood we found a place and parked. It was dark; I was starving and nauseated. Brian looked haggard, bleary, and generally undone. I felt I could sleep for months, sleep through the whole pregnancy and just wake up to the baby. Maybe that would do it. If Brian could see the baby, he'd want the baby.

"Do you want to come up?" Brian said.

"What do you mean by that?" I said. It was an old joke of ours, answer a question with a question.

"Just come up," he said.

I went up. We ordered food from our favorite Mexican place, took a shower together, and lay down on his futon, named the General for the way it dominated his tiny studio.

The next day we ate and walked and watched some TV. We did not talk about the baby. We avoided the future. All the while, the cells I housed continued multiplying. They were turning into things, tiny, barely visible things, but things.

For two weeks we walked this high wire. We were happy, almost. We had a present of breakfasts and afternoon strolls and writing in the same room. Every day was a clown act, starring us as clowns.

When we gathered enough courage to talk about the baby, Brian's answer was always the same: he couldn't see a way to live life as a father.

"You live it like this," I said, patting a space between us on the General, "only with a baby next to you. It's not like you have to become a whole new person. You just scoot over."

But scooting wasn't his strong suit. If a fellow diner knocked into his chair on the way to the bathroom, Brian would startle, scowl. Not out of annoyance with his fellow humans, but because his own borders were so porous that space was sacrosanct. I liked to compare him to Rilke, who couldn't even live with a dog because the dog's moods, its sorrows and triumphs, affected Rilke too radically. I had found this a charming image of Brian until I remembered how Rilke didn't live with his wife or raise his children.

Maybe I'd been viewing his resistance too narrowly. Maybe Brian's fear of being a father was not about losing his identity as a writer. Maybe he was afraid to love another human being as profoundly as one loves a child. He was empathic in the extreme; his child's worries, his child's trials, would be Brian's, millisecond by millisecond. It would be as if they shared a central nervous system. Such a symbiotic existence sounded almost unbearable, even to me. Maybe he was accepting himself for who he was, someone with finite limits in the realm of human attachment.

Brian had once told me about a dream in which he'd dug a moat around his house in order to protect his "fallen self." Good luck constructing a moat, I thought, big enough to protect you from this delicate, microscopic nervous system already under way.

* * *

After the 3 a.m. change of shift in the NICU, things got very, very quiet. Even the machines dozed. The baby made her high-pitched, barely audible squeaks. I believed I could recognize that singular sound from a million squeaks. As much as I enjoyed the more subdued hours in the NICU, it was also the time of night when the truth of the place grew loudest. Embedded in the soft purr of the distant generators, the muted thud of the nurses' rubber soles against the floor, the doctors' whispered instructions, the occasional blaring alarm, was this: your child could die.

Looking around that room, it was easy to list grievances with God: for-profit health care to the suffering of innocents, fluorescent light, the suffering of innocents, plastic footwear, the suffering of innocents, the suffering of innocents, the suffering of innocents.

When I could no longer hold my eyes open, I walked across the hall to the strange, skinny room I'd been assigned to sleep in. It was a cast-off room, oddly oblong, closet-sized, and off the grid; it wasn't nearly big enough to be a lobby or a lounge. It held just one narrow plastic couch and a single chair. I suspected this was the room where they took parents to deliver bad news. The worst news. I resolved to spend as little time there as possible, so as not to tempt fate.

The next morning the residents rounded through, a flock of uncertain birds clad in white, peering at my girl as if she was a mathematical problem they were tasked with solving. But not one of them could figure out why her red cells wouldn't hold together. This was "the Red Team," the group of doctors in training assigned to us, for whom I felt an immediate and irrational allegiance. "Go Red Team!" I semi-shouted when I saw them later in the day. One of them gave me a *what's-with-you* look; the rest kept on scribbling on their identical pads. *No jokes in NICU.* Write that down. *Nothing is funny here.*

* * *

Maybe if I'd been more patient, Brian would have figured things out. But pregnancy has a way of forcing the point, and I was getting more pregnant by the sliver of each second. One night after dinner I said, "I think I should go home."

"You mean to California?" Brian said. He sounded half panicked, half relieved. I had only meant downtown, to Twelfth Street. But he had a point. Why was I still in New York if his mind wasn't changing?

I would return to my apartment as a first step, a pause to give Brian a chance to turn this immense boat around in the water. And if he didn't, then California.

On the subway back down to my apartment, I took stock of my resources: I could rent out my apartment for a lot more than the mortgage, plus my dad's mom, bless her, had recently begun to gift money annually to each grandchild. Between grandmother money and Twelfth Street rent, I could patch things together in California without working for a time. Especially if my mom were willing to give me a deal on her studio. Which she would, of course she would. I'd be OK until the baby was born and Brian began to pay child support, if it came to that. I knew for certain that, no matter who we became to each other, he'd take full financial responsibility. So I could do it. I could go back to California. Only I didn't want to.

When I arrived on Twelfth Street, I looked east toward Sixth Avenue and west toward Seventh, beautiful, marbly prewar architecture in both directions. Brian had once told me that after we met, every time he stepped onto this block he thought of the song "On the Street Where You Live." *For there's nowhere else on earth that I'd rather be . . .*

My apartment smelled empty and stale, a cardboard box thinning in hot attic air. It had sagged into a funk of neglect. I opened all the windows and lay down on my bed. The cover was white crinkly fabric, very slippery. I'd once thought this duvet made my entire apartment more stylish. Now I could see its total impracticality; a baby would slide right off. I turned my head into the soft gauze and cried over the stupidity of my former self for buying such an item, the stupidity of my present self for continuing to care what my apartment looked or smelled like, and the stupidity of my future self for the myriad fuckups she doubtless had in store.

I tried to reverse the tide. I was not just a pregnant person whose partner wanted no part of her; I was other things. I was the daughter of an uber-caring mother. Beloved friend of a handful of warm, funny people. Someone who, at twenty, had lived in a Nepali village for three months, the only foreigner for fifty miles. I had two master's degrees. Count them, two!

I was a performer who'd trained in physical theater and improvisation for ten years. I had stood up on an empty stage, many times, without a script or a plan and made theater out of my imagination and an agile body, presto. I wasn't afraid to do that. In fact, it brought me joy.

But this—mothering alone—I was not made for this.

I cried until I ran out of energy, then got up and poured myself a glass of water. There was nothing in the fridge but a moldy lemon and a jug of apple juice with yellowish film on top.

I suppressed a wave of nausea and tried not to turn on the computer. If I didn't check, there was a chance that an email from Brian was waiting, saying, *I'm sorry, I'm in a cab, I'll be there in five minutes.* If I did check, the chance was nil.

My in-box held two notes from Suzi: One said, *Eat fruit first, then an egg.* The other, *Try not to be sad, Heath. Think about the wiggler. The wiggler deserves to have a good day.* There was a short note from my dad: *Take good care of yourself, kiddo. And take good care of my kiddo's kiddo.* There was an offer from a local theater inviting me to perform in the spring.

In the spring I would likely be the sole parent of an infant; could such a person perform?

I wrote Brian an email saying, *I'm sorry we can't seem to understand each other.* And deleted it. I wrote him another: *What an asshole you've turned out to be.* And deleted it. I wrote him a third: *Art and parenthood aren't enemies. Duh.* And deleted it. The fourth note said, *Sonogram is scheduled for Wednesday, if you want to come.* I sent it.

He called me. "I can't do the sonogram with you; that doesn't feel right. But I'd like to know how you are feeling."

"How superkind and amazing of you to ask," I said. "I am FANTASTIC. These have been the best few fucking weeks of my entire life, you phenomenal asshole."

Stunned silence. We didn't fight like this. We fought calm; we fought grown-up. We fought in full, well-punctuated sentences without obscenities.

"Did you hear me?" I said. "You are a PHENOMENAL ASSHOLE. You excel at being one. You have found your calling. Maybe being an asshole and a writer at the same time will be easier than being a writer and a father."

More silence.

I was in misery. And Brian was in misery. And there was no way for either of us to make the other one less miserable.

On a cellular level it felt like a minor sin, a venal sin, to call the father of your child an asshole.

The fact that I'd never witnessed Brian behaving like an asshole made it even worse. He was, in fact, an anti-asshole. The only man left in America to hold doors, cede the conversational right of way, wish everyone he knew a happy birthday, ask after your aunt. Seriously, he asked after aunts.

In the weeks when we were first dating, he'd occasionally need to adjust our plans so that he could visit Simone, an elderly woman he worked with at *Dissent* magazine and cared for deeply. When Simone was dying, Brian went to see her in the hospital every afternoon. Not in a showy "Hey, look at my act of charity" way. He didn't experience it as an act of charity; he just wanted to be there, with Simone, as much as he could be, before she was gone. If he was an asshole, it was only to me. I was in a state of cognitive dissonance so complete I could not speak.

I hung up.

* * *

I spent my second NICU night in the skinny room adjacent to the nursery, awake, holding my cell phone. I wanted to call Brian. Or rather, I didn't want to want to call Brian. But, more than that, I wanted to call Brian. It was midnight in California, 3 a.m. in New York. He'd called me shortly after I'd delivered; he knew the baby was a girl, but he didn't yet know we'd been transferred or why. Brian answered fully awake, as if he'd also been sitting with the phone in his hand for the sixty or seventy hours since we last spoke. I told him about the transfer to UCSF Med Center, the little hose in her torso, the (as yet unused) blood-cleaning machine, the doctors' inability to understand why her red cells lacked stability, and how she seemed mostly undisturbed by it all.

"She barely weighs five pounds," I said, "and that includes her central line."

"Central line?" I could hear the soft pencil scratch as he wrote this down. Brian, in doubt, taking notes. It was what he knew how to do: externalize worry into symbols and syllables. He said, "Will you call again in a few hours? Or can I call you?" I was relieved to hear his fear for the baby but also a little disgusted. He'd be waiting for my call? If I were him, I would get on a plane. But he was him, slow mover, deliberative decider, a man afraid of life beyond the moat.

In the few minutes before sleep overtook me on the plastic couch I tried to assimilate what was happening. I was with my daughter in the Intensive Care Unit for neonates at the University of California San Francisco Medical Center. She'd crossed the Golden Gate Bridge in an ambulance. She was small enough to fit into a handbag; how could you fit an entire soul into something smaller than a handbag? I was, for now, a single mom. I was living on cafeteria food, leaking milk through my nursing bra onto my shirts, I couldn't decide what to name her, Amelia or Grace. I was a disheveled waffler. *Misery Day Parade*, by all means.

But what leapt to the surface of my consciousness before sleep was her face. *Holy infant so tender and mild.* Thinking of her, I was sick with worry, alone and lonely for her dad. I was scared. But I also felt an intrinsic happiness. She had made it into the world and—though she might not cure plaguing diseases or quell the rage of nations—the world was a better place for her presence.

* * *

I went alone to my sonogram and listened to a lush galloping sound, the rush of blood, thrumming and syncopated, that is the human heartbeat. The technician showed me the moonscape of my uterus, where, nestled against the curve, a rambunctious, pixilated alien bobbed. Hello, little alien, welcome to earth.

She asked, "Do you want me to print this out for your husband to see?"

After our fight on the phone, days had floated past without contact. And then one night there was a message from Brian, asking to talk. He was calling from nearby. I called him back, buzzed him up. Walking down the hall, he looked like Brian, only worn and whippet thin. His face, always pale, was pinched and gaunt. Seeing that he'd lost weight, that he couldn't sustain the rhythms of daily life, satisfied me. At least he was suffering. But he was suffering from a great distance. When he drew closer I started to cry.

Stop, I commanded myself. *Have a little dignity, show a little pride, fuck him!* But the tears appeared at the same rate as I brushed them away.

"This is not what I want," he said. "I wish that it were."

I wanted to kill him, on the spot, not for his decision, which I disbelieved and rejected, but for the formality of his grammar, *I wish that it were.* Who the fuck did he think he was? The blameless hero of a Henry James novel?

At the same time that I was in a rage at him—and couldn't express anything toward him except a biting anger—I pitied him. I knew for certain that, in the long run, I would be happy. But for Brian it would never be OK. He could never live happily, having failed to parent his child.

"I don't want this," Brian said. "I am not able to give you what you want."

Sitting between us on the couch was my purse; inside was the sonogram photo of the baby, taken by the technician who thought I had a husband. She'd been delighted by the baby's energetic swimming; "Such active guy!" she'd said, in a thick eastern European accent.

I put a hand in my purse and felt around for the sonogram. I was waiting for the right moment. This was my trump card. I actually believed the baby looked like Brian. It certainly had a long sloping forehead like his. Maybe that was a signature feature of all fetuses, but I believed the baby looked like Brian because it was Brian's. If he would only look at the baby, he'd want the baby. Knowing that this was ridiculous and that it reduced me to a form of begging or guerrilla tactics didn't dampen my determination. The baby he was rejecting was a theoretical baby, a faceless thought-baby, not this wiggler, not an "active guy."

Brian's eyes had followed the motion of my hand, reaching into the bag. "Thank you," he said, "I should take my keys."

I looked up at him. Keys? What did keys have to do with the sonogram?

Then it sank in. Did he think I would break into his apartment? Light his computer on fire? Toss the latest draft of his novel out the window and watch the pages flutter down twenty-six floors to Amsterdam Avenue?

Would I?

I could certainly picture myself throwing his keys out the window, a casual, underhanded toss. With any luck they would land in the rain grate, wash out to sea. Or lie on the street, waiting for a stranger to pick them up; a nefarious stranger with warped intentions. He'd never know who. Nothing would drive him crazier than having a set of his keys loose in the world. He was key neurotic. It unnerved him to lose anything, but especially a key.

I lifted my hand toward the window. But I was too exhausted for the high dramatic gesture. Instead, I dropped the keys into the palm of his hand without touching him.

"Thank you," he said. His voice was cold and formal; he seemed to resent me for putting him in the position to hurt me. I'd made him choose between his own well-being and someone else's.

Brian stood up. "I should go." We lingered at the door. I had no idea when I'd see him again. Did we kiss? I can't remember. He left. I closed the door and locked it. In my bedroom I slid under the slippery white duvet, quiet. A bird was perched on the wrought-iron railing of the fire escape, twittering out a Morse code of undecipherable glee. "Shut up," I said.

My upstairs neighbor called from her balcony, "Are you talking to me?"

"Jane," I said. "No! I was talking to that crazy bird."

"What bird?" she called back. "Want dinner?"

I could smell marinated meat grilling on her hibachi. I knew that if I walked upstairs, Jane would feed me. She was a born feeder of the friendless, a hospice nurse, a maker of handcrafted cards, a pioneer in the movement to destigmatize AIDS, a person who appeared with wildflowers from upstate just when you needed them most. If I caught her up on my plight, she would cluck and tut and truly care, and serve me everything in her fridge. She was an older woman with cobalt eyes, and no children, who gave her maternal love to all. Could I be that? No, too selfish. I wanted one person to devote myself to, or three. I wanted my own tribe. I was feudal at heart.

"Thanks, Jane," I said, "I'm good."

"You don't sound good," she called back. "You sound rotten. Come eat meat."

I got up and quietly shut the window.

After about an hour, for no reason I could identify, I went out into the hall. I wasn't going upstairs to Jane's; I was just . . . going to the hall. Brian was sitting on the wide marble landing. I sat down beside him. The anger had drained out of the moment; we'd surprised each other out of it. After a while he said, "How did you know I was out here?"

"I didn't know I knew," I said.

If we sit here long enough, I thought, things will shift. We'll recognize that we're birds magnetized to the same pole. The pinging pole within me. But sitting on the steps of my landing, side by side in silence, we were the exact same people we'd been an hour ago. After ten minutes or so Brian stood up. "OK," he said. And he left. He walked down the stairs, through the lobby, out onto Twelfth Street, and over to Sixth Avenue, where he turned north, and away.

I woke up the next day knowing I would go back to California, to the studio next door to my mom's house. I needed my mom, like it or not. I was embarrassed to be a highly educated, unpartnered mother, but I was also hugely lucky to have support, on any coast, and it was time to move toward it. It meant accepting Brian's no; it meant flying away from the father of this apple seed; it meant facing reality. But the alternative was to moon around Manhattan in pursuit of a phantom figure who, however much he might love me, did not want what I wanted. At least he'd given me the gift of an unambiguous answer.

* * *

At 6:30 every morning in the NICU, our team, the Red Team, rounded through; discussing the baby, ignoring me. By our fourth day, I was determined to insinuate myself into their private conversation.

"Her bili is down, that's good," said one.

"But her crit has dropped too," said another.

I wanted to ask them to slow down, repeat, wait, how do you spell that? But their talk was like Philip Glass music, filled with repetitive, incomprehensible sounds, unstoppable and forward marching. Even when I asked, they seemed not to hear. They had eager, scrubbed faces and kept looking at the attending physician for validation. Did they know what the hell they were doing? The attending was calm, patient, a good teacher. But there was a room full of sick babies here, and she had to keep moving.

"Keep an eye on the crit, run it again in three hours," she said. In my notebook I scribbled, "Crit low (bad), bili low (good)," hoping this would make sense later.

That night a new nurse came on duty. She wasn't part of the usual crew and nothing like my Irish favorite. She introduced herself by saying, "These babies are so pissed off, that's why they're crying all the time." I moved the baby's box a few inches away from her.

She cracked open a small can of apple juice with vengeful force and drank it in one gulp, saying, "I need to hydrate." Were her hands shaking? When she stumbled on the edge of a rubber floor mat and muttered, "Fuck this place," it was so quiet I couldn't be sure that's what she said. And so what if she did? Could I report her for swearing? To whom? She kept encouraging me to go to bed.

If she were a cartoon character, I thought, she'd be surrounded by a visible force field of lightning bolts. In real life, she was a well-groomed brunette with razor creases in the sleeves of her uniform—evil wearing over-pressed cotton. I was aware that my impressions of her were likely exaggerated by a lack of sleep, maternal terror, and an all-vending-machine diet. That I might be using her as a totem, a repository for my rapidly iterating fears. But still, there was no way I was going to bed. I would not leave my baby under the care of a woman who interpreted the cries of the NICU as proof that the newborns sheltered here were "pissed off" rather than disoriented, fighting for their lives, or lonely for their mothers.

I pulled a rocker beside the baby's incubator. I could sleep there. There were limits to how long I was permitted to hold her, how long she was allowed out of her box, but because I was a nursing mother, technically I couldn't be kicked off the unit. I was dozing in the chair, struggling to stay conscious enough to notice if the wacko nurse was pinching any nearby babies, when she touched my shoulder. "I ran another crit, and it's not good." *Crit*, I'd discovered, is hospital slang for *hematocrit*—the baby's red cell count was dropping again.

"How low?" I asked. No answer. In my experience, if you don't get a factual answer to a direct question in the hospital, it means the facts are so unpleasant the staff doesn't want to say them out loud.

I repeated my question, "How low is her count?"

"Low enough that she needs blood."

"What does that mean?" I asked.

"It means we need to get in."

"In where?" *Into* the baby, of course. I immediately regretted asking.

In medical vernacular, accessing the vein with an IV is "getting in." The baby's low red cell count meant many other things. But to that nurse, on that shift, the primary thing it meant was that she had to thread a needle into a very, very thin vein. Placing an IV into a severely anemic five-pound infant is an art spun out of skill, luck, confidence, and faith. If only we'd left that rubber hose in her belly button; it had been removed just the day before. No central line. No obvious way *in*.

4

MY MOM AND MY BEST CHILDHOOD FRIEND, CASSIE, MET ME at the airport. Cassie had found a sublet for me in Berkeley until my mom could persuade her tenant to move out and let me have the studio. The sublet was a concrete loft, cold, dusty, but available immediately. Cassie had swept the floor, bought flowers, stocked food: roasted almonds, eggs, rice cakes, milk, juice, chocolate, and fruit (so much fruit, in a giant blue bowl). Under the flowers she'd left a note, "*Nothing thicker than a knife's blade separates happiness from melancholy.* Virginia Woolf." After the quote, she'd added, in her tiny, precise script formed with authority, "And vice versa."

I put the note in my wallet and zipped it closed. Cassie. My mom. Suzi. Maybe I would be OK.

I got into bed and picked up the only book that looked remotely readable, *The Hobbit*. I tried to focus on poor Bilbo's plight. I imagined myself ensconced in a hobbit house with a round blue door, not pregnant, not miserable, not even human. Sign me up. I'd be a microbe. Anything but what I was, 2,904 miles away from Brian.

I dreamt in fitful sequences, a string of thwarted activities—running in snow with no sense of direction, no destination. And then a baby, my baby, born healthy with a vigorous cry and pinkish skin, perfect in every regard except that when you held her up to the light you could see right through her. She was translucent and fragile, nothing more than a sheet of vellum.

If a baby is the unfathomable concoction of two people, what happens when one of those two, upon discovering a baby is under way, changes his mind? I was physiologically bewildered; carrying around, in my body, the genetic material of someone who had said no to fatherhood. Meanwhile his genes and my genes were sketching the blueprint of a person. If I was constructing a human out of a reluctant set of building blocks, with genes that lay themselves out with reservations and regret, in sequential order, step by step, but under duress, what then?

* * *

The nurse, drinking yet another can of apple juice, said, "I'll just call another nurse to hold the baby."

"I'll hold her."

"It's better if another nurse holds."

"No thank you."

First she tried to place the IV in the baby's hand, poking in multiple places without success. My job was to keep the baby's body completely still as the needle searched the vein. Every time she was punctured, the baby howled a new howl I'd never heard before. She'd been alive less than a week and was rapidly expanding her repertoire of sounds for pain.

After twenty minutes of jabbing various locations with sweaty determination and what I feared was the slimmest hint of enjoyment, the nurse reluctantly gave up and said she would call the pediatric IV team. The team? The TEAM! There was a fucking TEAM? Somewhere in this hospital was a *team* of people specifically trained to place IVs into children, and she'd just spent twenty minutes pincushioning her? Later I learned that hospital policy allows only two "sticks" per nurse. It is commonly understood that if you don't get in quickly, the building tension and anxiety hinder further attempts. Two sticks, and you're out. But I didn't know that yet.

When the IV team arrived, they were "in" within minutes.

The blood was ordered from the blood bank. "Make sure the blood is washed and irradiated," the resident on duty said. I wrote down, "Blood 2B washed and irradiated," again with no idea what it meant and no energy to ask.

"They know what they're doing," my mom had said the day before. "They are keeping all these babies alive."

The washed blood arrived, was hung, and began to flow into my girl. She'd been pale, but after a few hours she pinked up. My favorite Irish nurse, now back on duty, came to check on us. "They are running it slow, so as not to overwhelm her heart," she said. I liked this: *her* heart, not *the* heart. She was, I realized, even younger than I'd thought. Maybe twenty-two, twenty-three? Surely she didn't have kids, but she had a fantastically wide smile. Warm, genuine, with dimples. I was so grateful to her and so unsure of everything that I wanted to take her hand. I wanted to ask her to take mine too, while I held the baby's hand. In some alternate universe, maybe this was possible. We could sit in a circle, holding hands— she and I and the baby—and that would constitute healing.

In this universe, the best I could hope for was a chance, later, to thank her. In the notebook: "cookies 4 irish nurse."

* * *

On the night my labor began, I was living with my little sidecar, as yet unnamed, and my mother's dog, Lulu, in a studio (formerly the garage) beside the house I grew up in, on an acre of land my mom had bought for $70,000 in 1977 in San Anselmo, a small town at the center of Marin County. This was not the Marin of my youth. It had lost (almost all) of the funky cottages with flaking pastel paint and the hippies playing Hacky Sack in front of the health food store. It had succumbed to the abrading effects of money, chiefly: overly landscaped yards and overly sculpted people. But it was still Marin, rolling gold hills and eucalyptus trees and Lake Lagunitas. It was home and thus where I hoped to give birth.

By the time my labor began, I had adopted, publicly, the identity of plucky single mom but fell asleep most nights sobbing, wondering what Brian was doing. Was he washing his dishes? If so, his head would be propped against the cabinets above his sink, an oddly restive, thoughtful posture. As though, while washing, he was also working out a new social order. Was he wondering when he would meet his child?

None of this was as I'd planned. I had planned to be one of those pregnant women in baggy overalls with sinewy arms. Movie star pregnant. The fact that I was not movie star anything in ordinary life had no effect on my movie star pregnancy plans: I would bound around Manhattan doing yoga with my tidy fetus tucked into a discreet ball, eating organic. The father of my unborn child would beam as he rubbed coconut lotion on my belly.

Instead, I'd spent my final two trimesters alone, unless you counted Lulu (which I did). She had been a loyal stand-in for human companionship; another body in the bed when I needed one most. A body without demands, complications, or agenda. Lulu the Wonder Dog I called her. She, the fetus, and I spent each night as three creatures in a tight curl of sleep. But Lulu, for all her charms, was never going to rub coconut lotion on any part of me. That was a job for a man who, at the moment I entered labor, was almost certainly barricaded in his Upper West Side cubbyhole. I imagined him with his hands clamped over his ears, chanting *banana, banana, banana* as we had in third grade, to drown out the sound of anything we didn't want to hear.

I lay in bed, in the dark, with a bright band of tension around my midsection, ambivalating. I hadn't spoken to Brian in three months, maybe four. I could sense the phone on the nightstand, alive. Shouldn't I hear his voice before undertaking an event that would link us, backward and forward, through all time?

He didn't deserve to know, but I wanted him to know. And what about the baby, didn't she deserve to have her father know? I dialed from memory. He didn't sound surprised to hear my voice. "I'm in labor," I said, then went mute. There was nothing more to say, nothing more important or clarifying I could add. Brian went silent as well. This was at least one definition of misery. Silence on the phone.

"I think I better get off," I said.

"OK." Long, long pause. "I love you."

I think he said this. Memory is fluid and shape-shifts to our desires. But still, I think he said this.

I remember trying to suppress the hope that he might knock on the door.

When I tried to get up, Lulu pressed a paw on my chest and came in close for a nuzzle. I expected something more Lassie-like, a heroic leap through the skylight into my mom's house to rouse the masses. But she was more committed to preserving the status quo than saving the day. I heaved her off me and made my way next door.

Evan, the older of my two teenage brothers from my mom's second marriage, was up watching *Law and Order* reruns. He is sixteen years younger than I am, and we have a half-sibling, half-parental relationship. I asked him to go upstairs and wake our mom. "Go wake her yourself," he said, with the dismissive air of a nobleman waving away a peon.

"I'm in labor, Evan," I said.

For once, he had no ironic reply. At last, something to trump adolescent insolence: labor! He stood up, clicked off the TV, and shot upstairs.

My mom took one look at me and said, "Let's call the doctor," as though it would be fun, like ordering Thai food.

The doctor was unmoved to hear my contractions were seven, sometimes five minutes apart and very regular. "Don't rush," she said. "This is a first baby. You're in for a long haul." So we lingered. When we called again around midday, she said, "Stay on your side of the bay until seven tonight; otherwise you'll hit traffic on the bridge."

I was panting and grim faced. When I relayed the message, my mom, whose strong suit has never been obeying authority figures, said, "She obviously doesn't know what the hell she's talking about. We're leaving."

My mom and Cassie (who'd arrived, as usual, at the precise moment she was needed most) half-dragged, half-carried me out the door. "I can do it," I said. "Let go." It hurt to be touched, to move. It also hurt to hold still. As soon as they let go, I sank down on all fours. Four-point locomotion, there was no other way I would reach the car. My mom and Cassie dropped down on either side of me. We were doing this ridiculous dance as a team, three abreast. "Sweetie," my mom whisper-shouted, "a little faster!" Her voice had the urgency of a woman determined not to deliver her first grandchild in the driveway.

Between the studio doorway and the car lay a little Japanese path of pebbles and paving stones, which I'd always thought of as a tranquil transitional space. So wrong. When you are crawling on your hands and knees, nine months pregnant and perhaps fully dilated, *pebbles* is a cruel euphemism for *gravel*. "Someday you will laugh about this!" my mom said. "Maybe even tomorrow," Cassie added. "Fuck off," I said, to neither, or both.

I tried to remind myself of Mary in search of a manger or, worse, her wretched, weak-kneed mule. I felt for the mule! The mule had it hard. All I had to do was make it to the Volvo. And then to the nearest hospital, Marin General, which was legally bound to take us in.

"You can do this," my mom enthused. "We're almost there." A benevolent lie. The car was as far as Fairbanks, Mongolia, the moon. I'd still be crawling toward it when the baby applied to college.

When we arrived at the hospital, we were greeted at the ER doors with a wheelchair. I grunted and made faces and waved my arms about, and somehow the staff understood that I needed a gurney, not a chair. The gurney guy, whose name turned out to be succinctly, perfectly, Ted, wheeled me into an elevator and pushed the button for the maternity floor.

In the elevator I regained speech. "Ted, hello! Ted, listen! Ted! I have to PUSH."

"Don't push," Ted said. "Please don't push."

I was amazed at his confidence in me. He thought pushing was an elective activity.

To Ted's and my astonishment, I didn't deliver in the elevator. On the maternity floor, a small fleet of nurses and one midwife gathered around the spectacle: an off-the-street admission dilated to ten centimeters, fully effaced. The midwife had long silver braids; she stood ready at the end of the gurney, saying a few things I didn't catch. My mom took my hand, and said, "She says you are tearing; try not to push." Cassie held one foot with steady pressure. Every electron, every proton, not only of my body but of the gurney, the room, the hallway, the elevator shaft, indeed every electron and proton in Marin County with its show-offy hills, its serrated coastline sliding under the Golden Gate, the clouds above Marin, its undersea ledge—*all of it* shouted: PUSH.

My mom leaned in, "She's going to cut you, so you won't tear."

"Just do it!" I panted or screamed or maybe only said in my head. I saw a glint, a flicker of metal pass between my knees, and then a person shot into the room. Time of birth, 6:54 p.m.

My mom stared at her, looking for the penis. Maybe because we'd all secretly wanted a girl (it seemed so much easier to imagine raising a girl as a single mom), we'd hedged against disappointment by believing I was carrying a boy. Plus I'd dreamt it was a boy. Several sage-ish women had confirmed this. When the baby materialized, penisless, we were disbelievers.

"It's a girl," the midwife said again. A true girl. A brand-new girl. A girl totaling five pounds, five ounces. A healthy baby girl. The midwife lifted her to my face, and I touched her cheek, slick with wax and blood. She was not crying; her clouded blue-brown eyes were open, as yet uncomprehending, but open. We looked at each other. *Hi.* My heart leapt and sang and did an Irish jig.

* * *

Two days after the baby's first blood transfusion the Red Team decided we could go home. They still had no idea why the baby couldn't "hold her numbers," but they had stabilized her. She had enough blood to last for a few weeks and they hoped that, whatever her red cell problem was, it would fix itself. Plus they were tired of looking at each other with blank faces every morning at our bedside.

The blond doctor said, "I'm referring you to an excellent hematologist here at UCSF. It's quite possible your daughter will require another blood transfusion soon, but for now she's stable and she's taking up space." I wasn't sure whether to be horrified or relieved that we were leaving without a diagnosis. It was like a fable without a moral lesson. But I didn't argue.

At last I got to dress her in the outfit I'd bought months before, a white sack with small rosebuds around the collar and a matching hat. She was so petite the dress nearly swallowed her, but she was in store-bought clothes, a massive improvement over hospital issue.

When my mom saw the baby in her own clothes, she burst into tears. "She somehow seems more real," she said.

I knew what she meant. Stripped of the arm band and ID bracelets, the myriad wires leading to multiple monitors, the baby at last looked less like a subject in an experiment on pain and more like what she was: a week-old infant on her way home.

My mom and I rode the elevator down to the lobby in a giddy state, cracking jokes about getting away before they could change their minds.

Outside I was surprised to find weather. I'd forgotten about weather. San Francisco was draped in its famous fog. I kneeled, shivering, in the backseat of the car, trying to install the car seat, while my mom waited with the baby in the lobby. On one side of the seat was a small color-coded dial with a needle, which indicated if the seat's angle was safe; green was good; red bad. I put us squarely into green, but the steep hills complicated the whole procedure. As my mother drove, I sat in back, frantically adjusting the knob. This was a crash course in baby safety and also in the irrational fears that were now going to trail me, a collection of cans clanging at my heels.

If I had glimpsed the horror that lay ahead for this girl, I would have wanted to jump out of the car. But I couldn't see anything, except the baby as she was now, head tossed back, sleeping, listening.

What I had to give her included my useless, cyclical worry. True. But also joy. Happiness—slippery, mobile, sneaky, and spry—enters the most unlikely rooms, unbidden. It can sneak up on you nearly anywhere and likewise wisp away. She was alive; she was wearing her soft cotton clothes, her rosebud hat, breathing in the car in the dark as a light rain touched everything with what e.e. cummings once described as "such small hands."

SAN ANSELMO

5

Arriving back at the studio in the dark in the rain, with the baby asleep in her carrier, felt miraculous. Ten days before, I had crawled on my hands and knees out this door as, more or less, one person. Now two of us passed back through. It was a dove-from-a-hat act; the world's greatest magic trick.

I looked around the room. In the corner was the rocker I'd hoped to whitewash before going into labor. It was a hideous pool-floor blue, but it rocked. In my arms now, the baby was sleeping. My girl, Gracie. I had settled on a name, splitting the difference and hyphenating Amelia-Grace. I crept over to the bassinet and poured her down in the careful choreography that kept her asleep, head, shoulders, torso, legs, tiny feet, lowering her into gravity. Her bones, leaving my hands, were a set of fragile sticks.

I sat down in the rocker and tried to take in our good luck. The baby was OK, and we were home. Lulu was sniffing circles around the bassinet, sniffing the baby's carrier, sniffing the baby's stuff. It was an olfactory feast; a new creature to profile in her scent catalog.

"Lulu," I said, "she's a girl like you. Can you believe it?" Maybe Lulu knew this before I did. Maybe dogs could detect gender in utero? I gave her a dog treat. "Why didn't you warn me, wonder dog?" She looked up with her concerned eyebrows, her open-mouthed smile.

My mom came over with dinner, arms overfull with roasted veggies from Whole Foods, a steak ("The baby needs you to eat red meat," she'd said), and an entire chocolate cake. We clattered around the kitchen as the baby slept. The doorbell rang as we were eating, flower delivery from my dad and his wife. A huge bouquet of white lilies and a note: "Welcome home, Baby Grace." I held one blossom to her nose. "Smell what your grandfather sent," I said. But on she slept.

After dinner my brothers, Evan and Dylan, showed up, bearing gifts. They are almost a generation younger than I am; my mom had me at twenty-one and then had Evan at thirty-seven and Dylan at forty. They came in shouting at each other, punching arms, half wrestling, a couple of self-appointed, badly behaved Magi.

Dylan shouted, "Evan, shut up, the baby is sleeping."

"You shut up, Dyl," Evan replied. "I'm mad ninja quiet." He mimed tiptoeing. The baby still slept.

Dylan was carrying the oddest-shaped gift; it looked like a small, crooked man in a padded suit. "I brought her something," he said. "What do you call her, Amelia or Grace?"

"I don't know yet," I said.

"OK, for the baby." He handed me the gift. Dylan can make wrought-iron stairs, outstanding blackberry ice cream, an entire album of original folk music—pretty much anything. I couldn't imagine what this was. I ripped through the paper to find . . . a little hat rack. The bottom was shaped like a free-form pond, painted pink, and from that rose a sturdy white spool with lots of little pegs for her collection, already growing, of pint-sized chapeaux. I love hats, and he'd been teasing me, through the pregnancy, about how I'd impose them on the baby.

"Thanks, Dylan," I said, and tried to sound more gruff than teary. That's what my brothers liked, keep the sloppy stuff at bay.

Evan was less handy but equally devoted to being an uncle. He'd come with a gift wrapped in paper towels, tied with a rubber band.

"Nice wrapping, Evan."

"Don't mention it," he said. I unrolled a hand-sewn onesie, cut from an old T-shirt. There was a skull with a Mohawk on one side, on the other glittery letters spelled *Metallica*. This was a shirt he'd worn almost every day of high school, not because he particularly liked Metallica, but because he'd grasped, from an early age, that irony was the key to everything. It had been worn and washed and worn again so many times that the cotton was downy soft.

Evan looked down at the baby. "It's so tiny," he said, "and alive."

"You really have the gift of summary, Evan," I said.

"Dyl," Evan said, "check out its minuscule fingernails."

Dylan looked. "Cool."

As the boys talked over her, the baby didn't stir. Our discharge paperwork read, "Needs easily met," and it was true. She was easily comforted by nursing or a song. She'd wake up for a few minutes and then drift back to sleep. In the back of my mind I knew the chance that we were done with hospital life was wafer thin, but I simply refused to think about it. And that worked well.

Together, away from the hospital, we were a closed, reciprocal system of delirium and euphoria.

Each forearm was a cushion of plush velvet I could rub or kiss for hours. The only thing that alarmed me was that her body now existed outside my own. Harm could come to her without passing through me first; amateur design flaw.

Daily, hourly, Gracie and I were entranced by the essential acts of infancy; the trope, the trifecta, of babyhood: poop, sleep, eat. Repeat.

Our third day home, Cassie arrived with ginger soup, an Anne Carson book, and her wind of good cheer. After lunch she baked brownies for us (that is, for her and me since the baby would only receive brownie by-products in the milk stream). Cass and I sat in my mom's garden while Lulu ran up the hill pursuing a scent only she could smell, and the baby slept beside us. It was a gorgeous California day, light wind, puffy clouds at high altitude.

Cassie, in a red silk blouse and black jeans, was the most beautiful woman ever to sit in a California garden on an April afternoon. Not that she cared, not that she noticed. She was interested in ideas over surfaces; she always had been.

We met when we were ten, in an alternative classroom run by a daft but darling man named Bernie, a fuzzy-haired progressive educator who liked to inspire us with aphorisms ("The only way to take responsibility is to *respond* with *ability*!"). Cassie would roll her eyes at me; I'd roll my eyes back. She didn't try to embarrass Bernie; she'd respond to his suggestions respectfully. But she could think circles around him. In my view, a fifth-grade classroom was way, way too small an arena for her. She was meant for bigger things; she should be riding into battle to save the French or performing lifesaving surgery or writing a poem. Most of all, always, writing a poem.

Often, when I looked over, she'd be staring out the window, eyes darting or peering searchingly up at the ceiling. She was the quiet girl at the back of the class, thinking clear, deep thoughts everyone wanted to know but only a lucky few, like me, got to hear.

After school we'd walk across the street to Cassie's house, empty of parents, and pray to the Great Horse God, asking her to grant us Appaloosas, Palominos, Pintos, Mustangs, any creature with a shiny coat capable of a dead gallop. We wanted to have horses, ride horses, know horses, breathe horses, trade horses, sing horses, love horses, *be* horses.

Looking at Cassie twenty-five years later, I realized that she'd gotten our wish. She possessed the sprung, flexible energy of a lithe animal on the verge of taking flight. And such was her spirit of generosity that, beside her, you felt infused with the same set of live possibilities. Lumpen perinatal blob though you might be, next to Cassie you felt perkier, more artful. As if she might unscrew her long, articulate arms and offer them to you.

"Hey," Cassie said, "are you in there?" She was holding the baby, smiling at her, but talking to me.

"I was just thinking," I said, "that you'd probably lend me your arms if I asked."

"Only," she said, "if you promised to conduct a symphony with them." She picked up a brownie, took a bite, and handed it to me. "I've always wanted to conduct a symphony." I took a bite and handed it back. It was gooey at the center. We'd pass it back and forth until it was nothing but a crumb, and then one of us would bite the crumb in half and pass it back. This was what we did best, share. She took another bite, handed it back. A tiny piece fell off and landed on the baby's forehead. It looked like a *tika*, the mark worn by Hindus to indicate the location of the third eye. Thusly blessed by brownie, the baby slept on.

"How is she?" Cassie said. She was looking at Gracie so intently I had the feeling she might spontaneously diagnose her. Mystery illness solved.

"She looks OK, is she OK?"

"I'm not sure," I said.

"Well, she's got a certain something," Cassie said, "a definite certain something."

A handsome, sexy god in our high school had once said this to Cassie, "You've got a certain something." We'd been pretty sure he didn't know her name, and he definitely didn't have the vocabulary with which to describe her presence, falling, as it did, outside the high school box. But he knew she was unique, of note. Entirely original. At the time, we'd filed it under pathetic, backhanded compliment. Now, it was our highest form of praise.

"All babies have a certain something," I said.

"Maybe," Cass said, "but she's the somethingest of them all."

After Cassie left, the baby and I crawled up to the studio's loft and fell asleep instantly. New motherhood strips you down to the studs. Almost everything I enjoyed doing in the evenings, pre-baby, like reading books or writing emails or watching *CSI* or walking to the park, was now an irrelevant luxury. All I needed in this refashioned life were brownies and baby and sleep.

Through those early days, my mom was a pillar of motherliness. She did laundry, cooked meals, took out the trash, held the baby while I showered, and wiped the glop I hadn't noticed from my face and clothes. My friends Suzi and David (her college boyfriend, now husband) camped on our couch so that they could keep me company at 3 a.m. Suzi would lie beside me in the loft in the wee hours. "Fall back asleep, Heath. I'll make sure she doesn't roll off the bed." Even Evan and Dylan were useful. Every time the baby cried, one of them would shout over from the main house, "Help her!" And if she didn't stop crying instantly, they'd appear at my door, indignant on the baby's behalf.

Everyone chipped in, everyone doted. But at the end of the day, I was on my own. I didn't have to work, and I had enough of every necessity. And yet life with the baby seemed impossibly complex.

Just getting up to bed had become a comical ordeal. The studio had a sleep loft, reachable only by a built-in wooden ladder, angled at a sharp rake. Ascending the ladder, using one hand to clutch the baby to my chest and the other to grab for incrementally higher rungs, was a physical joke. At night, once I'd gotten up to the loft, I was loath to come down again. Did I bring the baby with me, fumbling in the dark? Leave her in the loft alone? She couldn't possibly wiggle off the bed and over the edge of the loft, right? It was impossible! It couldn't be done! And then the infant who had not yet learned to burp strikes a match and burns the house down.

Parenting, I discovered, invokes questions you never thought to ask: Are you willing to leave the baby to her peril, even imaginary peril, if you have to pee? What if you have to pee *really badly*? Will you pee in a cup, in a loft, in the dark? What do you do with said cup? How self-sacrificing are you willing to be? Define *peril*. Define *imaginary*.

Bit by bit, these questions hammer at your sense of self.

Finally, my mom said, "Just put the baby's bassinet up in the loft," and it seemed reasonable to assume that, unless the baby could defy the laws of physics, she would be safe in her bassinet while I went down to the bathroom. But the dilemma of conflicting needs had only just begun. If the phone was ringing, and the stir-fry was burning, and Lulu was barking to be let out, and my pants were sliding off, and the baby was crying—where to start? The baby, of course the baby, but that leaves one hand for all other competing priorities. I dubbed this dance—baby in the left hand, everything else with the right—the one-handed life.

One-handed as I was, I didn't miss Brian. I didn't rage at Brian. For the most part, I didn't feel he owed me anything in particular, now that the baby was born, except child support. It was as if, at the moment of her birth, my shock, my fury at being left while pregnant became a relic from another era. The hurt that had passed between us was beside the point. The point was her. I hadn't forgiven him; I just didn't feel intensely much of *anything* toward him anymore. I felt intensely for the baby, and the rest of life was white noise. My one-handed life was by design. I chose this girl, squeaky girl, sleepy girl.

Still, he was psychically hovering, more than I'd expected. He would call around eight each night, and I'd give him the update. She ate! She slept! She pooped! And he was as bowled over by these achievements as I was.

We never said, "Now we'll talk every day." We never said, "I forgive you" or even "I don't forgive you." We simply fell into a pattern of contact that reassured us both and, in my imagination at least, helped to form a protective seal around Amelia-Grace. Though we didn't discuss it, I imagined Brian was living inside a titanic clash of inner tides: know the baby, love the baby, and let all hell break loose; or stay three thousand miles away. I didn't envy him. She was an irresistible force.

I told him how her hair had begun to fall out in random patches. "She's nearly bald, with this weird, Hitchcockian hairline," I said.

I described the way she loved to sleep on her back with one arm thrown over her head, her chin stuck out at a contentious angle, daring the world to dish it out. Or how she'd fall asleep while nursing, leaving one eye open, a drunk too far gone to get comfortable. He wanted to hear everything, anything.

One night, after we'd chatted for a few minutes, Brian said, "Can I talk to her?" I held the phone to the baby's ear. What was he saying? Was he whispering or just listening to the light whistle of her breath? It seemed like a private conversation. Did he apologize for missing her birth? Missing her blood transfusion? Did he recount the events of his day? I couldn't know. I didn't know. She fluttered awake, seemed to listen for a beat or two, and closed her eyes. Back to sleep.

"Why do you sleep so much?" I said.

"What?" Brian said.

"Just talking to the baby."

We paused, a semi-comfortable silence.

"She's a decent-looking baby," I said.

I knew Brian would appreciate the understatement. That was his style. When we'd been together, if we shared a mind-blowing night, the next morning he'd say something like, "I had an OK time with you."

"What's so great about her?" he said.

"Well, Cassie says she has a certain something."

"Cassie is obliged to say that. But tell me, specifically, what is so great about this so-called baby?"

"For one thing, she has fantastic breath. I could sell tickets. In fact her whole body is really outstandingly fresh; it's as if each cell has been aired out at the top of the Sierras."

"That is impressive." Long beat. "I wish I could smell her."

Get on a plane, you've heard of planes?

I stayed quiet. Because you do not run out scolding the deer that peeks from behind the bushes. You hold still. You wait. Even when the deer is acting idiotic. If I opened up my anger and impatience, this would be about me. And, more than Brian was my ex, he was Gracie's dad. My job was to make room for him, at whatever glacial pace, to know his daughter.

6

MY MOM AND I THOUGHT THAT TWENTY-ONE DAYS OF LIFE ON earth sounded auspicious, and so we were sitting in the sun, at an outdoor café, celebrating the baby's three-week birthday when the full foolishness of my pretend-the-baby-is-fine-and-eat-Salade-Niçoise plan dawned on us. Or rather, it dawned on my mom; I wasn't even thinking about the baby. I was watching a pair of toddler twins, a boy and girl, play at the edge of a nearby fountain, both of them emanating good health like gamma rays. They had the sun-burnished skin and brown-gold hair of kids who spend their days collecting seashells. Looking at them, I ached. It was nearly impossible to imagine my fragile, pasty baby transforming into this kind of bursting, cell-dividing, condensed sunlight child.

I didn't say any of this to my mom. Instead, I held up *People* magazine and pointed at a picture of Halle Berry wearing ripped jeans, flip-flops, and a white men's shirt as she pumped gas not as a mere mortal but as a demigod whose body inspired an unwavering allegiance from any object it touched. On her, the button-down shirt was impossibly sexy.

"Look how buoyant she is," I said. "Her body practically floats. How is that possible?"

"Untold hours of yoga," my mom said. "Or, an all-raw, mostly nothing diet combined with salt scrubs and Finnish saunas. Whatever it is, regular people don't have time to be buoyant. Anyway, not everything is the way it appears; I'm sure there are unseen things weighing her down."

We routinely discussed celebrities as if they were extended family members. In fact, my mom believed celebrity culture had replaced tribal affiliations.

"She lost most of the hearing in her left ear from an abusive boyfriend," I said. My mom looked at me. I'd stepped into territory she preferred to avoid. I took a bite of my salad. "Maybe," I said, "she has a team of people who pull her muscles north, south, east, west, intoning ancient chants." No response. "I'd pay a thousand dollars to see her naked," I said. "Not to touch. Just to check her out, at my leisure."

Given her incredible levitating body, Halle Berry, it went without saying, would have a gorgeous and peppy baby. Not a pasty over-sleeper.

I waited for my mom to respond, but she was looking at the baby. Really looking at her. She touched the baby's cheek and looked up at me, "I think you better take her in."

We both knew where *in* was, even though we'd barely spoken of the hospital since we'd left. I regarded the hospital like a bad acid trip: the less said afterward the better. I glanced down at the baby, at the twins circling the fountain, at Halle Berry happily filling up her car, at the baby again.

I didn't want to take her back *in*. I wanted to take her home.

My mom was emphatic. "She's so pale. And she never really wakes up."

She wasn't only pale; she was nearly see-through. Her skin was parchment thin and transparent, like an anatomy doll. Beneath her skin a tributary of veins formed intricate, lacy patterns in violet hues. I was afraid to press on her, afraid she could be breached.

I looked down at her. She was just a little comma, a small curved thing, cupping air. Her face was peaceful, her hands quiet on top of the blanket, her moist lips pushed forward in the involuntary pout of infants. Her eyelids didn't flicker or twitch. Either she wasn't dreaming, or her dream was of an unmoving landscape.

"Don't drift off," I whispered into the curve of her ear, sunny yellow with wax at the core. She didn't stir.

My mother was right; she was a girl in need of a doctor, probably several doctors. But I hesitated. I didn't want to set the medical wheels in motion. I didn't want her examined or diagnosed or written up. I wanted to finish eating the goodies of Provence (anchovies, olives, bits of seared tuna) and decoding Halle Berry's sex appeal.

I wanted to be a person dedicated to earthbound pleasures. A person from another era—my great-grandmother, born in an olive grove before email, before permanent paper trails, with nothing to verify her birth except her. She raised her children outdoors with a minimum of medical interference. They ran through the olive groves and grew strong. End of story. The only trouble with this vision was that, back then, my girl wouldn't have lived twenty-one days.

I took a last look at the bronzed twins and at Gracie, still sleeping, hands motionless. I collected the diaper bag and hoisted the baby carrier into the crook of my arm. "OK. Fine," I said, and started walking toward the car, dialing the pediatric hematologist's pager. My mom trailed after me, saying, "Let me help, let me hold that." I shrugged her off, irrationally furious.

I got the page prompt and entered my number. I had no idea that the act of paging this specialist would be replicated dozens of times over the next year, or that Marion Koerper's number, even years after it was decommissioned, would remain in my consciousness, the one number I could remember without trying.

7

WHEN DR. MARION KOERPER, RENOWNED HEMATOLOGIST, called back, she sounded like a warm, chatty grandmother, like someone who might invite you over for raspberry scones. When I told her that the baby was see-through and slept most of the day, she gave me instructions in a calm, authoritative voice: "Take her to Marin General. They can check her blood counts. I'll call in the orders. Step one is to determine if we need to transfuse her." A pause. "This must be very scary for you."

I wanted to hug her through the phone. I didn't yet know what she looked like, that she had ungovernable silver hair that flew around her face in long independent-minded strands. I didn't know she had a wide smile populated by a band of unruly teeth. I only knew the sound of her voice made me want to curl up in her lap and sleep.

Eventually, I came to know that she'd wanted to be a doctor from the age of six, that she had two sons, both in medical school, that her husband was also a doctor. That she'd been raised in the Midwest, loved ice-skating, and didn't consider herself dressed without medium heels and panty hose. That she treated the nurses with respect, always, even in private.

And she came to know that I was on my own with my daughter, that I had feelings, of one kind or another, for the father, who lived in New

York. That I lived in a studio beside my mother's house, together with a dog whose white and black hairs clung to the baby's clothes, despite my occasional efforts to dehair her. That I was sometimes rude to the nurses, sometimes nice, and was the granddaughter of Greek immigrants, one of them a wrestler who went by the name of Pete the Greek. That I also liked to ice-skate. That I had not one doctor in the family. That I was a worrier, a hoverer, and couldn't be counted on to hand the baby over easily.

That first day, when she said, "Take her to Marin General . . . I'll call in the orders," I believed she'd take good care of Gracie.

The nurses on duty at Marin General, where Gracie had been born only three weeks before, recognized us. The kind-faced doctor who had transferred us to UC Med was there too, Dr. Eric Scher. "Call me Dr. Eric," he said, smiling. It made me feel like I was ten, but I was happy he wanted us to feel comfortable. "You remember us?" I was pleased. He gave a smile and a shrug. "Not many newborns need central lines or are transferred by ambulance to UC," he said. "Your girl is unique."

One good thing about having a sick kid: it confirms what you've secretly believed all along—what your mother repeated to you, like a mantra, all through your childhood—you are special. Well, technically, only your kid is special, but you're the mom. You made her. It's fame by association.

"Dr. Eric" had spoken with Dr. Koerper on the phone and taken down her orders. "Your hematologist asked us to transfuse the baby if her hemoglobin is under six," he said. "So let's see what her numbers are and then figure out what to do." He paused, surveying her like an engineering problem. "Does she still have the central line?"

"No," I said. "They took it out when we left UC."

"OK, then we have to get in. We might as well place the IV at the same time we draw her blood. Then, if she does need a transfusion, we will already be in."

Again, *in* was the key concept.

"OK," I said, unclear on what I was agreeing to or if my consent had even been requested.

A nurse came over to look at Gracie's veins. "Is she a hard access?"

she asked. I hesitated. I wasn't sure what a hard access was, and I didn't want to brand her as a difficult patient. She wasn't yet a month old. But on the other hand, what if being a hard access qualified her for special treatment? I remembered our experience with the brutal nurse the night of her first transfusion. If there was a team of crackerjack IV placers, we wanted them.

"She's very hard," I said. "Super hard."

"Most infants are," said the nurse. She was slight, waifish, a dishwater blonde with a delicate crucifix at her throat. She stroked Gracie's forehead and picked up one hand, bending it at the wrist so that the hand stretched flat at a ninety-degree angle. A padded layer of baby fat lay between the skin and the veins; no amount of stretching would disperse the fat completely. The veins, visible as they were, would be hard to hit at the precise angle necessary. From the way the nurse touched Gracie, looked at her, looked back at me, I could tell she was on the side of babies everywhere.

"What's your name?" I asked, making a mental note to write it down in my notebook later as "kind one with crucifix."

"Marybeth." Her attention was on the baby.

Marybeth put down Gracie's arm and picked up a foot. "I'm just looking," she said. "Just looking, baby." On the inside of the ankles are large veins, the saphenous veins. Over time I learned that nurses don't like to use them for IV insertion because it is hard to keep pediatric patients from kicking the IV off. Plus ankles are surprisingly sensitive, dense with nerve endings. But in a pinch the saphenous veins are your man. The ankle is easy to rotate, and its veins are big enough to enter. Marybeth liked the look of the left foot. She turned to me. "The more you can nurse her, keep her hydrated, the better," she said. "That makes the veins plump up. But don't worry, I'm usually lucky."

I didn't want to rely on luck; I wanted someone with skill. Someone stellar at threading a tiny needle into a tinier vein. But I didn't protest when she wiped the baby's ankle down with alcohol and picked up the IV needle.

She felt around the inner ankle with her fingertips, searching for the pulse. She took a short breath and slid the needle in. Done. Gracie, who had been dozing, woke with a scream and a jerk. She opened her eyes and shut them instantly in a wince, winding up into a rhythmic cry. The needle had an open back, and blood began to drip out that end. Marybeth taped the needle against the skin and screwed on a syringe to collect blood. I was allowed to pick up Gracie and comfort her. She quieted down.

"Thank you," I said. "The last time that took six or seven tries."

"Don't thank me." She twisted the delicate chain of her crucifix with one index finger and pointed upward with the other. "Thank him."

A sample of the baby's blood was sent to the lab. I waited with her in a rocker in the NICU. Once again, we'd landed in a room with plastic boxes holding sick babies.

A young couple nearby was trying to commune with their preemie son through the plastic incubator walls. They looked like they'd wandered off a movie set into the totally wrong room. The woman's hair hung in a sleek sheet halfway down her back; the man was tall, athletic, and wearing pale green suede loafers. Their baby was fit-in-a-teacup tiny. He had wires and leads running off every limb. The man glanced up at me. Even in his expensive shoes, he was rumpled and half-mad. I offered a wan smile. "They are stronger than they look," I said. But I thought, Nothing can protect you: not youth, beauty, true love, not money, not Italian loafers. Anyone can end up bent over their child, helpless and afraid.

Anyone.

At a little under six pounds, Gracie seemed huge in comparison to the preemie babies. I smelled her head, an intoxicating mix of curdled milk and burnt sugar cookies. I wanted to take a bite. Or swallow her whole, put her back out of harm's way.

The nurse Marybeth found us with Gracie's lab results. "Well, she's real low," she said. "But she's gonna be a whole lot pinker in a few hours."

I looked down at Gracie, about to receive her second blood transfusion at three weeks old. "This is becoming a bad habit," I said. "A really bad habit."

Dr. Eric came by to tell us what to expect. "Giving blood to infants is tricky," he said. "You have to be careful not to give too much blood, or it can overwhelm the heart."

"Right," I said, "I remember that from the first time." If the whole baby weighed under six pounds, how big could her heart be: the size of a prune or a cotton ball? How could they possibly calibrate the volume precisely enough to avoid overwhelming a cotton ball?

"Let them do the math," my mom said. "That's what they do."

"Plus," Dr. Eric continued, "the blood has to be typed and crossed, to make sure that the donor and the baby are fully compatible." He explained that this screening process was necessary because incompatibility could induce adverse reactions, including anaphylactic shock. He handed me a release form, spelling all this out. I signed in big loopy illegible letters, thinking, If this goes south I'll disavow the signature. Near the door was a crash cart, with the paddles, the electric current to restart the heart. "Don't worry," Marybeth said. "We almost never use it."

Dr. Eric added, "To reduce the possibility of a reaction, she'll receive washed blood." Washed blood? Wasn't it all washed? I definitely didn't want her to get dirty blood, off-brand blood.

I called Brian. "We've been readmitted," I told him. Surely the worry of two parents, even on separate coasts, was better than the worry of one. I added that the new hematologist seemed nice, like a Midwestern grandma, who happened to be summa cum laude from Harvard, and that we were waiting to be transfused, again, and that they planned to wash the blood even though washing a liquid sounded ludicrous, and that the baby's heart was no bigger than an apricot pit, so the doctor would try not to overwhelm it or chill it. Brian was silent except for the sound of pen on paper.

I waited for him to say, "I'll be right there."

He said, "I'll call you in an hour."

When our blood arrived, Dr. Eric said, "We'll run it extraslow, to give the heart a chance to catch up." I had an image of Gracie paddling furiously upriver in a canoe, chased by her heart in a tiny canoe of its own.

"Do I have to put her in the incubator?"

"Holding her is fine," he said. "Just keep her leads on." The leads were the only link between her interior and us. If anything went wrong, the leads would let us know.

But no alarms sounded; her cotton ball heart beat happily on, unoverwhelmed, filling with the blood of an anonymous stranger. Gracie was surviving, literally, on the kindness of strangers. This was stranger number two. I tried to fathom who these people keeping her alive might be. Winos in need of a buck? Handsome good Samaritans dropping by the blood bank on the way home from Google? Soccer moms with spare time? Whoever they were, I wanted to make out with them. Just for a minute or two.

The next day we were allowed to go home. Crossing the parking lot, I broke into a run.

At home she was a brand-new girl. She stayed up for hours at a stretch, looking at me, looking at Lulu, looking at the mysterious objects, unseen by me, that she saw in the middle distance. She was pink. Not yellow. Pink! She gurgled and cooed and swished her hands through the air. She cried. She was a proper baby, at last. A baby with enough blood, oxygen, and energy to make her needs loudly known.

"Baby," I told her as she nursed with force, "you are an Olympic nurser!"

Later Brian called. "We're home!" I said by way of answering. "Beautiful news," he replied. We'd begun to share an esoteric tongue made of medical jargon and new-parentese. "Is she still doing the toe bendy thing?" he'd ask, or "Have they mentioned an arterial access as a way to get in?" I could feel his worry, his attention, the force of his care beaming toward us. I fed him vocabulary from the doctor, and he spent hours on the Internet, looking things up, comparing medical sites, taking a crash course in transfusion medicine. Trying to figure out what the hell was wrong with her and how we could help her hang on to every one of her red cells.

I pictured Brian as Captain Kirk from *Star Trek* (for whom Brian, intellectual though he was, harbored an adorable, abiding regard). It felt as if he was returning via transporter, from a long journey, rematerializing in our lives, particle by particle.

8

The whole studio smelled like Nepal. Suzi was cooking a Nepali dinner for us. She'd made the basic—*dal bhat* (lentils and rice)— plus *tarqadi* (veggies) and *aloo ko achar* (potato relish). *Aloo ko achar* was my favorite, boiled potatoes covered in sesame seed paste with lime and chili and salt ground in. It was almost impossible to make the way we'd had it in Nepal when we'd lived there together. But Suzi, when she puts her mind to a particular project, is unstoppable. She once applied a faux finish of "fleck stone" to aging countertops and gross appliances throughout an entire kitchen, one spray can at a time.

I dipped in the edge of a spoon. "It looks legit, Suz. Yum."

"I know, right?" She smiled.

The three of us, Suzi and David and I, spent almost a year in Nepal together as college students at World College West—a tiny liberal arts college founded on the belief that all students should, by graduation, understand themselves to be citizens of the world.

World College West required you to pick a developing nation in which to spend your junior year. The choices were China, Mexico, the former Soviet Union, or Nepal. All the students coming back from China said it was freezing in the dorms and that they ate meat of indeterminate origin, three meals a day. The Soviet Union sounded too . . .

forbidding. And Mexico was somewhere we could go on our own, later. So, Suzi and David and I all picked Nepal, a lifelong happiness choice. And David came home as Dawa, his Nepali name, which we'd called him ever since.

Even now, ten years later, we often spoke Nepali to each other for fun or discretion or just because we could. Sometimes I dreamt in Nepali, speaking like a five-year-old. Nepali has a great sound, lyrical, rhythmic, and full of onomatopoeia. *Rungi chungi* means "colorful." *Geeli meeli* means "bright and sparkly." We were charmed by the entire country. Its physical beauty, the green terraced rice fields under the white peaks of the Himalayas; its cultural richness. There was a festival nearly every week, often complete with a festival princess clad in red silks, paraded above the celebrants' heads on a hand-carried wooden dais. Nepalis were, hands down and on the whole, the nicest people I'd ever encountered. If you spoke a few broken sentences of Nepali to a shopkeeper, the next thing you knew they'd be offering you milky, sweet tea.

Suzi and David and I longed for Nepal, and to make Nepali food was always an act of comfort-giving.

Suzi and I sat on the couch with Gracie tucked between us and tried not to spill spicy food on her as we ferried it to our mouths. After dinner I said, "Dawa, will you get us some New York Super Chocolate Fudge Chunk?" And off he went to the store, always ready for a mini-adventure.

Suzi and I sat in silence; we each rested one fingertip on the baby's stomach as it rose and fell.

"She's your child," Suzi said. "You have a child."

We'd known each other since we were nineteen and twenty-one. Since we stood in the corner at parties and gossiped, since we hitchhiked from San Diego to the tip of Baja and somehow survived, since we wondered whether or not to take Ecstasy with our assorted boyfriends.

"I guess we're grown-ups," I said.

"Do you talk to Brian?"

I hesitated. When it came to Brian, Suzi was not, at present, a fan. "Yeah," I said, "but never about us, just her. He takes a lot of notes. He looks stuff up."

"He takes notes?"

"He researches things I tell him. Like when I said the baby screamed when they placed the IV, he looked up *pain reduction in infancy*. Sugar helps, apparently. But how do you give an infant sugar? He's fretting about her."

"From afar."

I didn't tell Suzi that our conversations were often laced with wide, impenetrable silences. Places where we each refrained from saying anything, for fear of saying something incendiary.

After dessert we watched a movie. Something with guns, muscle cars, and explosions. I fell asleep with my feet on Dawa's lap and my head on Suzi's shoulder. The baby was asleep on top of me, and neither of them wanted to wake us. Lulu stayed on the cool tiles. When the movie ended the quiet woke me.

"Thanks, guys," I said. Not just for dinner, dessert, letting me sleep on you both at the same time as if you were a human La-Z-Boy. Thank you for this year of friendship. Thank you for all the dinners while pregnant and miserable when I spent the night on your huge and comfy couch. Thanks for buying a huge and comfy couch when I was pregnant and alone and you knew I'd sleep on it often. Thanks for walking with me to go get coffee, thanks for driving like crazy to make it to the hospital in time for Gracie's birth, even though you didn't quite make it. Thank you, thank you, thank you.

In Nepal people don't say thank you easily or often. Not because they are ungrateful but because assistance, casual acts of kindness, of community spirit are expected, woven into the fabric of everyday life. To say thank you is quite formal. And Suzi and David and I shared that understanding; thank you was not usually part of the currency of friendship we exchanged.

"You're welcome, Harpo," Dawa said, and hugged me.

Suzi stood at the door. "She's sleeping," she said. "Don't wake her up."

After they left I spent a good hour staring at the baby and absentmindedly petting Lulu with my feet.

The next few weeks, and months, passed much in this same fugue state. Dinner with my mom or brothers or Suz and Dawa or Cassie or even just Lulu. Days doing errands, rocking the baby, feeding the baby. The baby doing her three-step: eat, sleep, poop.

Amelia-Grace would be happy, pink, robust, and full of little squeaks. And then, as her red count dropped, she was a toy whose winding mechanism slowed to a stop. Pale baby. Nonresponsive. The very definition of *transfusion dependent*.

"At least I can count on her for consistency," I told my mom. "She's spunky with blood and droopy without it." We went through the same drill of paging Dr. Koerper and returning to Marin General for yet another blood transfusion. This was followed by a week or so of bliss when she cooed and flapped her hands at me and latched more vigorously to the breast. I could sleep without watching her breathe. And then exceedingly long naps, a de-energized bunny.

I'd check under her lower eyelid. Pink? Whitish pale? I'd press down on her fingernail beds. If they remained rosy, that was a good sign. Blanched white, bad.

As soon as my anxiety reached an unbearable level, I'd page Dr. Koerper. She would set up a blood check, and we'd find out definitively whether or not Gracie was "holding her numbers," a phrase that was thrown around like candy, the sweet possibility of something just out of reach.

Dr. Koerper was mystified over the cause of Gracie's unstable cells, but that didn't dim her optimism. She seemed willing to more or less make up possible answers if she didn't know them or at least to err on the side of psychic comfort over statistical probability. She kept making promises and then revising her own deadlines. "This will most likely resolve at three months," she started out. At four months, she said Gracie would "hold her numbers" by six months. When, at six months, Gracie still needed regular blood transfusions, she told us the disease might "spontaneously resolve" at one year.

I loved the sound of that, *spontaneously resolve*. I wanted to spontaneously resolve as well; to become more humane, more patient, less combative with medical staff, more intelligent, kind, sound, and if possible, an elegant lounge singer, overnight. But nothing resolved; no numbers held; the promised cure was always a month or two away, a wavering mirage that we marched toward without reaching.

By the time Amelia-Grace was three months old, she had had four blood transfusions. Four times she had been readmitted into the hospital. The staff poked and poked to obtain samples of her blood to compare with the samples of the donor blood. Poked and poked to get an IV into her infant veins. Hung the bag of blood above her head, attached the tubing to the IV, attached the leads for the heart and pulse/oxygen monitors to ensure her miniature organs were not swamped by the flood of new blood. Waited for the slow drip. Unhooked the leads, slid out the IV needle, and discharged her. Four times.

Brian hadn't been there for any of this. Not one second of one hour of one day. He'd heard about it all in detail. He'd looked at it from every angle on medical websites. But that was nothing, just words, images, information. Not a lived moment with a breathing baby.

And then one night he said, "How would it be if I came there?"

I wanted him to want to see her. I wanted him to *demand* to see her. I was determined not to poison Gracie's relationship with her dad with my own lingering anger or expectations. My mother had always, even when she was furious with my dad, fiercely protected my right to love my dad, to know my dad, free from her critique. I would try to do the same for Gracie. But personally, I wasn't sure I wanted to see him.

We'd been talking about the heat wave in California and how the baby had an angry red rash of minuscule raised bumps.

"What I want to know," I'd said a moment before, "is whether this rash is nothing or a serious symptom, heralding some exciting new medical problem."

"Chances are heat rash." And then, "How would it be if I came there?"

How would it *be*? Too late, insufficient, enragingly inadequate, confusing, and disorienting. It would be bad, the worst. And also the best. Nothing could be better. As long as we both understood, as Brian seemed to, that he was coming to see his daughter. Not me.

"That sounds like something to talk about," I said.

"We are talking," Brian answered. "What do you think?"

I thought I wanted to hate him for the pain he'd caused me. And that I wanted to forgive him for Gracie's sake. I wanted Gracie to have a dad in her life but not on his terms. I wanted her to have a dad who was there when she needed him. Regardless of whether or not he was "ready." But Brian was her father; she didn't have another. Even if he could only be there for her in a limited way, it seemed better than not at all.

"Meeting her is step one," I said.

"I want step one."

"You do?"

He repeated himself, not just then, but the next time we spoke, and the next, until I began to see that the balance of love versus fear had shifted in him, had created some psychic wiggle room. We made a plan; he would come in early August, when Gracie was four months old.

She was barely past blob status—when not smiling, she still looked, from certain angles, alarmingly like Alfred Hitchcock—but she was his.

9

BRIAN HADN'T SPOTTED ME YET. HE WAS LEANING AGAINST A lamppost, reading, eternally Proust, pausing to glance up and down the block. I thought, "Oh, there's Brian." I'd expected him to look fundamentally changed, but he appeared much the same: gentle bookworm with a loose posture. Not the monstrous guy who danced through my imagination, saying over and over, "I don't want what you want." Even from fifty feet away, the contours of his face filled me with the same diffuse sense of well-being that they had from the beginning. I turned the feeling away; this visit was for Gracie. I was tolerating his presence, at best.

He looked up again and saw me. There was something soft and unguarded in his face. I hoped I looked more reserved.

He stowed Proust and walked over to where I'd parked.

"Spiffy car," he said.

A faded blue Volvo, which he'd helped pay for.

"Glad you like it; you're a shareholder."

We smiled; it felt tantamount to moonwalking.

When we got to the studio I showed him inside and went next door to my mom's to get the baby. I had dressed her up for the occasion. Most babies are naked when they meet their father. Amelia-Grace was in her white cotton sack with rosebuds embroidered on the collar, the same dress she'd worn home from the hospital. It had swum around her as a newborn but fit her now. Somehow it seemed right that he should meet her in the first real clothes she'd ever worn. I carried her to the studio. "Believe it or not, behind that door is your dad."

Brian was standing in the galley kitchen, hovering by the door. He looked at her, looked at me, looked at her again. I can't remember what he said. Or if he said anything at all. I do know he cried. A discreet cry, so as not to alarm the baby, who remained cheerful and curious. She reached up and pulled off his glasses, batted at his face. He had brought her a plush rainbow hippo; she gurgled at the colors and reached for the ribboned edges of the hippo's ears. Brian watched her and watched her and watched her.

The visit was short, three days, maybe four. He spent most of that time staring at her, taking her in. When she cooed instead of her regular flute squeaks, he noticed. When she hiccuped or burped or sneezed, he noted it. When she smiled, his universe expanded. Surely no one had ever been looked at with more interest. Not Neil Armstrong bouncing on the moon, nor Muhammad Ali dancing around the ring, not even the little dude in his manger adored by his wise men. None of them had enjoyed a steadier, more absorbed gaze than the one Gracie received now, from her father.

His pleasure in her was matched by an equal or greater fear of inadvertently doing her harm. He wasn't really comfortable holding her, even sitting down, unless she was strapped against his chest in the Snugli. He held her like a man mistakenly entrusted with a rare, precious object.

The last day of Brian's visit we drove up to Lake Lagunitas, a reservoir in the foothills of Mt. Tam. We parked about a mile below the water and walked up, Brian carrying Gracie in the frontpack. I carried all the gear required to go anywhere with an infant. As we labored up the hill, Gracie pulled off Brian's glasses, flung them to the ground, and laughed. Brian stooped down, holding her with both hands. "Can you get those for me?" He couldn't let go of her, even with one hand. I put the glasses back on his face. Gracie laughed and threw them down again. And again. She seemed to enjoy watching this dance. Finally, Brian tucked the glasses into his pocket, after which Gracie laughed some more for no discernible reason. When she laughed, she bobbed up and down with the pleasure of it, a mischievous Harpo Marx. Through all this, Brian clutched her to his chest. She didn't seem to mind the extra security; it put no damper on her antics, her head bobbing, her nascent sense of humor.

By the time we reached the summit, it was late afternoon. The water's surface was an oblong gray oval, reflecting high silvery clouds and an occasional pocket of blue. There was no wind. We spread out a blanket and lay the baby down to gaze at the scythe-shaped shadows of eucalyptus leaves playing across her face and arms.

Until this moment we'd been in near perpetual motion, feeding the baby, walking the baby, changing the baby. Side by side but not face to face. Now we sat on opposite sides of a picnic table and looked at each other. For what felt like a long time, we said nothing. The birds chirped. The light pooled on Gracie's blanket in amber patches. Gracie produced an ongoing babble reminiscent of a fish tank, a comforting, steady stream of watery sounds.

"I am sorry I hurt you," Brian said, very simple and very direct, because that was his way.

"Thank you," I said.

We sat there a while longer, looking at each other, glancing over at Gracie on her blanket. She was asleep now, with her head tossed back, her ear cocked upward as though listening for an answer to a question only she could hear.

"Have you seen this?" I lifted the silky hair at the base of her neck. There was her strawberry birthmark.

"I hadn't," Brian said. "Thank you for showing me."

It began to get dark. The picnic table was wooden and old, splintering. I pulled at slivers of the wood, prying them free. Brian said again, "I am sorry." I stared down at Gracie, watching her chest move rhythmically with the deep breath of sleep. He was sorry? What did *sorry* even mean in this context?

What I wanted most from him was curiosity. I wanted him to ask me how it had been to be alone and pregnant. Ask about the day of her birth. Every blood transfusion. I wanted him to say, "Tell me everything." But he didn't ask, and I didn't say. Nor did I ask him what his time alone, as his daughter had been born across the country, had been like.

Still, some measure of forgiveness arose between us. Not much. Not a tidal wave of forgiveness, more like a capful, a thimbleful. We loved someone in common; that was a start.

The product of our mutual astonishment was lifting her head on the blanket by our feet, turning her face for our approval, our smiles. Her own smile was utterly undefended, a smile of abandon, a crinkle-eyed smile. She smiled like that every time, throwing herself into it. Now, for the first time, she added to the smile the slightest lift of her left eyebrow.

Brian laughed. "That's a very lofty gesture for an infant."

"It's your patented left brow lift!"

"Is it?" he said. But I could tell he agreed.

We packed up our things and headed down the trail. It was fully dark now, and the walk back seemed more treacherous than our jolly walk up. Brian held Gracie snug against his chest. The fact that he lived in fear of dropping her ensured, I hoped, that he never would.

There was no moon yet and few other hikers on the path. We crunched along in silence, branches tossing around over our heads, the reservoir a sleek black expanse at our backs. In a few hours Brian would be on a plane headed home to New York; the baby and I would go back to our studio, our sleep loft, our devoted Lulu, our beloved clan of friends and uncles and grandparents. None of them would feel as right as this: the three of us walking down the hill in the dark.

A young couple walking in the opposite direction stopped to admire Gracie. "Your baby is a cutie," the woman said. She was talking to us both, assuming, as anyone would, that she was ours. Not mine and sort of his. But ours. Neither of us said anything. Who would impose on strangers with a long, painful explanation of their relationship history? *Um, actually he left when I was pregnant, and he just met this baby the day before yesterday or the day before that.* We smiled stiffly, walked on; the spell was broken. We were semi-strangers living on separate coasts who happened to have a baby in common.

The next day we drove to the airport making halting small talk. We'd left the baby, loather of long car rides, at home with my mom. Alone together we were awkward. Without her burbling in the backseat, our whole premise for being in the same car was questionable.

"You did great with her," I said, to say something.

It was true. Brian had made it successfully through the entire visit, despite his worries or because of his caution, without injurious incident. Saying good-bye, he'd told Gracie, "I'm so glad I didn't drop you," and kissed the top of her head.

I thought that leaving her again, to fly back across the country, was a form of dropping. But I certainly wasn't prepared to ask him to stay. I was confused about what kind of time I wanted to spend with Brian, if any. Still, this visit was an unmitigated good for Gracie; she officially knew her father. And he knew her.

Standing beside the curb at departures, I felt as though anything were possible, as if Brian might fling himself back in the car and beg to stay; or get on the plane and lift out of sight for all time. Or that, lacking the courage to move definitively in either direction, we might grow old loitering, staring at the ground. We hugged briefly. Mumbled our good-byes.

Brian looked up. "Thank you for making room for me with her."

"You're welcome," I said. A traffic cop swooshed her hand through the air. Time's up. I got back in the car, Brian walked into the terminal. Everyone back to their corner.

By the time I arrived home, there was a message on my machine, left from the gate before he boarded. "Hi." Long pause. "I'm just calling because . . ." Dead air, followed by muffled airport sounds. "The last few days have been the happiest of my life."

10

IN THE DAYS THAT FOLLOWED, I PICTURED GRACIE AS A balloon and below her, holding the string, hand over hand, were Brian and I. We would tether her here, the two of us. But beside my hope was a destructive impulse of unsettling proportions. If I let the image linger, I could see myself stamping on Brian's feet, kicking out his knees, biting his face, scratching him off the string. *This girl is mine. Back, the fuck, up.*

Five pregnant months of falling asleep alone except for Lulu, four months of caring for Gracie solo, transfusion by transfusion. My one-handed life. The way he'd left without a clear plan of when he might return. Or even *if.* Fuck him, fuck him for saying such a thing. Only bless him too.

I didn't share that message with anyone. Not my mom, not Cassie, not Suzi, not even with my therapist, Virginia.

I'd known Virginia since I was five years old. She was my mom's therapist before she was mine. Fairly common in the '70s and '80s when there was a more gestalt approach. Frowned on today. But it worked for us.

My mom found her during a tumultuous time: she was in her mid-twenties with a young daughter to support, a drug-addicted boyfriend, marginal work, and overbearing parents who wanted, above all, for my mom to look, act, and be uncontroversial, which was the one thing my mom could not do, even if she'd wanted to, which she didn't. Enter Virginia, with her warmth, humor, tolerance for untidiness. She was the calmest, sanest person in my world by a wide margin but also antic, playful.

In the beginning my mom would drag me along to her sessions to be babysat by one of Virginia's teenage daughters or to linger at the pasture fence, chatting with her horses. My favorite was an obstinate pony named Loggermoss. Who would name their pony Loggermoss? I'd thought. What did that even mean? I asked Virginia once, and she'd said, "Oh, I can't remember, but isn't it fun to say?"

Virginia was often late, fluttering into her office with a coterie of bags clinging to one wrist, trying to fluff her wispy hair, apologizing. But when she sat down, you had her undivided attention. It was like sitting in direct sunlight. She illuminated whatever was in the room—the crux of your problem or apex of your potential.

As a rule, I told Virginia everything. But during my first session after Brian's visit I did not tell her *The last few days have been the happiest of my life*. I wanted to hold on to those words, to turn over the obscure promise in them, a stone in the palm, casting off heat. I wanted to think about what they meant without anyone else's voice in my head.

I did tell Virginia that Brian had spent every minute of his visit fretting about dropping the baby. Wasn't that courting disaster?

"I think that's called being Jewish," Virginia responded.

"Fine," I said, "if he cares so much, how can he tolerate being away from us now, again, even for a minute?"

"Are you asking why he can't turn on a dime?" Virginia said. "Do people operate that way?"

"I don't care how people operate," I said. "Why would I even consider taking a risk with someone who has already hurt me more than I even knew I could be hurt?"

"I don't know," Virginia said. "Why would you?"

I scanned her long, thoughtful face. I knew that Virginia had raised her (surprise) fourth daughter, alone. She'd gotten unexpectedly pregnant very late in life, and the father had opted out. Given her own history, I kept expecting Virginia to advocate for single parenthood over the more messy enterprise of partnership. Maybe even advocate against men altogether. But that didn't seem to be her drift. She seemed to be alert, as ever, for the possibility of growth.

In the 1980s, in the wake of Pol Pot, Virginia had traveled to the Cambodian refugee camps in Thailand. While there, she sponsored several Cambodian families for relocation in the Bay Area, where, ultimately, she helped them find work and settle into new lives. If people could lose everything—country, livelihood, identity, beloved family—and still find a way forward, however tentative, then surely there was hope for someone with problems as modest as mine.

Virginia carried this infuriating belief: no matter how bad things are, they might be made better.

I drove home in a state of disequilibrium. I kept turning the radio up to drown out my thoughts and then snapping it back off to hear myself think. Brian had once accused me of unconsciously orchestrating life as a single mother because I couldn't believe, given my family history, that any man could be a safe father. When he said this we were in a Cuban-Chinese restaurant, I was pregnant, and he had just reiterated his intention not to be my partner or to father this baby in any traditional way. Then he had asked me to split the check. I was so enraged at him, for everything up to and including his refusal to pay for my half of a Cuban-Chinese chicken, that I'd shrugged off his accusation. I'd assumed it was just his way of making himself feel better about his decision. But now, driving down the mountain, slow turn by slow turn, it dawned on me that there might be the smallest kernel of truth in this. My mother had lived with three men during my childhood, and each one, in his own way, had harmed me. Not one out of three or two out of three, but three out of three. It's hard to argue with those odds.

Had I entered into this unhappiness via my own unconscious imperatives? I had no idea. We act out of a Molotov cocktail of conscious and unconscious desires. And also, we just do stuff.

The next day there was another message from Brian: "Being apart while you were pregnant is the biggest regret of my life."

I called him back. By way of answering the phone, he said, "Heather Harpham."

"Hi," I said.

He handed the word back. "Hi."

And then we sat in silence. Not a silence from our typical repertoire of silences; not an angry or disappointed or repressed silence, infused with unexpressed resentments. This was a tensile silence, a charged silence. Possibility ran back and forth between us on the stretched, live wire of what wasn't said. Erotic silence.

Who knew such a thing even existed? Well, someone. Not, until now, me. For a long time we continued saying nothing.

Finally I said, "OK, bye."

"Bye," Brian said, and we put down the phone, I hoped, at the exact same moment. A synchronized dance, with a continent between us. Five minutes later, he called back. "I keep thinking about when I can come see you both again."

II

On brian's second trip out, gracie and i visited him at the San Anselmo Inn, where he stayed. Gracie was now almost six months old and still waking up at night. I didn't know how this was going to work, an infant at a small inn, but I wasn't ready to have Brian stay at the studio, to broach the idea of a reunion to my mom. I knew she'd be supportive of whatever I decided. I knew she thought I'd been, at times, too rigid in not communicating with Brian while pregnant, unbending. I knew she wanted, more than anything else, for Gracie and me to be happy, and if that meant a reconciliation with Brian, she'd be the first to leap for joy. But—given how miserable she'd watched me be for the last year or so—this would take some getting used to. But more than that, I didn't want to be subjected to the tide of her opinion when I wasn't yet sure what *I* wanted.

And so we hung out at the inn. The room was dark, too precious, and smelled of tangerine air freshener. But Gracie thought it was great. A whole new environment in which to be frustrated! She had been lifting herself up onto her hands and knees for the last few weeks, flirting with crawling by rocking back and forth.

Brian set a bright blue glass bottle on the carpet, a few feet out of her grasp. Up she went onto knees and hands, and the rocking began, the heaving, the straining, the spurts and fits of ill-coordinated forward motion. She was reenacting the water-to-earth struggle, trying to get her knees to cooperate. She inched toward the bottle; locomotion powered more by will than physical ability. Gracie craned her neck to look behind her. Was I still there? Yes. Was Brian? Yes.

"Go, baby," I said. "Go, Amelia-Grace." Brian said nothing but pushed the bottle farther away. More effort, a shuffling of knees, a stretched and retracting neck, turtlelike. Was she trying to head-butt the bottle? And then her hand went out, fingers open, and the bottle toppled. She looked back at us. We beamed at her; approval and pride ran the circuit of our little triangle.

"The great bottle challenge," Brian said. It was a garden-variety moment, first crawl, but it felt doubly sweet. Infinitely sweet coming from her in front of us both.

After her glass bottle success, Gracie and I packed up to return to the studio for the night. I leaned against the doorjamb, bags on an arm, baby on a hip. "Bye."

Brian leaned into the doorway. We were just a few inches apart.

"You could stay," Brian said.

At the end of our first date, two years and one child ago, we'd stood in front of my apartment on Twelfth Street, and Brian had declared, "I'm going to kiss you now." I felt the same rush of excitement. Only now it was shot through with sorrow, worry, uncertainty.

"Not with her," I said. "She's still waking up crying at night." It was a feint, a punt—we both knew that—but it bought me time to think.

"OK," Brian said, "call me if you change your mind." And he touched my shoulder. The first time either of us had reached for the other in almost a year.

* * *

That night I went for a walk up the fire trails with Gracie in the front pack and Lulu by my side. At the end of the paved road we walked past the metal gate that was never locked, past its list of prohibitions against fireworks, unleashed dogs, horses, cigarettes, open fires, beer bottles, and unaccompanied minors under the age of twelve. I'd been walking past this gate with contraband of one kind or another, including unleashed dogs and a defiant pony, since I was ten. Twenty-three years of hiking up this same hill, and it never got old. And now I had a companion.

Gracie kicked her legs and bobbed her head and made the loudest sound I'd heard from her yet. A piercing squeal of delight. What was exciting her? The fading light, the smell of eucalyptus, the two black labs running circles around each other at the top of the next hill? The fact that she was tucked against the mother ship and able to see a slice of world?

I tried to focus my thoughts on Brian, on what to do. What was best for *her*? Was she better off with just me or with a dad in the margins? What about a more central dad? What if that central dad turned inconsistent? Or harmful? Then what? Also, what did I want, and what were the forces behind what I wanted? Could I imagine something for Gracie beyond what I'd experienced?

I'd grown up as an only child with siblings. It's complicated; I'd need poster-size paper and a Sharpie to explain it all. But in briefest terms I am the only child of my two parents, both of whom went on to marry other people who already had kids of their own, and then to have kids with those people.

During my earliest years it was, on a daily basis, just me and my mom, an intrepid team of two. My dad was a weekend dad. A loving dad, but a distracted dad. A dad who remarried when I was six, to a woman who had three young children. Suddenly, every other weekend, I was one of four kids, and, then, with the birth of my sister, one of five. Partly it was fun. At last, other small people! My dad, in a last grasp at bachelorhood, kept his little red Karmann Ghia, from which our newly minted family poured out like clowns.

But mostly I did not like it at my dad's; it was chaotic and multi-spoked and no longer revolved around me. In one year my dad went from part-time parenting one low-key kid to full-time parenting a cabal of kids, several of whom openly resented him. Under stress he turned, periodically, into the kind of tyrannizing father I'd only encountered on TV. My dad, I saw, was too dazed by the turbulence in his own life to care about or respond to the turbulence in mine.

Life with my mom was equally unpredictable. Though it looked like a buddy movie starring a plucky, pretty single mom and her pigtailed sidekick, it also starred a rotating cast of boyfriends, not all of them well-meaning. When I was sixteen, and she was thirty-seven, she finally remarried. She was pregnant and in love with a man who, at month eight of her pregnancy, became so enraged by something she'd said that he badly bruised her right arm, shoulder to elbow.

One afternoon I came down the hill after walking the fire trails to piercing screams, the kind of screams people produce when they are under the impression that their life is in danger. As I began to run down the driveway, my mom tore past me in the car. "He's crazy," she said through the car window, "really crazy." And kept driving. I turned and walked back up the hill, back to the fire trails.

Later, from a pay phone, I'd called Cassie. We were both familiar with domestic drama of one kind or another. She came for me, as she always did, in her teal blue Mazda, circa 1970, with the white rag top. Her parents were on the verge of a divorce, but they did not fight loud. And their house was soothingly full of her mother's sculpture, oblique figures in alabaster. A good place to wait out any storm.

Except this storm had no definite end.

When my brother Evan was born, I stared at him through the window of the nursery at UCSF, crying. I must have cried for a long time because a nurse came by and said something to soothe me. I tried to tell her that these were tears of joy, which they were. But they were also tears of frustration, and shock, and an annihilating impotence; my mom was going to keep this man around. In fact, she was going to have another son with him, my brother Dylan, just a few years later. I couldn't imagine choosing a violent man to father my child. But then her own father had been violent both professionally (he was a boxer and a wrestler) and domestically, and so the circle goes.

My family of birth—extending outward from my two parents in a complex web of attachments—contained multiple fissures, outlying siblings, half-attached parents, unclear rules, an abundance of love, but also true harm. Family life with a father, as created by each of my parents, looked at best unappealing and at worst outright dangerous.

The calmest and easiest years of my childhood were early ones, those years that count most and shout the loudest, when I lived in a kid/mom dyad. That was my map, and consulting my map, I couldn't figure out where Brian fit, much less whether I could trust him.

While I'd lollygagged along, Lulu had dashed off to join the two black labs on the adjacent hilltop. The baby and I trudged after her. As we watched Lulu play, Gracie squealed again. I kissed her head; she grasped two of my fingers and squeezed. Not a reflexive squeeze, an intentional one. "You are mine," her squeeze said. "I couldn't agree more," I said. But our world was insular, an airtight system of singular authority. And too familiar. I'd already lived this story from the role of the little girl.

I wanted to know how it felt to be a family of three, two stable adults with a child between them. Maybe I would fail, maybe I would not be able to forgive Brian, or maybe unconscious motives I couldn't envision from the top of this hill would derail us. Maybe Brian's nature was not roomy enough to accommodate change on this scale. Maybe mine wasn't either. But at least this would be a new plot, something beyond mom-and-girl versus world. It held the potential for being a surprising life, a life that was the product, the gift, of multiple imaginations.

I started back down the hill. What was the worst that could happen? Something bad, I thought. The worst, from what I knew of fathers and father figures. Unbearable. But maybe that wasn't Brian. He was reactive and selfish when cornered. But who wasn't? He was not like the fathers I grew up with. Not dangerous in the ways I feared. He was in good faith. And he was smart, kind, funny. The trifecta of marriage material. And Jewish! Jewish was a bonus.

Lulu was trotting along beside us, sniffing the perimeter for anything untoward. I kissed Gracie's nose, cold from the night air. "Do you have a general position on fathers?" She pulled my hair. Affectionately.

I took out my cell. "Okeydoke," I said when Brian answered. "You can come over."

By the time we reached the top of our street, Brian was leaning against my mom's mailbox, holding Proust. When he and Gracie spotted each other, he broke into a grin and she kicked her feet. At least these two were unambivalent.

"Hi, Gracie," he said. He leaned in and kissed her cheek, leaned in further and kissed mine. In the studio we put Gracie to sleep in her bassinet downstairs and went up to the loft. "It won't be long until we hear from her," I said. "She's still waking up every few hours."

"That sounds nice," Brian said. "I'd like to hear what she sounds like at all hours of the day."

"You say that now, but it's not really that fun to pull yourself out of REM and fumble down the ladder."

"Actually, that sounds fantastically fun."

We lay down side by side in my loft bed. Brian lifted my hair away from my face. I put my hand into his hair; I loved its texture. It was wavy, coarse, athletic, outdoorsy hair, antithetical to the rest of him. Hair I'd wanted to sink my hands into, even before we'd spoken.

"Salt-and-pepper hair," I said.

"I think the color you're looking for is brown," Brian said.

"It's salt-and-pepper, and it's outstanding. No intellectual deserves hair like this."

"You're my kind of gal."

"What kind is that?"

"The you kind."

"That's circular logic."

"I know," Brian said, "all roads lead to this." He ran his fingers up my throat, to my lips.

We lay still for a long time. Looking at each other, then drifting in and out of sleep.

Brian asleep smelled like Brian awake. This was a man who mysteriously had no body odor, ever. He smelled like warm cotton cloth. I moved my face into the cubbyhole between his shoulder and neck. He put an arm around my waist and pulled me in.

I was aware that whatever it was we were doing, we were doing it backward. Couples usually decide to have a baby together before they have the baby. First we had the baby, and now we were deciding whether or not to have it together.

Every once in a while, if something is troubling me, a phrase will appear in my mind as I wake up, a floating sentence. Like those inexplicable visions of Christ on a piece of toast. This never happens when I ask for it. But it does happen. When I woke up beside Brian the next day a one-word sentence appeared: *try*.

I turned to face him.

"You again," Brian said.

We were exhilarated to be together but exhausted. Gracie had woken multiple times in the night, and each time Brian had gotten up in sympathy with me, with her, and been kept awake for the thirty minutes or so of shuffling and snuffling downstairs, until I came back up to the loft and lay down, a bag of lead.

I'd occasionally, over the last month, tried to "Ferberize" Gracie, but I could only tolerate her cries for a minute, three max; upsetting her in any way seemed too cruel given all she'd gone through medically. I'd cave and rush down the ladder. This undermines the Ferber approach, which explicitly calls for no caving.

She was almost six months old, big enough to sleep through the night, to comfort herself, and I was wrung out from climbing up and down a ladder in the wee hours, but I had been unable to change the status quo. Brian, after listening to me sum up this situation, expressed faith in Gracie's ability to learn. "Let's try it," he said. "She's a tough cookie."

The next night, when Gracie cried, Brian laid an arm across my chest, "Hang on," he said. "Give her a minute." Though I'd asked for his help earlier, I was stunned: where did he get off? Alarm bells were trilling in my head: *GET BABY*. Brian's arm was a steady, warm weight on my chest.

"She can do it," he whispered. Who the hell was he to tell me how to respond? He'd already missed more than half the movie. Did biology alone entitle him to chime in?

Inside this queasy miasma I was the smallest bit grateful. He considered her cries his problem too. Within a few minutes her cries wound down. Maybe she sensed his determination; his faith in her. Whatever she felt, or didn't, she flopped over and sighed. Snuffled and grunted, but did not cry again.

12

We leapt, in a series of small leaps. brian came for visit after visit, staying a day or two longer each time. He made plans to bring his mom, Tasha, out to meet Gracie. I told my mom that we were in the process of figuring things out, and told Cassie and Suzi and David and my dad the same. All were a little cautious, or a lot cautious, but also wanted what was best for Gracie and me, and seemed willing to accept that the best might be Brian.

On his third or fourth visit, we started to see Virginia together, to work on our reunion, but also to work through all the fears and ongoing questions we had about Gracie's health. Our world was dominated by one question: How could we make our girl better? Nestled inside that question, like tiny, nefarious Russian dolls, were sets of other questions we were afraid to ask: Was it our fault? Would she survive?

She continued to be hospitalized, transfused, and monitored. She settled into a schedule of needing blood about once every three to four weeks. The doctors insisted we let her hemoglobin drift down to five or six. At that point, with very little oxygen in circulation, she'd become wan and listless, a dollop of baby who said and did very little. Letting her red count drop so low, said her docs, might "kick-start" her marrow into making red cells on its own. But that was a mirage. No matter how low we let her levels fall, she never made new cells in significant numbers. The older cells disintegrated one after another. She was our darling wind-up toy, who, after each transfusion, was funny, active, and chirpy for two weeks and then grew increasingly inert as her cells diminished and she wound down.

Gracie turned one in March, and Brian was finding it harder and harder to come and go, to worry about her from afar, and to be apart from me. I was finding it harder and harder to parent on my own when he was gone, and to sleep without him. We'd already lost irreplaceable time; it felt urgent that we not lose more. Brian suggested he move to California at the beginning of May when his teaching semester was done, and then take a sabbatical for the next fall. That would give us a solid eight months of living together. I was nervous but ready to try. I found us a new apartment, still in San Anselmo, but bigger, with two real bedrooms, a vaulted ceiling, and a wooden deck over a creek. I would miss Lulu, who would stay at my mom's. I would miss my mom and the coziness of living next door. But this was a path forward. I hoped.

On the day of our move into the new apartment, Gracie discovered the joys of an empty box. She crawled in, shrieking with excitement. Over the top of the box, she bobbed her head up and down, the happy seal, the classic Gracie. She was fifteen months, not yet walking or talking, but on the cusp of both. She looked, to all the world, like a healthy child.

During our first few months in the new apartment, Gracie was everything you could ask for in a toddler. She learned to toddle, for one thing. Toddled from the bedroom to the kitchen, from the kitchen to the bathroom, shocked and pleased by her new powers. She still loved nothing more than to snatch the glasses off Brian's head and lift them above her own, a height she perceived as impossible for him to reach. Or she would grab my hats and throw them across the room, then careen after them like a drunken speed walker.

She began to speak an invented language all her own; she called water *nangi* and carousel ponies, slides, indeed anything you could ride (which, from her point of view, also included Lulu) *wha wha*. She was an imp, into everything. An imp with a hospital habit. The only good thing was that she seemed to have a fantastically short short-term memory. Whenever we entered the hospital, she would waddle in, waving at strangers as we walked toward the lab, toward the blood draw. She would greet the nurse on duty with her porpoise grin. It was not until the needle appeared that she would try to climb me like a tree.

We were no closer to an answer as to what exactly was wrong with her. At various points, Dr. Koerper believed she might have: Diamond-Blackfan anemia, a malfunctioning spleen, megaloblastic anemia, thalassemia, autoimmune hemolytic anemia, pernicious hemolytic anemia, Biermer's anemia, and on it went. She had none of these, but to be fair to Dr. Koerper, neither did she have anything else with a name and a prognosis. What she did have, more every day, almost every hour, was personality.

She loved horses and feared tigers. If you showed her the scene in *Spirit* (the Disney movie about wild Mustangs) where the herd thunders over the horizon, she would shout, "Dey go! Dey go!" Her first two-word sentence. Their exhilaration was her exhilaration. Some months later, she would begin to call out to us from bed, perhaps reflecting on some of the more invasive things she'd experienced, "I not afraid of tigers. I safe, I safe!"

Our clown, our playful sprite. Our terrified girl who denied her fright.

That she was not safe, that there was nothing we could do to keep her safe, was the vein of misery running through our lives.

Because we were in California, we approached this problem as Californians. We tried everything: cranial sacral therapy (touch the head and hope for the best); moxa treatments, in which one lights a thick bundle of herbs and holds it near various pressure points (accidentally burnt her leg); homeopathy ($400 to walk in the door and hear homeopath's thoughts, $300 for actual remedies to support baby's constitution); visits to a Brazilian faith healer, who said, "She is very sick, and she will get well" ($100); visit to the cranial sacral guru in a hushed hall where we awaited him, with restless toddler, for over two hours (he arrived, wearing a sleek black turtleneck, and instructed us to address him in the honorific). We were hoping, hoping, hoping. In vain.

As cynical as I sound, I'm a believer. I've been helped, many times, by complementary medicine. But whatever Gracie had lay beyond its fragile reach.

It astonished and moved me that Brian tolerated all this. In fact, he endorsed it, sought it out. What more vivid sign of his desperation to help Gracie could there be? This highly rational man with the aristocratic forehead, this man who did not believe, even, in God, was willing to believe, if briefly, in a cure predicated on skull tapping.

* * *

One Sunday after two long days at the hospital "getting blood," Brian and I took a drive out to Bolinas Bay. I wanted Gracie to see the water, wanted her to play in the sand. Wanted her to forget about indoor life. But she was her father's daughter—deeply suspicious of any situation that requires removing your shoes.

Before Gracie, I'd once taken Brian to a California beach; I was excited to show him the Pacific Ocean. It was a clear, bright, windy day. At the edge of the sand I took off my shoes and ran toward the waves. Brian followed hesitantly. When I looked back he was trudging toward me still wearing his black "work shoes." I was a little alarmed.

"Are you going to take off your shoes?" I'd asked, laughing, hoping it was a joke.

"What do you mean?" he said. "Why?"

It seemed to me that if you were a person who would walk across the sands of a California beach on a beautiful day, wearing office shoes, then you must be alienated from your true nature. It didn't occur to me that Brian was in fact being himself: an Upper West Side Jewish intellectual, at the beach. It wasn't that he didn't want to be there; it was that he had to be there as who he was.

The first time we ever sat in a room together, alone, in his cramped office at NYU, Brian asked me what I had planned for the summer. I told him I'd applied for a writer's residency in Maine.

"Maine," he said derisively, "what's there?"

"Nature," I said. "You've heard of nature?" I gestured out the window to his view—a solid brick wall. "What's there?"

He glanced outside. "Every one of those bricks reflects human intention."

At the little beach on Bolinas Bay, I slipped off Gracie's sandals; she clung to me, refusing to touch her feet to the sand. Sand, from her vantage point, was unknown, unstable, and strange. I walked half a mile along the shore, trying to set her down from time to time; each attempt ended with her clinging to my shirt, trying to climb me, always trying to climb me, to get away from the perceived threats of her world.

"Don't force her," Brian said. "Let her figure it out."

I took her to the edge of the lagoon and crouched down so she could, while perched on my knees, lean over to play in the water's wake. Brian squatted down beside us, picked up a sand dollar, and showed it to Gracie. He didn't say, "Look, a sand dollar!" just handed it to her. She turned it over and considered its smooth round shape, shook it. The sand inside rattled. She put it in her mouth. We offered her a cracker as an alternative. She threw the cracker into the water and laughed. After a few minutes she touched a toe down on the wet sand; it yielded to her weight. She lifted her toe back up again and put an arm around Brian, an arm around me, swinging from our necks, feet above the sand. "Look at the birds," I said, spotting a few sandpipers skittering away from the tide.

"Dey go!" she laughed. "Dey go!"

Driving home, Brian and I were quiet, waiting for her to fall asleep. When we heard the deep metronome of her breath, he said, "This is good. We're onto something." I smiled at him, silent. Feigning mystery, feigning elusiveness, but we both knew he was right.

If I wanted to have children with anyone, he'd said, *it would be with you.*

And now she existed. But our world still rested on the slender shoulders of two letters. *If.* If we could count on her to go on being her.

13

We were still trying to solidify our gains, to feel fully back together, when Brian's mom, Tasha, arrived. This visit could go either way. Mothers-in-law can be a force of division—but maybe they could also be uniting, the way Democrats and Republicans cozy up under external threats. I was leery that it was too soon; we weren't ready. But she wanted to come, and she was unaccustomed to accepting no. She'd spent fifty years as an educator, fighting first to racially integrate the schools of Teaneck, New Jersey, and later to introduce progressive education principles into a closed-minded system; she does not suffer fools.

In the days before Gracie, she and I had a mostly nice relationship. Then, when I'd been pregnant on my own, Tasha had reached around Brian to contact me, to let me know that whatever role he decided to take on, she was this child's grandmother. Which had meant a great deal. But still, any conversation with her had the potential to ignite. She had strong opinions on virtually every subject, from child-care methods to whether or not one should shop at Trader Joe's (first no, later yes). And she was a fighter by nature; she'd been on her own from the age of sixteen. Now, she was almost eighty. I thought, how complicated can a visit from a little eighty-year-old lady be?

Tasha arrived upbeat and ready for action, bearing, as was her wont, a million gifts that we did not want: clans of Tupperware, rolls of tinfoil, tiny egg cups. They spilled out of her suitcase, which she opened in the middle of our living room. Brian had procrastinated telling her she'd be staying at a hotel. We'd booked a room at a place a few miles away. It was clean and nice, had free breakfasts and a pool.

When Brian finally told her, as she opened her bag, Tasha balked. It was her right, from her point of view, to stay under the same roof as her granddaughter, earned by many hours of hard flying and ordained by Jewish mothers everywhere. But we didn't feel up to having her. We had a sleeper sofa in the living room, true, but we didn't want anyone on it.

That first night, in protest, Tasha slept in our car. She would rather cramp up in the Volvo than check into the Marriott. The next day I sat with her on the couch and tried to understand her, and to help her understand us. I started by saying that we didn't want her to sleep in our car again, and that if she was going to sleep in the car then she should come on inside the house. But that we'd really appreciate it if she'd try the hotel. Please. Just try. And, shockingly, she did.

Later, in bed, Brian said, "You are a magician."

"I am?"

"You worked magic on Tasha Morton."

The rest of her visit was mostly sweet. We drove around the Bay Area pointing at landmarks we didn't have the energy to get out and look at. From the car we oohed and aaahed. And that was fine with Tasha, who, anyway, only had eyes for Gracie.

When Gracie asked for water with a gesture and her secret word, *nangi*, Tasha said, with genuine grandmotherly pride, "She obviously gets her intelligence from Dick." Brian's dad.

Though he would never meet her, Dick had provided at least a quarter of the genetic material that comprised this particular girl. It moved me that Tasha, who'd been living as a widow for over twenty years, still wore her wedding ring. And that she'd claimed a little of Gracie in Dick's name.

14

"HAVE YOU CONSIDERED HAVING ANOTHER CHILD?" DR. Koerper shifted in her seat.

Brian and I stared at her. When you have one sick baby, the absolute last thing in the world you want is another sick baby.

"Listen," Dr. Koerper continued, undaunted, "Amelia-Grace could be cured." Full stop. "With a bone marrow transplant. The first step is to find a donor. The better the match, the higher the success rate. A sibling match is best. Kids with a sibling match have the highest rates of survival."

A sibling match? Survival rates? She seemed to be speaking in tongues.

"We don't know what is broken, but if we take out the old engine and replace it with a new engine, the car will run."

"The car will run?" Brian said, making her analogy sound as banal and useless as it was inscrutable. I gave him a murderous look.

"The transplant gives her a new engine, new bone marrow. Gracie is the car," Dr. Koerper said.

After a year and a half of constant blood transfusions, after a year and a half of false hope and wrong turns, Dr. Koerper had finally stopped promising that this undiagnosable disease would spontaneously resolve. She was admitting defeat: the disease was not going to get any better. Gracie would continue to require blood transfusions for the rest of her life. Unless . . . we could eradicate the disease. Cure her. We could *make* her better.

"Amelia-Grace can be cured with a transplant," she said. "I can refer you to the pediatric transplant team here for a consultation."

Brian looked stricken. "A bone marrow transplant," he said. "That sounds like an extreme solution to a problem we haven't even defined yet." His tone, as he said the words *bone marrow transplant*, made it sound like a terrible thing to do to a child, like leaving Gracie by the side of the road with nothing but a cardboard sign that read "Toledo" and a warm can of Dr. Pepper. I, on the other hand, only heard *cured*.

I squeezed Brian's knee, momentarily euphoric, until I remembered that this undertaking, outlined by Dr. Koerper, rested on the premise of having another baby.

Out of the question.

Dr. Koerper knew our history; she'd been Amelia-Grace's doctor before our reconciliation. I'd had the vague impression that she was pulling for us as a couple, but surely this had nothing to do with that. Surely she was in earnest.

"But," Brian said, "we've assumed that having another baby would risk having another sick baby."

Dr. Koerper was quiet for a beat. Was this little hitch in the plan only now occurring to her? "Since we haven't been able to diagnose Amelia-Grace, it is true that we can't give you reliable odds on your chances of having a child with the same disease," she said. "But think it over. She'd never need another blood transfusion; she'd be cured. And you could go back to being a normal family."

I suppressed a snort. *Back*?

My thoughts flew in confused circles, tangling and looping through each other, doubling back. How could we put our daughter into a situation with published survival rates? I didn't want a transplant for my child, or anyone else's. But I also didn't want to have a very sick kid who grew into a very sick adult, *if* we were lucky.

The one question I'd been afraid to ask, and had put off asking while we searched for a diagnosis, was no longer avoidable.

I made my whole body still and took a breath. "If she doesn't get better, if she needs lifelong transfusions, what are those survival rates?"

"I don't like to give those kinds of statistics," Dr. Koerper said. "People become very attached to the numbers."

"Please," I said, "we know they are just numbers."

Dr. Koerper looked from me to Brian and back again. "Transfusion-dependent patients, in the last available data, have a fifty percent chance of reaching the age of thirty."

I thought I might slap her; one sharp blow to bring her to her senses.

"OK," I said. "We'll be in touch." I gathered my purse, Brian stood up and took my hand. I knew without looking at his face that he would be tight-lipped, foreboding, knew he shared my view that Dr. Koerper's statistics were unnecessarily hostile. Never mind that I'd pressed, almost begged for them. How dare she say that out loud.

I wanted to be with Gracie, immediately. I needed to touch her pudgy hands and smell her thin, silky hair, to inhale her sweet toddler breath. When we got to the lobby we found my mom alternately reading *People* magazine and watching Gracie cruise around the perimeter of chairs. Gracie was wearing a summer dress with giant pink and orange flowers. As she moved, the hem kept riding up; her small legs, plump and strong, propelled her around the lobby at top speed. What kind of creepy statisticians would bet against such a girl?

I chased her and kissed her and smelled her. She squirmed to get down, as if I'd interrupted her at work. I wanted to whisper in her ear, "You *will* be thirty. And then forty, fifty, sixty, seventy, eighty. You will be ninety and then a hundred. You will be so old and so decrepit, you'll be baggy with age and decay. Doesn't that sound nice?"

Walking to the parking garage, hand in hand, Brian and I said nothing. We were suddenly the parents of a girl who might or might not see thirty, and that somehow seemed like a personal failing. We'd made someone with an expiration date.

My mom said good-bye to us in the lot; she was off to do errands, her eternal errands. When I hugged her good-bye, she whispered, "I don't know what the doctor said to make you two so grim, but doctors don't know everything. Look at her, she's perfect."

I looked at my daughter. She was chubby, currently pink, and humming a wordless, happy opera. She was a baby from central casting.

With a time bomb inside.

I thanked my mom, and we got into the car. I was driving. As I pulled out of the garage, the city spread below us, a rippled, silvery skirt, rising and falling with the hills, hemmed with the blue of the bay. It was an infuriatingly perfect day. Why would the weather never corroborate one's mood? The bay sputtered with light, transmitting its secret code in a series of blinks and flashes—blue, blue, blue, silver, blue, silver.

Relax, the signals said, everything is OK. The baby might be sick, but she is going to get well. Someday she is going to get an apartment at the top of one of these hills; she'll count herself among the supremely lucky who get to live in Northern California. She'll hike the Marin Headlands, get coffee at Caffe Trieste in Sausalito, kayak. She'll bike through the marina, fly kites at Fort Baker. She'll do laundry and read trashy magazines and eat cold tofu chili out of the can. Fall in love. Maybe have a baby of her own. She'll waste time, someday, in a beautiful place because her time on earth won't be precious. It will be ordinary, disposable time. Just wait.

I was on Lombard Street, approaching the bridge, with both hands on the wheel, when a midnight-blue SUV swerved fully into our lane. The driver seemed to hold a beautifully naive belief that two objects can occupy the exact same time/space. I pulled hard to the right and our car jumped the curb. Thank God, the sidewalk was empty. The SUV driver drove merrily on.

At the next stoplight, she was chatting on the cell phone, head tossed back, laughing. If you are going to nearly kill us, I thought, at least have the courtesy to do it on purpose. I put the car in park, got out, and walked up to her window. She kept chatting. I knocked. Finally, she turned to look. I pointed behind her. "Do you see that car?" She nodded her head. "There is a baby in the back of that car who needs blood transfusions to stay alive. Can you see her?" The woman made the universal palms-down, calm-down gesture. "Do you see the baby or not?" She just stared at me; risk assessment. "That baby has enough trouble surviving without your fucking murderous phone calls."

Brian got out of the car. "Heather," he said, "you've made some fine points. Now it's time to go." I looked at the woman; she didn't seem like she got my points at all. The moment the traffic light turned green, she was gone. I walked back to the car; Brian was behind the wheel.

"I'll drive," he said, sounding casual.

"I can drive," I said. "I'm a great driver."

"You are," Brian said. "You are a legendary driver."

But he didn't get out. I walked around to the passenger's seat.

"She tried to kill us with her Lexus," I said.

He put one hand on my knee. "I'm always so impressed by the way you know the brands of cars."

"But did you *see* that?"

"I did, I saw that," he said. His *that* seemed to encompass my actions as much as the woman's.

Thankfully, Gracie had slept peaceably as I'd wandered around in live traffic, cussing people out. As we crossed over the Golden Gate, I remembered some pop psychology book I'd once read that said anger, searching for an appropriate target where none exists, will aim at whatever is handy. *Maybe* the Lexus woman was handier than a blood disease. But I said nothing of the kind to Brian. Chances were, he'd be my next target, and I didn't want to help him disarm me.

After dinner—something veggie for Brian, something meat-ish for me, and minuscule pieces of both for Gracie—we put her to bed with her favorite book, *Goodnight Moon*. "Goodnight kittens . . . Goodnight mouse . . . Goodnight stars. Goodnight air. Goodnight noises everywhere."

This book, once beloved, now sounded sinister. *Goodnight* was uncomfortably close to *good-bye*.

After Gracie fell asleep, Brian and I sat on our narrow deck overlooking the stream and talked about everything Dr. Koerper had said. Each of us, in our own way, was trying to metabolize the shock of her statistic. If we did not give her a transplant, we had a 50 percent chance of knowing our daughter at age thirty. She had only a 50 percent chance of knowing herself for thirty years.

We calculated her odds of reaching various ages. Did she have a 100 percent chance of reaching the age of twelve, fourteen, eighteen? A 75 percent chance of reaching twenty-five?

"Fifty-fifty chance of reaching age thirty," Brian said. "I didn't expect to hear that."

"Bone marrow transplant," I said. "I didn't expect to hear that."

"Me either."

"But *cure* sounds good. I am crazy about cure."

"Yeah, but to get to cure you have to take your kid through hell. And there is no guarantee she'll walk out."

"Also, what would we cure her with? We have no sibling!"

"And even if we wanted to give her a sibling, we can't be sure that the new baby would be born healthy. Can you imagine having two sick kids at the same time?"

"No," I said, even though I was picturing two wan, limp babies side by side in a double stroller that Brian and I, side by side, pushed uphill, never down, for all eternity.

"Besides," Brian added, "we only have a one-in-four chance of having a kid who, if they were healthy, would match her well enough to use the cells for transplant. Twenty-five percent. Those odds stink."

I looked at him, my glass-half-empty guy, who I suspected was secretly a glass-half-full guy. We were doomed. I did not want to be doomed, I rejected doom, but I couldn't see a clear path through the numbers to daylight.

And there was this: was it ethical to have a second child to save the first child? Who wants to arrive on earth as a parachute, a backup plan?

"We can't risk it," Brian said.

"We can't," I said. "And we won't."

Brian put his hand out for mine and stood up. "I'm going to putter for a while. And then, do you want to watch *24*?"

By *putter* Brian meant *write*. Despite his worst fears, he had been, miraculously, inventively, finding time to write inside family life. Sometimes he brought his computer to doctor appointments and wrote as we waited, which made me both thrilled and jealous. Now, from out on the deck, I could hear the beginning taps on his keyboard.

I sat listening to his rhythms and to the creek's. I was waiting for some kind of epiphany, which I knew wouldn't come. In the Greek Orthodox tradition, the Feast of the Epiphany is sometimes celebrated with *vasilopita,* a bread baked with a lucky coin inside. Whoever receives the slice containing the coin will have a blessed year. But there was no way to slice our loaf for the lucky coin. Unless the present moment was luck enough; Gracie asleep in her crib, Brian puttering, and waiting for me, in the bedroom.

The next morning, as soon as I woke up, I tried to suppress my consciousness. I'd noticed lately that Gracie seemed to intuit when I woke up, and to wake in response. Even though she slept in her own room in our new apartment, she knew within seconds when I woke. Even if I lay still, made not a sound, I'd hear her stir and coo and call out. She had some kind of special Spidey sense. You could not slip out of sleep, into consciousness, without her knowing.

When I walked into her room, she was standing up in her crib, holding her arms out over the railing. "Mama," she said, and broke into her award-winning grin. She began to bounce up and down in excitement, squeaking the mattress, jiggling the whole crib. *Mama.* Just two syllables, but they kick-started another revolution around the sun. I picked her up; she clung with all four limbs in a tight wrap, her baby head tucked under my chin. Tiny primate clings to bigger primate. Pure joy.

"Good morning," I said. "Did you have dreams?"

I set her down on the deck and went to make coffee. She loved to pick up dried leaves, stray earrings, errant keys, anything she could get her hands on to drop through the wooden slats into the stream below. When I came back out with my coffee, she was disposing of an entire box, one by one, of expensive gluten-free cookies. She seemed decisive, sure of every move. I envied that. "Gracie," I said, "I'm sorry we can't give you a sibling. I'm sorry we don't have a donor for you." She looked up at me, grinning, scooted on her diapered butt, placed one hand on each of my knees, and began to bob up and down.

"What are you two up to?" Brian said.

"Dancing and wasting food."

"Sounds like an ideal morning." He stepped out to join us on the deck and sat down beside me. I inhaled. Being close to him made my entire nervous system downshift into a lower gear. When he sat close, the concept of purring made sense. He rubbed Gracie's back. "Hello," he said. "It's nice to see you both." And he meant it. With Brian nothing was ever an empty gesture, nothing was phoned in.

"Will you watch her while I run?" I asked.

"I will be very happy to watch her while you run—or pay bills or stroll town aimlessly," he said. "Watching her is a privilege and an honor." His answer, meant to charm—in fact charming—annoyed me. I wanted him to watch her because he was her dad, not because it was a privilege but because it was his job. Still, I'd asked. He'd answered.

This was the seesaw quality of my internal state: I love you, you infuriate me. You infuriate me, I love you.

"Thanks," I said, and grew angrier still, at him, for making me thank him.

I loved to run even though I was slow, inconsistent, and prone to injury. Sweating and listening to music and running past the eclectic houses of my hometown made me happy. I'd been running for the last few months, and people had begun to say, "Hey, you are getting your body back," which, though I was flattered every time, also offended me. It sounded as if my body, while pregnant, had been missing. On hiatus.

But I was a physical person, a performer, a quasi-dancer (real dancers don't run), and I wanted to be able to leap around in the same old way I always had. Half appreciating Brian, half resenting him, with equal measures love and anxiety over Gracie, as ever, I laced up my shoes and headed out onto the tree-lined streets of San Anselmo. Normal life. Or close enough.

When I got home Gracie was napping. Brian was back in bed. I climbed in beside him. Sweaty, smelly, probably muddy. He didn't seem to mind.

Later, after a day, after dinner, after putting Gracie back to bed, we sat out on the deck with wine, with the time to talk and to decide.

We would not have another baby. One sick kid was enough. We would try to find a way to cure her, but we would not, we could not, risk having two sick kids. It felt like a door shutting, but it also felt right.

15

Two weeks later, I was pregnant, which was impossible. It was a defy-the-laws-of-physics-common-sense-chemistry-and-the-rules-of-reproduction pregnancy. A throw-your-hands-in-the-air-and-demand-to-know-who's-responsible-for-this pregnancy.

"That day you went for a run," Brian said.

"I've gone for runs before," I said, "and not gotten pregnant."

"After the run. The . . . you know . . . remember how it . . ."

The fact that we were people who would rather not say *condom* aloud was maybe why we were always one step behind the best practices in birth control.

But this had truly been an accident. We'd been using "barrier contraception," but it had gone AWOL. Way, way AWOL. It had gone on a walkabout. We *knew* that. We'd been a little worried, but it wasn't a particularly fertile point in time. Still, I'd called my doctor, and she'd prescribed Plan B. I had picked it up, for Christ's sake, and—even though I was ridiculously, almost superstitiously, drug-averse—I'd taken the damn thing. Our decision had already been made, out on the deck, over the stream. No second kid. No *potentially sick* second kid, especially not via accident or subterfuge or the heavy hand of fate or whatever the hell this was. We'd decided no, and we were in charge.

Plan B was an innocuous white tablet. Two of them, a set of twins, to be taken twelve hours apart. I swished down the first dose. My doctor had assured me that Plan B worked by preventing conception, not interrupting a process already under way, and (reproductive-rights-supporter though I am) I'd found this reassuring. I did not want to send any souls packing. I just wanted to discourage them from settling in.

While the first pill did its work Brian and I lay down with Gracie between us. Brian stroked her hair and wrote and stroked her hair. I read and stroked her feet and read. Poor toddler, as she slept her parents treated her like a toy they adored but were rarely allowed to play with.

"Guess what I'm doing right now?" I said.

"What?"

"Not conceiving." Pause. "Aren't you proud of me?"

"Very proud indeed," though Brian sounded more subtly sad than proud.

"We are well within the time frame listed on the box. It said seventy-two hours, and we're only at thirty-two hours."

"Phew," Brian said.

Only, not *phew*. Because as we read and wrote and adored our toddler, another soul was settling in.

And now here I was—a mere two weeks after going for a run and getting sweaty and being outmaneuvered by barrier contraception and taking Plan B—staring at the stick. The all-knowing stick that tells your future. I stared open-mouthed. Brian called this expression "the Garfield." It usually encompassed indignation and shock, both directed at him, but this time it was pure inability or refusal to believe the facts. Even though I'd been fretting about this enough to go to the drugstore and buy the test, it hadn't occurred to me that it might read positive.

I did not say, as I'd said with Gracie, "Oh, my God," fifty times in a row, out loud. I did not put my shoes on to walk into the fire trails. But I did have the same vertiginous feeling of having been pushed into unincorporated space, of cartwheeling through air.

I should not have been surprised: there is no better way to get pregnant than to decide against having another child. Probably even as we had sat talking and watching night fall over the creek, settling on an understanding that a second child was out of the question and beyond our limited powers, I got pregnant.

"Brian," I said, walking out onto the deck where he'd been peaceably reading, "look!" I was welling up but had no idea whether these were tears of incipient joy, fear, regret, excitement, or disbelief.

He looked at me, looked at the stick, shot to his feet, and embraced me. Exactly the response I'd hoped for when pregnant with Gracie. In reverse proportion to his fear and avoidance then, was his authentic joy now. "This is wonderful," he said. Here was the reaction I'd once longed for but could no longer reciprocate. I was on the wheel of panic.

Somehow, in the space of seconds, our magnetized poles inverted, and the alchemy of intimacy reversed. Brian was thrilled, beyond thrilled. Meanwhile, I was an untethered astronaut.

"Is it wonderful?"

A second child now would seal my fate to Brian's. I felt a rising feral terror of being trapped with two small children in a disintegrating relationship. Even a non-disintegrating one. How could I decide *if* I wanted to stay with Brian when I *had* to stay with Brian?

And what about my work? Soon enough Gracie could go to day care, and I'd be able to figure out if my post-baby body could still bend in all the ways necessary in order to perform. Or look for a teaching position within a college theater department, a long-held dream. I'd be able to make a solo performance piece about all this medical insanity instead of just living it.

But most of all, I wasn't sure if I could trust Brian to be a stable mate, a good father. I lacked a good-father template to compare him to. True, he was patient and tender with Gracie, holding still while she pulled off his glasses fifty times a day, fetching the toys she threw down into the creek over and over again. And he was devoted to decoding her gibberish, repeating it back to her syllable by syllable, until they understood each other. He was the one who'd figured out that *nangi* meant "water" and *baas* stood for "pasta." But could he love another child as much? Could he and I stay sane together under true pressure? What if Brian had a dark side, a superdark streak, which had yet to show itself?

I remained silent, clutching the stick, stupefied. Brian stood beside me.

"It is wonderful," he said, "and terrifying. It's both."

"I'm no good at both," I said. "I'm good at one or the other."

At our next visit, I shared the news with Dr. Koerper. "This is thrilling," she said, pushing her gray-blond bob behind her ears. "This is really delightful news."

Sure it was thrilling; so was ice-skating across a thawing lake.

"What about the new baby being born sick," I asked, "what are the chances of that?"

Dr. Koerper picked up Gracie's chart and held it against her chest like a shield. "Well, as we've discussed, it's difficult to say without a diagnosis. Until we know what is causing her symptoms, we can't calculate genetic heredity."

Here, for once, Brian emerged as the optimist. "But we have a one in four chance that the new baby will be a match for her. Right?"

Dr. Koerper looked visibly relieved to be back in safe waters. "Yes, a twenty-five percent chance," she said, "that the baby will be a perfect HLA match, and you'll be able to cure Amelia-Grace." She looked so happy at this prospect, saying the words *cure Amelia-Grace* aloud, that I was moved. Dr. Koerper cared. As frustrating as it was to get her on the phone, as much as I resented her many false starts at a diagnosis and her unrelenting optimism, she had this rare trait: at her core, she cared. She was with us, shoulder to shoulder, in our hopes for a healthy daughter.

We drove home in silence, thinking side by side.

Our new baby might provide a bone marrow match that could cure Amelia-Grace. Our new baby might be born with the same enragingly undiagnosable blood disease. Or our new baby might be born both sick and a match. In which case, tragically, being sick would render the match useless. We were back to the same unsolvable calculus that had made us decide against this plan.

A new unspooling ribbon of worry laced through every act; it was no longer just how can we cure Gracie but what if the new baby is born sick?

We decided to go away for a few days and stop thinking. My dad offered us a house he'd once rented, up the coast in Gualala. "Water is good," he said. "Take the baby and play on the beach. My treat." It was a two-hour drive of switchback turns, which might have been awful but instead was heaven. We were on Highway 1, tracing the northern California coastline where the mountains' ragged edge touches the ocean. High drama for hundreds of miles. If there is a more beautiful landscape, I have yet to see it.

It was a fabulous house, huge and clean and modern, set a few hundred yards away from a cliff that dropped down to the beach below. We unpacked and settled in. Gracie fit her hands into a pair of decorative wooden clogs and clomped them on the wooden floor, laughing at how much sound she produced. Her hair was growing; she had the beginning of toddler curls on the back of her neck. Her face was rosy (recently transfused) and her smile easy, immediate. Who would not want a second one of these? Brian did. He'd made that clear with every look and touch on our drive here.

But . . . everyone said the second kid was exponentially harder. Kid to the power of twenty. It would swamp us—time, money, energy— we'd drown.

We unpacked, fed Gracie lunch, then stood around on the many decks looking at the expansive views across the ocean toward a dark blue horizon line. Gracie went down for a nap; I soaked in the hot tub in the middle of the day, under a searing blue sky, to the sound of breaking waves. I was bobbing in the tub, and bobbing in me was the beginning of a second someone. Grain of rice with a heartbeat. A cluster of cells, clumping and grabbing on, trying to differentiate themselves from one another, from me. I figured by now my body knew the drill. It could grow a kidney or an earlobe or any other human component, even without my explicit consent. I wanted to embrace this process. And yet.

I walked into the house dripping hot tub water, padding around on bare feet trying not to wake Gracie. I found Brian in a downstairs bedroom reading and listening to Van Morrison. I love Van Morrison. Brian loves Bob Dylan, but he'd put on Van. We lay down side by side to listen. *She's as sweet as Tupelo honey, she's an angel of the first degree.* I'd been listening to this song since it came out, in 1971, when I was four, and now, thirty-one years later, it made a new sense to me. Gracie sense. That's what kids do, they remake the world.

"Are you happy?" Brian asked.

I laid my head on his forearm. "I might be," I said.

I wanted to be happy.

I was scared and poorly equipped for hardship, that much was certain. Happiness is episodic; it's hard to know when you've caught its coattail. When searching for a parking place on a hot afternoon while cycling through endless contingency plans for Gracie's health—not so happy. Sitting in my mom's garden at the end of the day watching Gracie chase Lulu in circles, imagining her with a sibling, romping after—happy.

When, anyway, did happiness become the one golden ring we reach for? How about being guided by what is right or ethical or meaningful? Or by making—as Brian sometimes called it—the "growth choice." That sounded good, but I wasn't that mature. I'd always aimed for what brought me the most joy.

The safer, smarter, maybe even wiser choice was no new baby. But the joy choice was yes. Or at least that was the choice with the highest probability of joy. True, a pile of potential anguish lay on the opposite side of the scale. But this is the deal in life: the inevitable twofer of joy and misery in their boxer's clinch.

This new baby, two or ten or thirty years from now, might make me hear a song in a brand-new way; surely they would dilate someone's understanding of the world along the way. Likely many someones.

"OK," I said.

"OK?" Brian said.

"OK. Yes."

Brian broke into a smile and took my hand.

Yes to another child who might be sick, yes to having two children under two years old at the same time, yes to Brian. Yes, yes, yes to drool, late nights, mutual accusation, yes to euphoria, yes to the probable, the impossible, the impractical, yes to boy, yes to girl, yes, if need be, to a cabbage patch kid. Yes to the whole crazy, doomed mess. Yes, to whoever had chosen us, yes, we chose you back, yes. Yes to life, yes to the flower of the mountain, yes to yes. I say yes. Come on and come little soul. We accept you.

16

I WAS DETERMINED THAT IF THIS BABY WERE SICK, SHE wouldn't take us by surprise. Gracie had been most acutely sick at birth. That was when she'd been riding around in ambulances and living in the NICU and people had begun taking snapshots of her, "just in case." We would not end up in that situation again.

Dr. Koerper reassured us that if, during my pregnancy, the baby was discovered to be seriously anemic, the fetus could be transfused. This seemed like the kind of well-meaning lie doctors make up on the fly. "But," I said, "how would you get *into* the baby?"

"By threading a needle through the amniotic sac. We run the needle through you, into the sac, to reach the baby *in utero*."

"That sounds complicated and risky," I said.

"It is."

Stop asking questions, I told myself, when you really don't want to know the answer.

Brian gave my knee a squeeze, steady on. I focused on calming my heart rate and sending the baby good vibes, whatever those were. You'd think that having grown up in California in the '70s I'd have a near-encyclopedic understanding of vibes, but I drew a blank.

Dr. Koerper was her usual encouraging self. "Remember, this baby has a one-in-four chance of being a perfect match for Amelia-Grace," she said, "and if so, you can harvest the baby's stem cells at birth and use them for her transplant." I liked the way she put things. *One in four* sounded so much more optimistic than *25 percent*.

I didn't pause to bog down our conversation with details like the morbidity rate for pediatric transplant patients; to do that would seem ungrateful. I just nodded as though all this sounded great: If the baby is anemic in utero, transfuse right through me! If the baby is a match, transplant Gracie! I nodded and smiled and inwardly wilted. Too much information, too many variables.

17

BRIAN'S SABBATICAL LASTED THROUGH JANUARY 20; THE baby's due date was February 10. Even for artsy math illiterates like us, the inherent conflict of these dates was obvious. He beseeched me to look at our situation with cool logic and to move back to New York.

All the hands on the clock of reason pointed toward New York, but I was unmovable. I wasn't ready. I was scared to leave our doctors. I was scared to leave my mother, my brothers, Suzi and David and Cassie, our apartment, the deck over the creek, the whole of California, including Lulu. I knew it couldn't last forever, but I insisted that the new baby would be born in Marin, at the same hospital where Gracie had been born. I trusted them. Even though it was more and more obvious that eventually we would head back East, first, I wanted to have one more California-born baby.

And so, we stayed. In my final trimester I went weekly to a local sonogram lab where they measured the baby's blood levels, in utero, exactly as Dr. Koerper had said they could. Amazingly, each measurement came back normal. The baby appeared to be the picture of health. We were in clover, more or less. And yet our puzzle had a million unplaceable pieces.

When Brian's sabbatical ended—as crazy and untenable as it sounds—he began commuting to work. As in commuting from California to New York. Weekly. Four days in California, three days in New York. For a man who had once resisted family life so violently, he was incredibly willing to do whatever it took to be with Gracie and me and the new apple seed. It was his writing, in large part, that made this possible, that paid for it. Within the last year he'd gotten both a Guggenheim grant and a book contract, enabling us to run this kooky experiment in bicoastal domesticity.

Brian would leave for work Sunday night and return Wednesday night in a state of utter exhaustion. If, as has been said, the soul travels at the same rate as an unburdened mule, his was perpetually trailing behind him, somewhere over the Midwest. Before his soul could make it as far east as, say, Idaho, he'd be on another plane, flying in the opposite direction. And the poor, exhausted soul-mule would have to turn around and go the other way. I imagined it forever zigzagging the same few interior states.

All the while, I was on my own, seven, eight, then nine months' pregnant, with a toddler. Lifting Gracie up and down, carting groceries from car to house, riding out the daily emotional ups and downs of a nearly two-year-old human. Responding with calm understanding to the mood swings and serial desires of a toddler is a two-parent job, but there was only one of me, plus the baby in the belly. Millions of people are executing much worse tasks, I reminded myself. But I stink at relativism.

The girl wants peanut butter on the cracker; no, wait, she wants jam. You *already* spread the peanut butter. Are you insane? A terrorist? Why would you use peanut butter when she wanted jam? No, you can't get a new cracker and put jam on it; she wanted *that* cracker. That was the good cracker, and now it has been polluted. No! Don't try to wipe the peanut butter off. You cracked it. It is a cracked cracker with a corner missing. It can never be made whole again. But look, there's a bag of gummy bears on top of the fridge. Of course gummy bears are good. Cracker? What cracker? Give her the red gummy bear, not the yellow gummy bear. What are you, crazy?

In the witching hours of late afternoon, I'd call Suzi, now also a new mom. She and Dawa had conceived a little boy, she believed, on the very day Gracie was born (as if Gracie's birth were not a cautionary tale).

According to Suzi, their infant son, Liam, was "a world-class expert on nonproductive nursing."

"Bummer," I said.

"Remember that girl who danced in her wet T-shirt on the Indonesian boat?"

"No."

"She was dancing on deck, and all the boat guys started clapping. I want boobs like her again."

"Suzi, you never, not for one minute of your life, had boobs like her. And your boobs are not the problem. The babies are the problem. Blame the babies! Why am I having another one? Infant-toddler combo—worst idea ever."

"Bummer." Then a long pause. "You might be the luckiest person I know."

As dreamless, dehydrated, and deprived of our youthful selves as we might be, we were lucky and we knew it. Suzi was madly in love with Liam. The week before, she'd told me that he smelled like her favorite food, pizza.

"All the time," she'd said, "good pizza. Brick-oven pizza."

"Is that maybe because you eat a lot of pizza?"

"No!" She'd been indignant. "He just smells like pizza. Naturally."

On Wednesday nights Brian would arrive home after traveling nearly six thousand miles round-trip and teaching nonstop for three days.

His first day back the best we could do, typically, was to sit side by side on the couch, like a pair of catatonic zombies, while Amelia-Grace frolicked around the living room, drawing bright pictures on the walls, sketching new faces over our faces with her scented markers. We said nothing. Our little Picasso. If she got really bored, she'd begin to reorganize our possessions into like-minded clusters. All the lamps in one place. All houseplants in another. All wooden things together. Days later we would find a clump of toothbrushes behind a chair. It was adorable and heartbreaking, her wish to impose order on her unorderable world.

Sometimes she would sit on my lap, patting my belly, half amused, half mystified by its size. When we tried to explain to her that a brother or a sister was growing inside me and would soon come out, she'd wriggle off to play. We were too ridiculous to take seriously.

As my due date approached, we were painfully aware that if I called Brian at work and told him I'd gone into labor, the chances he'd make it to the hospital in time for the birth were slim to nil. From phone call to walking onto a plane would take two hours at least. The flight itself was five plus another hour at best from airport to hospital. That gave us, tops, an eight- or nine-hour turnaround time. Even though Lewis and Clark would leap out of their buckskin boots to learn that one could cross an entire continent in hours rather than bone-cracking years—it was too long.

Brian could not miss this birth. He had a special role to play. He was the cord blood guy. When Dr. Koerper had first explained how we would "harvest" the new baby's cord blood for a possible transplant, it had sounded so rinky-dink that I thought she was joking. But this was the very early days of cord blood collection, and it was still a largely do-it-yourself operation. You first had to special-order a collection kit from one of the private cord blood banks. They would then mail you the kit in a big cardboard box, and you would bring this kit with you to the hospital, having carefully read the directions for cord blood collection, and then *you* would explain *to the doctor* how to do the actual collecting, which involved a syringe and the baby's umbilical cord and timing things just right. The responsibility for this entire operation fell on Brian.

All this would be done in the hope that the baby would be "a match" for Gracie.

The only truly terrific aspect to this method of harvesting the cells was that it would be totally painless for the baby. When I'd asked Dr. Koerper if it would hurt, she'd said, "No more than cutting your fingernails."

The more traditional method of harvesting cells for transplant is to extract marrow from a donor's biggest bones, typically the hip or pelvis. It's not hugely dangerous, but it is painful. And we were so happy to have another option. Plus cord blood stem cells are superior in purity and adaptability to cells extracted from the marrow.

And so we ordered our kit and received in the mail a cardboard box full of tubing, bags, and a Xeroxed sheet of instructions to share with our doctor, which Brian memorized word for word.

Though Brian's presence at the birth was crucial, there was no way to communicate this mandate to the baby. The baby, however, seemed to understand and went about being born in a way that facilitated not only Brian's speedy return home, but also some calm pre-birth time together.

My contractions began on a Wednesday morning, while Brian was in New York. They were steady and strong; when I called to tell my OB, he said that labor had begun. I called Brian, he rushed to the airport, caught the first flight. And then, while Brian was over Nebraska, his soul-mule snapped to attention, willing the plane to go faster, my labor stopped. Not tapered off or slowed down. It stopped.

When Brian landed and called from the airport, frantic, I told him to take his time driving home. When he arrived the baby in the belly and I were watching *Seinfeld* and eating sour cream and onion Kettle chips. We all slept well through the night. The next day we made breakfast for Gracie; Brian wrote for a few hours in the morning. I checked my bag for the hospital, double-checked our checklists and birth plan. Brian triple-checked the cord blood box. My mom came over and took Gracie to the park. Still nothing: no contractions, no labor.

Brian and I decided to run to the local indie book store, Book Passage, where we liked to lurk. On the way there mild contractions started again; I insisted we push on.

"We'll never go to the bookstore alone together again," I said. "This is our last hurrah."

We browsed the new fiction section side by side. Between looking at books, I would freeze with a contraction, gaze into the middle distance, and then straighten up and go back to browsing.

"Heather," Brian said, after I dismissed his first few suggestions that we go, "great idea! We're leaving now!"

I thought of my little skirmish, oh so long ago, with the ambulance driver who'd wanted me to ride in front with him, rather than in back with Gracie, and how I'd tried to make my refusal sound like an acceptance of an offer he'd made. I was pretty sure Brian was using my own tactics on me.

We drove to the hospital. After I was admitted we were left alone in a room together. I wasn't hurting too badly yet. We put our foreheads together, saying nothing. We breathed the same small cup of air, waiting.

People began to arrive. My mom. Suzi and David (with an inflatable tub in which I hoped to labor). Cassie. My dad and his wife. Our spell was broken. Real labor began. Hours went by during which I shouted, every thirty seconds or so, "Where's the fucking tub?" Dawa—dear friend, ever the man for any job, the world's best fixer, a guy who once located and rented a live donkey for our college play with only four hours' notice, a guy who, in essence, could do *anything*—could not fill the tub. It was unfillable because, as he later put it, "the water pressure was for shit." It took three hours to achieve ankle depth, and by then the water was stone cold. But David was a paragon of optimism. Every time I asked, he would shout back, "Tub is filling, Harpo!"

I stopped caring about the tub. I wanted drugs. Any drug, up to and including whippets or roofies or polluted street crack, but I was in too much pain to ask. And I'd told my people not to offer me drugs, so no one did. Which was a crying shame.

"I can't do it," I told an orderly wandering by with linens. To Brian and my mom and David and Suzi and Cassie, I repeated my new mantra, "I can't do this!" And they nodded pseudosympathetically. "I'm not kidding," I said. "I can't do this!"

On TV babies are born so fast. And Gracie, my sole experience to date, had been born just twenty minutes after we arrived at the hospital. This baby was taking hours; I was out of oomph. I'd never have oomph again. I'd be laboring in the pre-push stage, until this hospital fell down around me.

Brian said, "You can do this."

And then, presto, a baby boy, seven pounds seven ounces. Huge lips; he looked like Mick Jagger. And he was pink, so pink. He must be healthy, I thought, to be so pink. Inside his body every red cell must be holding together; veins thick with beautiful, fat, blessedly stable red cells.

Moments after his birth, the doctor inserted a long needle straight into the umbilical cord and pulled a stream of crimson stem cells up into the syringe. If our boy matched our girl, these cells would save her life.

Brian squeezed my hand and said, "They got it, they got it all." The two of us, more than anyone else in the room, knew how much this mattered. It wasn't only a match that we needed; it was volume. The more cord blood you had, the better your chances at a successful transplant.

Finally, everyone left us alone, the three of us. Me and Brian and our huge-lipped, pink-skinned son.

No one came by at 2 a.m. to say the words *blood, brain, barrier, bilirubin, permanent,* or *damage.* No one came by the next day with bad news, either. He was precisely what he looked like, a healthy beautiful boy. We named him Gabriel. Angel of annunciation, who arrived bearing the good news of himself.

18

THE NEXT DAY, IN THE LATE AFTERNOON, BRIAN WENT TO pick Gracie up from day care and brought her to the hospital to meet her brother. Even though we'd told her that there was a person in my stomach and read her every sibling book on the market, she'd remained unconvinced. She was twenty-two months old; her ability to conceptualize a person, in the absence of that person, was foggy at best. She'd parroted back our words, *baby, brother, sister, yours, mine,* but she had no idea what was in store.

When Brian brought her into the room, she ran to the bed. She seemed happy, surprised, and a little alarmed to find me lying down in the middle of the day. My mom had Gabriel out in the hall. Gracie climbed over the bed railing to snuggle with me. When she was settled, we told her that she had a brother. She said, "Where?" We smiled and called out to my mom who brought Gabriel in and put him in my arms. Gracie looked down at his face, looked back up at Brian and me, looked back down at Gabe. She picked up his hand; he was asleep and stayed asleep. She put her face down into his face and rubbed nose to nose, squishing; curiosity or dominance or a tincture of both.

"What do you think of your brother?" Brian asked.

"Soft boy," she said, stroking his hand, more statement of fact than appreciation.

My mom cried. Brian cried. I cried. Gabriel slept. Gracie looked at us all with baffled amusement—what were we so worked up about?

Later we loaded both kids into the car to take Gabriel home. We carefully packed him into an infant seat right beside Gracie's toddler seat. He was rear facing to her front facing. I liked the look of those two seats, touching, two siblings face to face, side by side. Brian pulled out of the hospital parking lot with the greatest of care, I could feel the sense of responsibility coursing through him, and it put me at ease. For today, he could worry, I could enjoy.

We were about halfway home, cruising happily along, when Gabriel let out a piercing cry. I turned to find Gracie pressing her foot, clad in a smooth leather sandal, into Gabriel's face. She was a premoral creature, happily stomping on his mouth and nose. I shrieked, Brian jumped, Gracie pulled her foot off, and Gabriel fell silent. I was starting to scold Gracie in some new and phenomenally loud way, when Brian pulled over, got out, and separated the carriers so the middle spot opened between them. Problem solved.

Brian smoothed back Gracie's hair. "Gracie," he said, "we don't want to hurt the baby."

She gave us a winning smile. "Yes," she said. "I do want to hurt the baby."

I could relate to her irrational urges, her free-floating aggression. Not toward the baby—I was besotted with this boy of big lips, thick blood, powerful heart—but toward Brian. Almost instantly after Gabriel's birth, I'd descended into a murky, cold tank of anger.

I knew I should shake it off. I'd already ruined our first night with our son, for myself at least. But my joy over Gabe's arrival was cut with a resurgence of fury toward Brian, in part because of an inherent conflict of interest.

We'd been told that getting the "full volume" of cord blood was critical, the more stem cells the better for transplant. Each cell, in a sense, increased Gracie's chances. And so, in the minutes after Gabriel arrived, when I'd experienced a minicrisis of continued bleeding and pain,

Brian had needed to focus on collecting the cord blood, rather than on me.

As much as I understood this rationally, I was plagued by a lingering sense that Brian had turned away at the crucial moment.

When we'd finally been alone with Gabe tucked into the sling of my arm and Brian peering down at this astonishing development, I'd said, "I was scared." I said it accusingly, as if he didn't know, and should have known.

"I'm so sorry you were hurting and scared, my love."

I could feel his apology reach backward in time, to embrace Gracie and me, without him, on the day she was born.

19

"LET'S PRETEND WE'RE IN HAWAII," I SAID. "HAWAII IS LUCKY and warm." Brian and I were sitting at the lonely end of Stinson Beach, where it nearly touches Bolinas. It was getting dark, and we were shivering. It had been over three months since we'd sent Gabriel's cord blood for analysis to determine whether it was a match for Gracie. Brian didn't look convinced that pretending we were in Hawaii would have a direct effect on Gabe's matching outcome, but he did offer me a bag of almonds we'd packed as a snack: "Care for a macadamia nut?"

We were staying at my mom's cottage near the ocean. She'd bought it for a song years ago and now rented it out by the weekend to supplement her income. People drove from San Francisco and paid all kinds of money to fall asleep to the sound of waves. She'd offered us this place for a whole week. To be nice, to take our minds off waiting. We were lucky; but I didn't feel lucky. I felt sick with the possibility that Gabriel's cells, being split and analyzed, would reveal not only an incompatibility with Gracie's but also some scary, hitherto undetected, defect of their own.

"Let's go make sure the babies are still breathing," I said. A passable joke in another family. We got up and dusted the sand off our butts and walked the fifty feet back into the cottage, where both babies were, happily, alive and napping.

By our fourth day out at Stinson, Gracie had made peace with the immutable fact that sand is inedible. She dug and threw, threw and dug, with the gusto of a dog allowed off leash. She showered us with fistfuls and laughed, bobbing her head. Gabriel slept in his carrier, on the sand, under a wavering circle of shade, dreaming of what, we had no idea, but his lids pulsed back and forth, ferocious dreamer.

My mom had driven out to bring us lunch. After we ate, Brian walked back up to the house, "I'll be puttering if you need me." "We're good," I said. Gracie was trying to bury my legs; the dry sand slid off, a thousand silky hands.

My mom handed me a book of Sharon Olds poems and *Star* magazine; "to distract and inspire, in any order."

"Thanks, Mom."

Her phone rang, and she wandered off to chat. Then my phone rang, one ring too many, and woke Gabriel; his crying sparked Gracie's crying. I could see from the number that it was Dr. Koerper. I tried to sound composed, not like a crazed lady camped on the beach reading *Star* magazine to two screaming kids.

"Hello?"

"He's a match," she said. "Gabriel's an *extended* match. A perfect match."

I wanted a better, more potent word than *thanks*. Even *thank you* felt inadequate. The match might not be her doing, per se, but Gabriel himself felt semi-attributable to her. She'd been the first one to say *sibling*.

"Dr. Koerper, you have given us something amazing." I said. "Thank you."

"You're welcome," she said. "I am so happy for your family." And we got off the phone.

I looked over at my mom, still chatting. I waved my hands in the air. "He's a match," I said.

She started to cry. That is my mom—perpetually ready to share misery or joy with anyone on the beach.

Brian was just a few hundred yards away, in the house. I wanted to tell him face to face. Mom said, "Leave the kids. Go!"

When I opened the door to the cottage I could hear the percussive sound of the keyboard. Brian had a particular rhythm. Bursts of sounds, brief silences, and then renewed bursts. I stood and listened: Brian, writing, happy. And I had more happiness to bring him.

I couldn't see his face; he might have had his eyes closed. I made a noise, and he turned to me and smiled. Seeing me unexpectedly, Brian had a certain smile. Everyone in the world should be smiled at like this, at least once.

"Hi," I said. "Dr. Koerper called."

He sat up straighter, every neuron on alert.

"He's a match," I said. "A perfect match. An *extended* match."

"Wow." A long pause. "Wow. My god. Wow."

And then his face fell, an infinitesimal slackening around the eyes, the corners of the mouth. A shadow thought.

"What?" I said.

"The risk."

We both sat for a while, living with *risk*, nestled against our hope, the yin/yang of possibility and danger, inextricably linked, coexisting. Cure and threat, clinging and inseparable.

We could cure her. But only if we were willing to risk her.

20

TRANSPLANT CAN CURE YOU. OR IT CAN KILL YOU. THERE'S not much middle ground. If we chose transplant, we would be, as one doctor put it, taking our "risk upfront."

If only she were a hedge fund, or an annuity, it would be easy to take our risk upfront. But she was a girl. A single, unique, irreplaceable girl. A girl who bobbed her head when she laughed, who squealed every single time the Disney logo appeared on the screen, who dreaded water but loved sand. A girl who, when I spoke to her in a severe tone, would sometimes say, "Smooth, Mama, smooth."

Without the transplant she would stay a sick kid whose life, however brief or long, would revolve around medical care. Or we could grab for the ring of health. Normalcy. A life not dominated by doctors or blood counts or needles or experimental drugs.

"Look," I said to Brian, "when your hair is on fire, you don't stand around debating whether or not to put out the flames!"

"You do," he said, "when the only way to put out the fire is to clobber the flames with a brick."

I knew what he meant, but I didn't want to admit it.

I was essentially for the transplant, and Brian was essentially against. We squared off in our default positions, optimists to the left, pessimists to the right. But this could turn on a dime. If I suddenly pulled away from the idea, he'd push forward, and vice versa. We couldn't seem to sit on the same side of the seesaw for more than a second or two. We were suspended in the stasis of indecision. It was our luck to be able to decide, but also our constant burden, and one without a clear deadline. The cord blood was safely banked; it would not expire.

We weighed the relative pros and cons while making dinner, folding laundry, driving to the beach, flossing teeth, changing diapers, answering emails, brushing Gracie's hair, while zipping up our coats for a walk, sitting down with a glass of wine after dinner, while making love, while silent in the car riding home from yet another transfusion, while Gracie slept, refreshed, re-pinked, in the backseat. No matter what we were talking about, that's what we were talking about.

21

MEANWHILE, THE CLOCK WAS TICKING ON OUR TIME IN California. Brian had been commuting cross-country for a whole semester. There was no way we could afford to continue our quixotic two-coast life. For the foreseeable future, my work was caring for a sick toddler and an infant, unpaid. We needed an income, and Brian had great work, in New York. Case closed.

Come September, we decided, we would move back East. Gracie would be two years and change, Gabriel only seven months. They might not remember California, but I hoped they'd been there long enough for some of its golden light to seep in.

The worst part of leaving California was leaving my mom. Given how miserable our leaving made her, she was incredibly gracious. In late August she threw a big good-bye party for us in her garden.

Toward the end of the night, Dawa sat down beside me on a low stone wall. "How's it going, Harpo?" he asked.

"I'm sad," I said. "I don't want to go."

"I don't want you to go either," he said. We watched people chatting. Van Morrison drifted out from the house speakers, *Well, it's a marvelous night for a moondance.* Suzi was standing in a corner with Liam. "You,"

Suzi had said, when she'd told me she was pregnant, "are contagious." How could I go when we were finally poised to do the thing we'd always said we would do—raise our kids side by side?

Suzi carried Liam over. "Scoot your butt," she pushed me.

"Wanna move to New York?" I said.

"Not now," Suzi said. "And how can you?" She seemed to have accepted my reconciliation with Brian, even to be rooting for us, but she saw our move back East as an outright betrayal. She took a chip with guacamole that I'd been holding out of my hand and ate it.

"Basically," she said, "you suck."

Cassie wiggled in between us. Our good-bye would be easy; she had independent plans to move to New York in a few months.

"Suzi," I said, "Cassie's doing it. I'm doing it. You and Dawa and Liam can do it too."

"Look around," Suzi said, "you're going to leave this?" My mom's garden had never been prettier; everything was green, the jasmine trellis she'd planted when Gracie was born was in full bloom. We were insane to leave this place.

My mom sat down on the stone wall beside us and began to cry.

"Jessica, no," Suzi said. "You'll set off a chain reaction." But it was too late. I was already crying, Cassie too. If you cry, she cries; that's how she's wired. Only when Liam began crying did we pull ourselves together.

Later I drifted around my mom's kitchen helping to clean up. "I guess you're really going," she said, "and I am happy for you. But I am going to miss you so, so much."

This was the kitchen where, as a teenager, I'd accidentally left the water running while sunbathing for an hour on the garage roof. When my mom had come home to find me vacuuming water out of the downstairs carpet, she'd forgiven me almost instantly. When I was pregnant and alone, heartsick and at bay, she'd given me everything she could. Food and money and time and most of all the spirit of camaraderie.

I thought about the Billy Collins poem "The Lanyard," in which the protagonist laments the impossible project of repaying our mothers.

She set cold facecloths on my forehead
then led me out into the airy light
and taught me to walk and swim and I in turn presented her with . . .
a lanyard.

We would have the phone and email and planes and whatever could be sent through the mail—spoof cards and See's Candies and eucalyptus leaves and heirloom china and bagels (if not lox)—but it would not be the same. And we both knew it.

I put my arms around her. "Thank you, Mom. I'm going to miss you too."

It was more true than I knew how to say. My mom had a way of looking at the world that moved me; she saw the light, no matter what. And she'd taught me that. We were expert at laughing through the worst. In the Marin County flood of '83, we'd laughed ourselves sick as water poured under the doors of our green Corolla and pooled around our ankles. We'd laughed as we waded through thigh-high water toward the refuge of a nearby playground.

"This place will always be here for you," she said. And with that, I tipped out of tenderness toward irritation. Was she implying I would need to come back? That Brian and I wouldn't make it?

I was determined that we would; I was moving cross-country to stay with him. And yet I did not pack. I did not plan. I did not book flights. Because, as much as it made logical sense, moving back East with Brian felt like lunacy. Like leaping from a moving train onto a speeding boat. Like asking history to repeat itself.

When my own parents moved East together, in 1969, it was the beginning of their end. They relocated to Stony Brook, New York, for my mom to attend graduate school. Right before they left, my dad had passed the California bar; unable to practice out of state, he was miserable in New York. He took odd jobs as an insurance salesman, junior high school history teacher, tree cutter. After a year he told my mom he couldn't do it anymore, and booked a ticket back to California. Why he didn't just take the New York bar exam was never explained. My mom was only halfway through her graduate degree but decided to quit and leave with him. The day before they were scheduled to fly, she got her first and only migraine. The pain was so intense she sequestered herself in the bathroom, where she lay down in an empty claw-foot tub for three hours. When she came out, she'd made a decision: she would stay in New York and finish her master's.

"I knew that if I left," she said, "I'd be completely dependent on your dad, and that would be bad."

This story had an iconic power in my imagination. It wasn't just an act of self-assertion for my mom; it was the turning point for a generation of women. So why was I leaving my base of support to return to New York, scene of the crime?

I waited for my migraine. I waited as I dropped off stuff with Goodwill and gave oodles of baby gear to Suzi, as I bought going-away gifts for my brothers and had a good-bye dinner with my dad and his wife. As I nuzzled Lulu good-bye, "Thanks Wonder Dog. You're solo pregnant woman's best friend." As I scheduled the movers for a Sunday, I waited for my head to split with pain. But it did not come. And, finally, the obvious dawned on me: I was not my mother. Brian was not my father. Together, we were not anyone from the past. And, as potentially unsound as our little family of four was, we were in fact a family of four. Our unit was primary. Trying to make a family is a gamble, and if I was going to bet on something, I would bet on what I wanted, what I hoped for, what I believed in. And that was a life with Brian.

It was a leap of faith, and I was already midair.

BROOKLYN (briefly)

22

"WHY DO YOU DRESS UP TO FLY?" BRIAN SAID.

I was drinking tomato juice in a plastic cup, red sludge on ice. Brian had a Coke, always a Coke. At forty thousand feet, wedged among rumpled strangers, we toasted each other.

"My grandmother flew in silk stockings and patent leather heels," I said. "This is a pale imitation."

We were over Oklahoma. Both kids had been asleep for a blissful, overlapping hour. I took his hand. I didn't tell him that I also dressed up to fly because I still wanted to feel like a contender in the realm of attraction. I didn't want to be written off, to disappear into the wallpaper of people. Even with two small children. I wasn't trying to be the prettiest person in the room—my shot at ingenue was long over—but I wanted to register, even a faint blip, on someone's sexual radar.

I squeezed Brian's hand again. I had my legs crossed. Brian slid a hand between my knees. We exchanged a look; we'd been reduced, mostly, to looks. There was very little time, energy, or space for more. But at this, looking, we were world-class. A solar system of desire and insinuation sprang up between us, holding everything we had inside the gravitational pull of our bond: one chubby seven-month-old son; one sickly two-and-a-half-year-old daughter, connected to me by a strand of spittle, thin and delicate as spider silk, strung from the corner of her mouth to a spreading pool of drool on my blouse. We didn't look away.

But there was also a virus in our gaze. What we passed back and forth was not only desire, commitment, and respect, but a needling, constant anxiety. We were building our lives on marshland. The primary unknowable was whether or not Gracie would be OK. Neither of us had the first foggy idea how that would go. We didn't say, "This could go wrong in so many ways." We didn't say, "This will all be fine." We just touched plastic rim to plastic rim and drank.

Outside the window, a pastel city of lilac clouds and dark gray columns grew upward at asymmetrical angles, like a collection of misty, artfully arranged skyscrapers. I wanted to get out and walk around. If nature was capable of beauty on this scale, why allow for mutation? The rogue nations of autism, faulty heart valves, cancer always, forever, cancer, blood disease—what the hell was their point?

"Wake up and pay attention," I said.

"Are you talking to me?" Brian said.

"Um, are you God?"

"Not that I know of."

"Then I'm not talking to you."

I leaned back in my seat and pushed Gracie's damp bangs off her forehead.

"Before she was born," I said, "it never occurred to me, not once, that I might have a sick kid."

Brian was quiet for a while. "I never once thought about having a kid without worrying that something would go wrong."

I was stunned, and a little spooked.

Unlike me, who disliked articulating the darker possibilities for fear of inviting them to manifest, Brian had to plan for the worst, as a form of preemptive exorcism. That meant that, more or less, every bad thing that transpired in his life was something he'd considered ahead of time. Of course lots of bad things he'd thought of hadn't come to pass. But this one had.

I started collecting all our garbage and shoving it into the diaper bag: half-eaten animal crackers, soiled baby wipes, a bottle of coagulated milk. I looked for Gabe's favorite toy, a plush elephant. He was waking up, cooing in a pleasant way that might or might not turn into high-pitched screams during descent.

Gracie stirred and looked around her. "Where are we? Are we up or down?"

"We're almost in New York," I said, and kissed the crown of her head.

"Is New York up or down?"

Good question. We are about to find out.

23

"IMAGINE TEN CHILDREN CROSSING THE STREET," BRIAN SAID. "Five boys, five girls, in a line holding hands. They cross. On the other side, only nine arrive."

We had been in Brooklyn for about six months, without Gracie getting any better. We were having an argument—*the* argument—in our Brooklyn bedroom. I wanted to transplant Gracie. Brian did not. At least not now.

The transplant doctors—we had seen many, on both coasts—had told us that one in ten children didn't make it through. Transplant carried a mortality risk of least 10 percent, maybe higher—15, 20 percent. What level of risk was unlivable? I didn't want to think about it, but I knew Brian wasn't arguing for argument's sake. He was terrified.

I tried not to picture the children, but it was too late; they had sprung to life. A chatty throng of kindergarteners: five boys in Velcro superhero sneakers; five girls with plastic pastel barrettes holding their limp bangs in place.

"Are you willing to send Gracie across the street?" Brian said.

For Brian, the possibility that Gracie could die from the transplant was real. In reality, it was real. For me, to say such a thing aloud was a sacrilege.

"Go away!" I went into the bathroom and locked the door.

"Answer the question," said Brian. "Would you send her across the street?"

If transplant was a huge risk, so was doing nothing. When I thought of Gracie's future without the transplant, the screen filled with silent, gray snow. I could see her at four, maybe five years old. But that was it. Beyond that, she wavered out of sight. My gut feeling was that she needed this cure to survive. If we left her sick, I felt sure she'd get sicker. "Failure to thrive." That phrase was never far off. She could dwindle down, sputter out.

He was afraid she would die if we transplanted her. I was afraid she would die if we didn't. The fact that we were both very wise to be afraid didn't help us decide. And we needed to decide soon. Not this week or month. Not even this year necessarily, but before Gracie got a lot bigger. A successful transplant depended on having a high volume of stem cells for every kilo of body weight. Gabe's cells, stored in the cord blood bank, were finite. Gracie, meanwhile, was only gaining kilos.

If Brian won't agree to this, I thought, *I'll go back to doing everything alone.*

"Heather, unlock the door." Brian tapped rhythmically against the wood, Morse code or maybe the William Tell Overture. I didn't respond. I wanted to stay mad; I would stay mad. We would wake up in the morning, nothing resolved, in a fugue of resentment, him in bed, me in a nest of towels in the bathtub.

But we were actually on the same side. We both wanted our girl to live, and to live a good life. I unlocked the door. Brian sat down beside me. He ran his thumb along my inner wrist. I felt my shoulders relax.

"What are we going to do?" I said.

I wanted him to say, *We'll follow your instincts. We'll use Gabriel's cord blood. We'll do the transplant. We'll hold on like hell and keep her with us.* "I don't know," he said. "I really don't know."

We were confused. We were scared. This was a trial by fire, and we were in the middle part, where you burn.

24

Six months earlier, when we'd arrived in Brooklyn, I had seen a Craigslist ad that sounded too good to be true. "Charming 2-bdrm purple Victorian on Webster Pl., quaint block of Painted Ladies," whatever those were. This rental was at the top of our range, over it. But our range had acquired a terrifying plasticity.

I'd read the ad aloud to my mom over the phone. "Too good to be true, right?"

"Just go check it out," she'd said. "You have nothing to lose."

When I think now at how close we came to missing out on Webster Place, I cringe. I shudder. We could have missed Kathy. We could have missed Eden, Chloe, Steve. We could have missed out on Marty Markowitz, borough president of Brooklyn, standing on our front porch to deliver a short speech to the crowd below.

Painted Ladies turned out to be brightly colored Victorian row houses with wide connected porches. Ours had two floors, huge in comparison to everything I'd seen before. Even before I looked upstairs, where two big bedrooms were divided by heavy wood pocket doors, I was leaping around with excitement saying yes. A backyard, a washer and dryer in *a laundry room*, "parlor floor" windows taller than Brian, double yes.

The owners had to leave town before we could meet to swap lease and keys, so they left the key with a neighbor. Brian arranged to meet her one day after work, but when he arrived at her house, she wasn't home. She was eight months' pregnant at the time, and in the fog of making a new human, simply forgot. He phoned her up, and all was arranged anew. That night I asked how our new neighbor seemed. He said, "She used the word *mortified* about forgetting to meet me. Can you believe someone would be so considerate in 2004 as to be *mortified*?" That was Kathy, day one.

The next morning, as I dragged the garbage out to the curb, an energetic blond woman walked by, pulled by her pug. Eight months' pregnant. Had to be her. She glanced down at our pile of broken junk, including a decrepit hobbyhorse and broken toilet brush.

"The glamour of domestic life," she said, "knows no bounds."

Later I'd know her as a forgiving daughter to inventively demanding parents, a calm and antic mother to two daughters, a tireless and wide-ranging reader, a scattered and funny partner on urban adventures, a haphazard cook, a lover of a slightly messy house, a secret player of strip poker with her mate, a pretty woman unvain in the extreme, a profoundly unpretentious person who grew up in the thick of one pretentious milieu after another without losing sight of what mattered—kindness. I'd know her as the holder of an MFA in fiction, a prize-winning playwright, and someone madly in love with her pug, Monkey. But all that was icing. The cake I found out within the first three minutes: the sight of her bright silhouette walking down the street toward our house gave me a good feeling.

"You must be Kathy," I said, and held out my hand. "I'm Heather, Gracie and Gabriel's mom."

"Kathy," she held out hers, "mother of Eden and whoever is in here."

We were a matched set: two mothers with a toddler and an infant (almost) apiece, aspirational creatives bogged down by small people. When we shook, it felt as if we'd brokered a deal: we'd help each other.

The next day Gracie met Eden, Kathy's daughter, a serious strawberry blonde with a narrow chin and wide-set blue eyes. She wore glasses, which she pushed back into place frequently and with great care. She arrived via a plastic car with a bright orange roof, like an emergency vehicle. Behind the wheel she was calm and self-possessed. When Edith Wharton drove, I thought, this is how she looked. When Eden got close enough, Gracie rushed the car and tried to climb in. It wasn't designed for two, but Eden scooted enough to make room. "Hi," Gracie said, pointing to the nonexistent space between them. "This is Doo Doo." Her imaginary friend.

"I know Doo Doo," Eden said.

And with that, they, too, were friends.

Neither girl had ever made a friend before, and the idea that they lived only a few houses apart was intoxicating. Each would rush outside in the mornings, stand at her end of the block, and shout down to the other end, "Eeeeeeeeeden!" or "Graaaaaaaacie!" They'd run to the middle and throw their arms around each other, a pair of lovers reunited after a tragic separation.

A month or so after we arrived on Webster Place, Kathy delivered her baby, another redheaded girl, Chloe. After that, we began to walk, almost daily, in any kind of weather, because it was the only way we could restrain/entertain all four kids enough to talk.

We would push our merry (or not so merry) clan to Prospect Park, past brownstones, rows of mature trees, and the many, many moms in muted-color, million-dollar active wear. In contrast, we were slobs, who shlumped to the park in anything clean. But we had a good time.

I never mentioned Gracie's illness. I didn't tell Kathy that the toddler kicking her feet with faux hunger as we passed the ice cream truck had thus far visited UCSF Medical Center, Oakland Children's, Stanford, NYU Medical Center, Weill Cornell Medical Center, Memorial Sloan Kettering, Columbia University Medical Center, Long Island Jewish Hospital, Hackensack Medical Center, and Boston Children's. I didn't tell her that we'd recently sent slides of Gracie's blood to a specialist at the NIH and several doctors at the Mayo Clinic.

I didn't share with her the oodles of conflicting advice we'd gotten.

How a famous transplant doctor who'd worked with over nine hundred patients in Italy emailed to say, "Transplant as soon as possible."

While the genius doc at Boston Children's whom we waited months to see wrote to us after the appointment to caution that younger patients see "overall higher rates of peri-transplant morbidity and mortality."

Peri-transplant morbidity and mortality. Really? You had my attention at hello.

With Kathy, our medical life was invisible, and I was just another Brooklyn mom. We talked about *whatever*: the pros and cons of Fresh-Direct; how not to strangle the brutish biters of the playground; our refusal to care about "the baby weight"; books we remembered from back when we read; our own writing, equally distant; our mates' foibles and failings (infinite) compared with their charms (finite). *Whatever* did not include life-threatening illness.

I didn't even tell her that Brian and I weren't married because that part of our story invoked the whole: the unsettling fact that we looked like one thing but were another.

One drizzly morning Kathy called. "Do you wanna go to Coney Island?" Least likely plan for a bad-weather day. Perfect. We arrived somewhere that was, if not Coney Island, then close damn enough. Two parking places on one block, what were the chances? It was now pouring, sheets and sails of pelting rain. Another friend might have said, let's turn back, or insinuated a bit of unspoken blame. We parked and ran toward a neon sign, "Nathan's Famous Hot Dogs."

Inside, I dried off Gabe with paper napkins. Kathy gently patted Chloe's ears and nose. Gracie and Eden, infected with the giddy absurdity of running through rain, shrieked, "We're wet," flailing their limbs. "We are so wet!" As if wet were rich or beautiful; a small victory they'd achieved by collaborating.

Friendship, with its inexplicable alchemies, is hard to parse. Something had drawn Cassie and me to worship the same horse gods, as ten year olds. Had drawn Suzi and me to the same grungy couch at college parties. Something made Kathy and me click at first shake, and that same unknowable something looked to be alive between these two toddlers.

They said it again, practically singing, "We are so wet!"

"This is great," Kathy said, "in the worst possible way." Her laughter transmitted goodwill, a sense of camaraderie in adversity, a little benediction on bad fortune. It was an antidote to Gracie's illness, which Kathy could not see, but which was omnipresent.

I thought of the Auden quote, "Among those whom I like or admire, I can find no common denominator, but among those whom I love, I can; all of them make me laugh."

We ate our soggy hot dogs, in our soggy clothes, then drove home. A nothing afternoon that meant everything.

If you are lucky, you meet four or five people in a lifetime who you're totally comfortable with. Comfortable in a way that causes your best self to surge forward. With them, rowing through life's quotidian mess is an adventure. I thought of my mom and me, twenty years earlier, cracking up as the Corolla filled with water.

That night after the kids were asleep Brian said, "You look like the California you."

"I look different in California and New York?"

"In New York, you sometimes look like a person visiting from another planet and this planet's gravity is too intense for you."

"In New York, everything is heavier."

"But tonight it's lighter?"

"It was a good day. Kathy and I dragged the kids, through rain, to Coney Island, for stale hot dogs."

"That is a good day. Did you talk to her about Gracie?"

"No. I keep thinking that maybe if Kathy and Eden see Gracie as well, then she will be well."

"Sweetheart." Brian put his hand on the small of my back and drew me in.

I put my hand on his cheek and left it there.

"Bedtime," he said.

Bed, where the trick was to stay awake long enough to enjoy it.

25

MIDWINTER, GRACIE BEGAN TO SAG, RUNNING A SERIES OF mysterious fevers, 104, 105, with no discernible cause.

I was already overtaxed by this crazy Brooklyn existence. East Coast winter, with young children, sucks. Leaving the house requires a complex layering of clothes onto baby and toddler that would try the patience of the sanest and most organized person (not me). Once I raised my voice at Gabe, not yet one year old, for squirming out of the snowsuit I'd levered him into. Gracie gave me a dark look and said, "He was just born, give him a little time."

Around four or five each afternoon, I considered placing my head in the oven and turning on the gas. Just to make the place nice and toasty. And then, blissfully, Brian would return home. He'd put down his brief-case. He'd lift Gabriel out of my arms. He'd make Gracie laugh. We would kiss, a nothing kiss. An end-of-day, I'm-home-now kiss, a kiss to make the world go round. A kiss that contained and tried to refute the truth—that our girl was a listing boat in the waters of toddlerhood.

About her fevers, our new New York doctor was cavalier: "Kids do unexplainable things, especially kids with underlying illness, like yours." Did she even know Gracie's name? Also, I didn't like the description, *underlying*, as though Gracie's entire personhood was built on the sickness, rather than the sickness being a footnote to the way she touched her fingertips to my eyelids at night and said, "Can you see me when you sleep?" Or the way—when Brian set her shoes on his head and walked around the house saying, "Where are Gracie's shoes? If only I could find Gracie's shoes!"—she'd laugh until she doubled over, touching her forehead to the floor. A tiny, davening supplicant to her dad's idea of funny.

It was also true that two or three times a day she would collapse with fatigue, a puppet whose strings had been cut.

At the park Gracie would quietly watch the other kids tumble through space, zigging, zagging, squealing through the play structures in wild, energized circles. She seemed to consider their play an enticing, alien task for which she was not fully equipped.

If she climbed to the top of a slide, it was with a devoted, intense focus. As the soul of caution, every step considered. Foot up. Stop. Breathe. Look around. Push up her sleeves. Wave to me. Wave to Kathy. Step. Stop. Breathe. Look around. In the time it took her to climb halfway up, an impatient mob would coagulate behind her, hoping to pass.

Eden would be up and down the slide five times before Gracie summited. Gracie was forever calling after her, "Eden. Wait. Wait, Eden. I am coming."

Kathy never mentioned Gracie's lethargy. If I did, she tried to be reassuring. "That might be her nature," she'd say. "She's a prudent kid. Like Brian!"

Gracie's fevers, her general lack of zest, fueled my sense that we needed to act. One night as I took off Gracie's shoes, I noticed they were tight.

"Oh no!" I cried out. Brian pounded up the stairs.

"What? What is it?"

"She's outgrown this." I held up the guilty red boot.

"And that's bad because?"

"If she's outgrowing her boots, she's outgrowing her donation."

"What donation?"

"Gabe's donation! His cells. They said for transplant the more cells per kilo the better. And she's gaining kilos. Look at these huge feet."

"*If* we decide to transplant her, the cord blood we collected from Gabe is sufficient for many, many shoe sizes to come. You know that."

Gracie, who had been ignoring this conversation in favor of looking through a picture book about baby ducks, turned her attention to her feet.

Brian looked at her. "You're growing, sweetie."

He looked at me. "That's generally perceived to be a good thing."

He picked up the red boot and placed it on his head, glanced anxiously around the room. "If I could only find Gracie's missing shoe, I'd be a completely happy man."

Gracie giggled and touched her forehead to the floor, then turned serious, helpful. "Daddy, look up."

26

THE NEW HEMATOLOGIST, WHO MIGHT OR MIGHT NOT KNOW Gracie's name, was Dr. G. She had come highly recommended by virtually every doctor we'd encountered. In theory, she was amazing. In practice, meh.

On our first visit she'd kept us waiting for almost four hours. "If this is the first date," Brian had said, "I shudder to think how she'll treat us on the second." But her hospital had the best facilities, the best blood. The *washed and irradiated* blood. We would wait.

On our second date, Dr. G told us that we needed to begin chelation. We'd known for a while about the need for chelating transfusion-dependent kids but had put off learning the details of the process in the hope Gracie would be cured before we had to deal with it. No such luck.

"Can you explain the process?" I asked.

Dr. G spoke to us while looking down at her pager. "Children who receive blood transfusions accumulate iron in their tissues. Red cells have an inner iron core. When the transfused cell disintegrates its iron is released into the bloodstream. Over time, this interferes with heart and liver function."

"What will this require from Gracie?" Brian asked.

Dr. G looked at us briefly and then back at her pager. "The patient is hooked up to a pump which delivers a chelating medicine over a twelve-hour period each day."

Until now, Dr. G had evidenced no sense of humor; the chance that this was a cruel joke seemed slim. Her foot bobbed, restless; she was ready to move on to the next room, next customer. *Were those Jimmy Choos?* A gauche display of conspicuous consumption made possible by the for-profit health-care system. Or maybe she came from money, and medicine was just a hobby. Maybe I would like to think about anything except what she had to say.

"Twelve hours?" Brian had said. "Isn't that a long time to constrain a three-year-old?"

"Most parents do it at night."

"How long will she need to do this?"

"For the rest of her life."

Silence on our part.

"As long as she gets blood, you will need to pull the iron out. Otherwise, eventually, the lungs and heart degrade."

My brain locked; I was post-verbal. The heart. The lungs. As though they were free agents, objects separate from the girl, with agendas, frailties, whims of their own. Parts that could rust, decay.

"When should we begin?" Brian asked.

"This week. I'll write you a script for the chelating agent and the pump. A visiting nurse will come and help you learn how to operate it. You'll see, it'll soon be as routine as brushing your teeth."

I wanted to scream, *Do you spend twelve hours brushing your fucking teeth?!* Killing the messenger was too good for Dr. G. I would torture her first, with the spikes on her Jimmy Choos.

From then on, every night, our primary mission was to successfully "hook her up" to the pump.

I was the designated mixer. The chelating medicine, Desferal, came in powder form, which had to be reconstituted into a fresh liquid solution with sterile water, dose by dose. The nurse who taught me the procedure emphasized the danger of overagitating the mixture and creating air bubbles, which could travel to the heart. I lived in fear of accidental effervescence.

The first night had been harrowing. *Wait . . . swirl gently, swirl gently.* I could hear the nurse's voice. *Wait . . .* When it was fully dissolved, I drew the liquid into the syringe, locked the syringe into an evening clutch–sized pump, and primed the tubing until drips came out the end of the needle—careful not to leave any segments of air in the line. And then came the hard part. We had to get numbing cream on the girl, and the needle in the girl, without waking her. It was not a big needle, more of a thumbtack, but, like a thumbtack, it had to be pushed straight down. Pushing a thumbtack into your child is a counterintuitive act.

We put the cream on Gracie and waited for her to fall asleep.

When the needle pierced her skin, Gracie sat up precipitously and looked at us. "Be very careful," she said, then toppled to the left, asleep again.

We crept out of the kids' room and into ours.

I could hear Gabe's quick whistling breaths in the next room against Gracie's slower deep breaths. Hopefully, the pump's medication was pulling iron out of her heart and lungs. Hopefully, they were not "degrading" right this second. It was hard to believe that chelating was a job for us, laypeople.

A week earlier, after a walk without hats in which the kids had been badly snowed on, Brian had said, "We don't deserve these kids." It was true, we didn't, because no one does; a child is an unearnable grace. There is no way to deserve or earn a child. But Brian wasn't being existential. He'd meant that *we* did not deserve *these* kids. And this infuriated me precisely because it was partially true. We were artists, easily distracted, epically unorganized. Acting as her medical team seemed a dubious undertaking at best.

Still. However much we fucked it up, life with these small people moved me beyond words. Their smells, the way they lifted their arms for "uppy" with total confidence that Brian or I would reach down, the velvet of their inner wrists, the translucence of their ears—little shells held up to the light. It was too much to bear. I turned to Brian in bed.

"We might not deserve them," I said. "But we cherish them. That must count for something."

"You did an amazing job with the chelating thing," he said.

"Thanks," I said. A beat went by. "I don't want to leave her like this. Do you?"

Brian didn't fidget; he didn't look at me. He stared at the wall. I knew if I waited, he'd say something meaningful. If I interrupted with another question, another accusation, we'd move backward.

I wanted to push the argument, but at the same time I was scared he'd agree with me. The alternative to a life with the pump was to send her across the street in the group of ten chatty children, each irreplaceable, one of whom would not arrive.

Our bedroom was on the parlor level. Indigo shapes wavered in the tall windows, shadowy tree wraiths whose branches made fleeting, indistinct hand gestures. If only we could decipher the signs.

After a while the wind died down and the branches quieted.

"We're so lucky to have that tree," I said, breaking a long silence.

"We are," Brian said. He pulled me toward him; I tucked my face into the crook of his neck and inhaled him.

As much as we were at a loss over what to do with our girl, I was calmed by our essential togetherness.

If my past self—pregnant and alone—could have glimpsed this moment hovering in the future, she'd have been floored. And surpassingly reassured. But she couldn't. All I could do for her now was to try and persuade her to let go of her resentments, her grudges, her niggling doubts. To remind her that the father Brian had become—one who offered both kids the full measure of his kindness, patience, playfulness, a near limitless attention to their boring, endless needs—had been embedded in the reluctant father all along. I stroked Brian's face with the back of my hand.

"You surprised me."

"I surprised you how?"

"With how much you like being a dad. Does it surprise you?"

"I wouldn't really put it that way. It's more like Gracie kicked down a door and released a tidal wave of love for you. And her. And then Gabe."

"Not everyone can accommodate tidal waves of change."

"Not everyone waits for it."

"I only waited because of your leprechaun dance."

"My leprechaun dance?"

"Remember that time you did that weird little dance, imitating David Letterman imitating a leprechaun?"

"Oh, yeah." And I knew he did, because he remembered everything. Every single thing.

"I thought that any man who wears button-down oxford shirts and believes in political morality and can correctly punctuate nearly any sentence—and who can *also* do a leprechaun dance—had to be the one."

"That's all it took? Any guy dancing a little jig could have scooped you up?"

"Any guy who was you."

27

Throughout our time in brooklyn, brian's college roommate, affectionately known in our house as "Stooch," would periodically urge us to call his ex-wife's sister, a pediatric transplant doctor down in North Carolina. Though we loved Stooch and knew he meant well, we doubted that the key to Gracie's well-being lay in contacting Stooch's ex-wife's sister. Everyone wants to help. Lots of people point you in different directions.

We didn't need another doctor in the mix.

But Stooch kept bringing it up, and so finally one Sunday we called, mostly to say we'd done it and be done with it. The doctor we reached, Dr. Joanne Kurtzberg, was a total surprise. First of all, she happened to be on vacation when we left a message, but she called us back within an hour. She instantly gave us her pager number and cell. She talked with us for almost an hour. It seemed impossibly generous, someone willing to interrupt their fruity cocktail to chat about HLA tissue matches.

Brian began Googling and ended up in shock: Kurtzberg ran the Cord Blood Bone Marrow Transplant unit at Duke Medical Center in Durham. Using cord blood was relatively new in 2004, and most of the places we'd consulted with had done fewer than twenty CB transplants.

Duke had done over two hundred. Cord blood bone marrow transplants were Dr. Kurtzberg's frontier, and she was Annie Oakley.

Dr. Kurtzberg had no doubt whatsoever that Gracie could be cured using Gabriel's stem cells, especially given that he was "an extended match." Of the six key markers that must match, Gabriel and Gracie matched all six, and then matched another twelve markers beyond the six. Given such an ideal scenario, Dr. Kurtzberg urged us to transplant Gracie immediately. The fact that this would require us to move to North Carolina for at least six months, likely longer, and that it meant accepting a serious mortality risk right now, didn't diminish her confidence. She knew she could cure this child and, she implied, it was our duty to let her do it.

This sent us spinning.

In contrast to other physicians who'd advised us to wait, who'd emphasized the risks in transplanting younger patients, Dr. Kurtzberg had one clear message: do it now.

Her perspective was that every blood transfusion Gracie received was weakening her transplant chances, as it weakened her liver with iron overload. The liver is transplant's hero, the star, the strongman who does the heavy lifting—filtering and disposing of all the toxins from the chemotherapy drugs necessary to prepare the body. Kurtzberg liked to bet on young, healthy livers, the younger and healthier the better. My intuitive sense of what was best for Gracie flowed in the opposite direction. Gracie's liver was so little; it was barely three. How could such an inexperienced organ be expected to do such a complex, demanding job?

Talking with Dr. Kurtzberg intensified my confusion to a near frenzy.

"This is nuts," I said to Brian. "They all say different things. Who are we supposed to trust?" I was manically chopping onions; crying for nonemotional reasons had become a strange pleasure.

"Us," Brian said. "We should trust us."

I spun to face him, onion knife in hand, "Why us? Do you have some secret scale we can use to weigh life with medical torment that lasts maybe, maybe, to age twenty-nine against a chance for a cure which might mean she only lives to four?"

Brian took the knife from my hand and began to chop in my place. Later, as we were falling asleep, he took my hand. "We are the two people who love her more than anyone else on earth. We're the scale. We'll decide."

In this state of agitation, in constant and unresolved conversation, under the shadow of *if*, fearing, constantly, that by making no move we were making the wrong move, but equally afraid to act, Brian and I passed out of winter through spring (unnoticed by us) and into summer's beginning.

28

On a saturday in early june, kathy and i walked to the Brooklyn Museum. It was hot, and we were desperate for the cool spray that blew off the fountain in front of the museum. As we watched the kids play in the water, I was thinking of whether to tell Kathy about Gracie. We'd been friends for three seasons, and it had been so nice not to tell. To pretend, even to myself, that there was no story. To put on this puppet theater, starring Gracie as a healthy child. Now, though, I wanted Kathy's counsel.

I dithered until it was time to head home. We each pushed our double strollers toward Webster Place. On the slightest of inclines, we wheezed. We weren't really young moms; we were just moms with young kids. It was a soft night; the kids were cooling down, drowsing off.

I took a breath. I was afraid she'd be mad at me for withholding something so big for so long.

"Kath."

She kept walking, pushing uphill, looking toward me. "Yeah?"

"Kathy."

She looked over at me.

"I've been meaning to tell you this thing, but I don't want to freak you out . . ."

"Yeah?"

"Gracie is sick."

"Sick how?"

I looked down into the strollers; both my kids were sleeping. So was Eden. Only Chloe, redheaded eight-month-old, was awake. "She was born sick," I said. "She has a blood disease." We were walking along the edge of Prospect Park, under the deep shade of old trees. Benches lined the sidewalk.

"Let's sit," Kathy said. "The kids won't wake up." She handed Chloe a graham cracker. Chloe grasped it in both hands and drew it to her mouth lovingly.

"She doesn't make red cells. Or she makes them, but they fall apart before they mature, so she has to get blood transfusions every three or four weeks."

Kathy kept looking at me. She didn't shout, "Are you kidding me? Is this a weird joke?!" She didn't glaze over. She was quiet and calm and curious. "So what does that mean? Can she do that forever?"

I explained that people could live into adulthood like that, always getting transfused. But that the problem was every time we gave her blood, we were also giving her iron, and over time that iron would accumulate in her lungs and heart.

Kathy reached over to Gracie and pulled her sundress over her knees, a protective gesture. A small act of ownership. I wanted to throw my arms around her or burst into tears. But we weren't like that. Even if we wanted to be sloppy, we would hold ourselves in check. We were the moms now, not the kids.

"OK," Kathy said, as if accepting the facts could abrade them, shrink them. "What can you do? What are you going to do?"

"We can transplant her. That would be a cure. A bone marrow transplant," I said.

"A bone marrow transplant?" She looked like someone who'd received an electrical shock; her spine went straight, she lost her air of languor. Her look said, *Let's not lose our heads*. Bone marrow transplant is drastic; it *is* losing one's head. Every bone marrow transplant is essentially a Hail Mary pass. And still, it was what we had.

"Isn't there something else you could try first?" she said. I shook my head.

"This is our only card," I said. "We can play it or not play it, but it's the whole deck."

I stood up, pulled my shirt away from my chest. It was still hot, and my skin and brain felt coated and clogged. Kathy stood too, and we walked on subdued. I told her about Gracie's chelation regime, how we had to pull the iron out of her organs, the little evening clutch of a machine we hooked her up to every night. The conflicting advice we were getting from other doctors in contrast with Dr. Kurtzberg's confidence, which had a synergistic effect on my fears and determination, making me both more afraid of transplant and more convinced we should do it.

"When are you going to decide?" Kathy asked, as we turned the corner onto Webster Place. I looked down its length of cheerful pastel Victorians. Some had rockers on the front porch. This was a special block. I reveled in our luck at landing here.

"I don't know," I said. "If Gracie keeps spiking mysterious fevers, and going all rag doll, it might be decided for us."

Kathy's house was first, near the corner, and we paused in front of her door. She reached to hug me. We were busy people, always handing things to each other or to the kids. We didn't bother with actual hugs very often. But now she held on. Her hair smelled good. I knew she used Pantene, but she smelled like Herbal Essence—which gave me a hopeful, serene feeling.

"I'm glad you told me," Kathy said. "I'm not glad it's true. But I'm glad I know."

29

As we were leaving the house for Gracie's first blood transfusion of the summer, our neighbors across the street happened to be climbing into their car. Gracie looked at them, waved, then asked, "Are they going to get their blood?"

Yes, we wanted to say. Instead Brian said, "Probably not, sweetie. Not everyone gets blood."

"But when you and mommy were little, you got your blood, right?"

Brian and I traded a look.

"Well," I said, "some people don't get blood. And other people do, like you." I was hoping this sounded as if she was not alone in her situation.

"Who gets blood that we know?"

We faltered. Why had we not—in anticipation of this question—befriended a few hemophiliacs? Then I remembered accidents. Fabulous, blood-spilling accidents.

"Uncle Dawa needed blood when he had a crash in the car!" I said.

"Did he like getting blood?" Gracie said.

"I'm not sure. Is it fun for you?"

"No." She seemed unsure of whether to pity or disdain me. "It's not fun."

We were forever trying to figure out how to talk with Gracie about her sickness. She knew she had it, but she just hadn't known, until then, that not everyone else had it too. We wanted her to see herself as normal, as essentially fine. But we didn't want to sell her a story of herself that was untrue.

As we waited at the hospital for Gracie's blood to be washed and irradiated, she and Gabriel stacked plastic cubes with realistic beach scenes inside. Each cube contained real sand, mini–palm trees, tiny beach balls that rattled against the clear walls. They fascinated Gracie. She was transfixed by a world miniaturized enough to fit into the palm of her hand. She shook the cubes gently to make the palm fronds sway. While Gracie stacked, Gabe sat beside her, handing her cubes one by one as she built upward. As she placed a block on top, Gracie peered down at Gabe. "Gabe!" she said, as though she'd just remembered to tell him something important. "Guess what? You don't need blood!" As a reply, he handed her a tiny ocean encased in plastic.

On the way home, with two pink and sleeping kids in back, I asked Brian to stop at the food co-op. I wanted to run in while he waited with the kids in the car, but Brian resisted. He hadn't written all weekend. He barely had time to write at all now that he was teaching so much to support us, and he wanted to get home to the keyboard while he still had mental power. He had the jagged energy of an addict deprived of his fix. But we were out of bread, milk, my favorite sharp cheese.

We negotiated, compromised. "I'll run in for essentials only," I said. "Ten minutes. Fifteen tops."

Walking around alone—without a person hanging from my hip or arm, without sticky fruit leather fingers in my hair—felt so luxurious. I lingered over the imported olives and popped wasabi almonds from the bulk bins in my mouth, aware that I was over my time limit. After a while, I didn't care. I decided to get everything we needed, or even wanted, so that I wouldn't have to come back later in the week.

When I got back to the car Brian was livid. It had been nothing remotely like fifteen minutes, more like forty. Maybe forty-five. Both kids were still sleeping, but he'd lost his window for writing. He started to say something condemning, but I had been practicing a preemptive counterpunch in the checkout line: "I was shopping *for our family*," I said before he could say anything. In my head this phrase had sounded like a moral home run. Who could argue with that? But I'd miscalculated. You can't slip sloppy moralizing past Brian.

He'd gotten out of the car to help load the groceries, so we stood face to face. "How noble of you, to shop *for our family*." His voice was tight, derisive. As he said this, he bowed, a full-body, bent-knee bow until his forehead touched the concrete.

"Oh fuck off, Brian," I said.

If I'd just said *fuck off*, without the aggressive casualness of *oh* or without using his name, that might have been OK. As soon as I said *Brian*, I knew I'd made a mistake. Saying *Brian* proclaimed my anger as not only free-floating anxiety, desperation, what-have-you, but as a force I was willing to leverage against him.

The grocery bags were sitting next to the car. Brian reached into the closest one, grabbed an organic pear, and chucked it over the car, onto Seventh Avenue. "Was that for our family?" he shouted as he threw it. Not at me but over me. He picked up a sourdough baguette and hurled it into the middle of the street. He kept on pitching groceries, one after another, over the car into the road, "What about this? Is this for our family?" A container of organic maple yogurt arced up and over the windshield, splattering where it landed near a storm drain.

This was Brian as I'd rarely seen him. Not never but hardly ever. He once told me how an old girlfriend described his confrontational style, his fuse, as *nice, nice, nice, nice—boom*.

I was trying to gauge how out of control he was. He seemed to be sticking to the soft foods. Nothing was hitting the car, only arcing over it. He was a decent shot, even in a fit of rage. Was he dangerous? He shoved one of the bags out of the way, to reach into another. A glass bottle of juice broke.

"Get out of here," I shouted, pointing down the street. "Get away from us."

Brian didn't move. I didn't move.

"This is over," I said, operating on the level of primary risk assessment. I grew up watching my mom tolerate a man who flew into rages. A violent man whom she allowed to go on living with her and with me and with my brothers. My small, vulnerable brothers. I didn't want that. I didn't want a grocery thrower, even if the groceries weren't aimed in my direction.

"This is over," I said again.

I didn't know exactly what *this* was. It might have referred to the relationship, the fight, the ill-fated trip to the co-op. All I knew for sure was that I meant something, and that I wanted him to get away from me, from the car, from the kids.

A tentative crowd had gathered. Or rather a few people exiting the store lingered, hoping not to get involved but also feeling obligated to make sure all was OK. Brian had begun to calm down, and he looked as if he wanted to help clean up. He hesitated, then began to walk away, down Union Street, in the direction of Manhattan. The kids, fabulously, were still asleep.

A man and woman approached me as I picked up food items off the street, "Can we help?" I brushed off their help, embarrassed, and got into the car as quickly as possible, leaving our mess. Worse things had surely been spilled on Seventh Avenue, but I felt as if I was fleeing the scene of a crime.

I'll move back to California, I thought. I can leave now. Tonight. I have credit cards. I have options. I can drive West. The kids are already in the car! This seemed like a viable plan. I could drive cross-country with the two of them in the back. They were a complete system: problem and solution, donor and donee. Brian and I could disassemble this family as fast as we'd assembled it. Fuck him. Seriously. Fuck him.

But then I would be in California with two small children. Without Brian.

I called Cassie, hyperventilating into the phone. She understood maybe every third word. She said calming things. In her calming voice. She reminded me to breathe, which seemed reasonable enough. I slowed down. I didn't get on the highway. I drove toward Webster Place, sobbing. "You are under stress," Cassie said, "too much stress. One of you, or both of you, is bound to blow up."

I relaxed a tiny bit. If this fight was not about grocery shopping or Brian's writing time, we might be OK. As I sat in the car, parked in front of our house, Brian appeared at the end of the block. I told Cassie it was all right, and I'd call her later.

I was surprised to see him. Any other time I'd pushed Brian away, he'd gone away. He wasn't one to be disinvited twice. The old cold shoulder never worked with him; he'd drift farther off. But, this time, he'd come home.

"I'm sorry," he said. "I'm really sorry. Do you want me to go sleep at Mark's?"

"Yes. I do." Not because I did, but because I thought I should err on the side of distance, sequestration. Time in my own head.

I carried the kids to bed and tried to figure out what on earth was happening. Who were we if we could fight like that? If Brian was willing to have a public tantrum when his writing time was whittled down, was he capable of family life? Maybe he'd understood himself better than I had, all along. And what about my hyperbolic *This is over*; was I that unsure of our life together that I could end things over a single fight, even a bad fight?

The next day Brian came home early from work. We didn't say much to each other. It was a Monday night. We fed the kids dinner, then ate peanut rolls and Thai soup. I felt reassured. If we could drink from the same soup bowl, there must be some mutual understanding. We put the kids to bed and went through the routine of med mixing, numbing cream, needle in, pump on. Gracie didn't wake up, only stirred enough to roll on her side and mumble vowels. Her light brown curls clung to the back of her neck with night sweat.

When she was hooked up, we went downstairs to talk.

We sat side by side on the couch, bent double, head to the knees, and turned to each other. This was the ultimate posture of defeat, no stamina to even hold the body upright.

I looked at him for a long time, and he looked at me.

"You frightened me."

"I know I did, and I'm sorry. I would never hurt you."

"You threw groceries at me."

"I threw groceries. Not at you."

"You frightened me."

"I was really angry, but I wasn't trying to scare you. I'm sorry I scared you. If you want me to go to an anger management program, I will. I will go somewhere where they teach you not to throw organic yogurt, no matter how mad you are."

If someone is volunteering to go to anger management, chances are they don't need anger management. I was wary of him but also comforted that he still looked like himself. Brian's face, even with the greenish cast of fatigue and worry, was so very Brian. His high forehead; his twice-broken nose that, midlength, bends right, as if, having considered its options, chooses to turn this way; his full mouth, with the sensual lower lip bestowed on lucky Jewish intellectuals. A line from a Sharon Olds poem drifted to mind, in which the iris of her lover's eye has a calm like "the dignity of matter."

This was what we could offer each other when we were lucky enough to stay awake for a few minutes beyond the children. Looking. Seeing. Being seen.

We were touching along the length of our sides: ankles, knees, thighs, hips, arms, shoulders. We laid the backs of our hands together, an old intimacy. After a while Brian looked down at the floor.

"Gracie is sick," he said.

"I know she is."

There was a long quiet, broken by sounds outside. Teenagers at the end of the block, throwing their voices for dramatic effect. "She fucking lied! What the fuck!"

"I'm ready to take her to North Carolina," Brian said. "Are you?"

"Yeah," I answered, "I am."

We sat for a while longer, listening to the street. Ten p.m. on Webster Place. Faintly, from a few blocks away, the ice cream man's insanity-inducing jingle. The brisk river of traffic on Prospect Avenue. Beneath this a chorus of harmonic chirps and rubbed notes. "Do you hear crickets?" I sat up. Brian shook off my question with a lift of his left shoulder.

He looked as if he was bracing himself for something painful and inevitable. Like someone trapped inside the lucid, elongated moments between losing control of the wheel and impact. Those baggy, expanding seconds in which you realize that even as the humped, dark shapes at the edge of the road draw closer, grow bigger, you have no idea what the hell it is you're about to hit.

30

LIFESAVING MEDICAL CARE IS THE KIND OF THING YOU BUY whether you can afford it or not. And so we prepared to go disastrously broke.

Shortly after deciding to go to Durham, we received a letter alerting us that, upon reviewing our insurance coverage, the Children's Organ Transplant Association (COTA, the family support agency we'd been referred to by the hospital social worker) estimated we would need $85,000 to cover uninsured medical expenses and Brian's commute during the transplant period. I could hardly believe that Brian would once more be living in one state with us and working in another, but we had to keep our health insurance, no matter what. And that meant he had to teach full-time, in New York, while Gracie got treatment in North Carolina.

Raising $85,000 in a couple of months sounded about as likely as Gabriel translating *Moby-Dick* into Arabic, tonight. I pictured $85,000 in the form of the kids' blocks: a stack of plastic cubes towering over Brooklyn in a long, skinny, tilting line.

Brian was working as hard as was humanly possible. I was taking Gracie to the doctor, watching the kids, my mom was in California, my generous grandmother's money was long gone. Who exactly was going to raise this money?

When Brian arrived home I'd said, "Are you ready for this? It turns out we can't afford a transplant!"

"What do you mean?" he came toward me for a kiss, with a kiss.

A kiss between two people in need of $85,000, neither of whom had a clue where to find it. A kiss to keep the world spinning. Brian's lips were soft and warm, brief and promising.

I showed him the letter. "Eighty-five thousand dollars," he said. He wasn't as shocked as I'd been. He was more of a realist. He knew we were raising money for Gracie to join the ten kids crossing the street.

We were capable of going $85,000 into debt, or more, if that was what it took. We had credit cards and health insurance; that would get us in the door. But unless we raised money for Gracie's care, and plenty of it, we would come out the other end in bad shape. An absolutely American story.

If you had told me ahead of time that Kathy would raise the money, that her husband, Steve, would make it happen, that a handful of Brian's longtime friends and colleagues from *Dissent* magazine and Sarah Lawrence College and my friends from World College West would rally around in the most astonishing ways, that two *separate* millionaires would offer to pay the entire thing, I wouldn't have believed you. But that was what happened.

On the West Coast, Dawa organized a Westie fund-raiser with two weeks' notice at the community center in Stinson Beach. On the Upper West Side, Brian's dear friends Mark and Melissa hosted a fund-raising party/brainstorm session in their big, beautiful apartment for Brian's *Dissent* and Sarah Lawrence College colleagues. And in Brooklyn, Kathy dreamed up, organized, and galvanized an entire neighborhood into a block party.

And then it went wider. Kathy's husband, Steve, had worked as a journalist. He got in touch with a few media people interested in Gracie's story, they ran short pieces, and then suddenly, and briefly, her story caught fire. She was on the cover of the *New York Post*, on NY1 (the local cable TV station), in almost all of the Brooklyn papers. Every paper ran COTA's website address for donating. Donations began to pour in.

At Kathy's block party there were clowns, face painters. The local fire truck drove Gracie and a gaggle of pals around the block. An older couple came up and introduced themselves; they had read about Gracie's story, and the man had built her a Victorian dollhouse, complete with gingerbread trim. They brought a photo of it. "Gracie's Mansion" was hand-lettered above a light blue front door.

"When she comes home, swing by and pick it up," they said. I love their optimism. *When.*

Around five o'clock, as the party took on a mellow vibe, Marty Markowitz, Brooklyn borough president, arrived. He stood on our porch to address the crowd. He declared this "Gracie Day" and wished her well. I cried and said something inarticulate. Brian welled up and said something articulate. Gracie shrieked and ran in circles and generally embarrassed us with her appearance of good health. "She really is sick," I wanted to tell people. "I swear." Gabriel fell asleep over Brian's shoulder.

All afternoon Gracie, who'd only lived in Brooklyn for one year, was claimed by folks all through the neighborhood and beyond, claimed by the working-class guys who drank at the bar where they ran a fifty-fifty raffle for her. Claimed by a young man from the DMV. How could he know how much his generosity meant? He was barely more than a teenager, with his teenage girlfriend by his side whom he called "my fiancée," both of them barely looking old enough to drink, much less marry, or care about sick children they'd never met, but there he was with an envelope stuffed full of cash. He'd taken up a collection at work and wanted to deliver it in person. Claimed by the mother and daughter who rang our doorbell, long after the party was over, with two fluffy stuffed chairs they'd bought at Target—one Elmo, one Dora—to take with us to North Carolina so that, as the mother put it, "your little ones can be comfy at least."

Without the block party, we might have raised enough money, *maybe.* But we would have missed out on knowing the full kindness of strangers, the power of a few determined friends, and the deep heart of Brooklyn. And it was also good that we raised the money because, as it turned out, we needed every cent.

At the end of the night, exhausted and grateful beyond all measure, I hugged Kathy. "You did this. You are superhuman. My God. How are we ever going to thank you?"

"Come back and be my writer-mom friend again. Let the girls grow into truculent teenagers together." Pause. "OK?"

That she posed it as a choice was her parting gift.

DURHAM

31

THE DAY BEFORE THANKSGIVING, WE FLEW TO DURHAM. Brian and I held hands across the narrow aisle. Gabriel stood on Brian's lap, peering up his nose, convinced that, given enough time, he'd find treasure. Gracie kept up a happy running monologue of questions and assertions.

"I am going to see Eden again. You know that, right?"

"I do."

"Look, Mama, we are up. We are going up." She was obsessed with the clouds, their fluffiness. Were they cold? Were they scratchy? Could they hold you?

"If you jump high enough, can you get from the ground to a cloud?"

"Maybe," I said, noncommittal, wanting to promise nothing, wanting to get off the subject of clouds, uncomfortable cousin to heaven. But she was curious.

"If I called 'Mommy' from the sky, could you hear me?"

"What do you think?" I don't know, don't want to know.

"*You* say the answer."

"Yes, I would hear you." I hope.

"Are the clouds soft? Will they snuggle you, like a blanket?"

"Look," I said, "here comes the lady with snacks."

"I want a fuzzy drink. Daddy! I see animal crackers. Get me animal crackers. Don't give Gabriel the elephant. No! I want the elephant, Daddy!"

Gabriel is giving you his stem cells, I wanted to say. Let him have the ever-loving elephant.

After a very long time, we were nearly there.

"We are going down, Mama. Look down!"

Down was the gentle green of Raleigh-Durham, a mild landscape. No dramatic cliffs, no edge of ocean, no peaks, no dense tangle of buildings. Just a few lakes, lots and lots and lots of trees, and a modest-sized city in the distance.

Gracie was pulling on Brian's collar, "Did Gabriel eat my cookie?"

Quiet, hush, hush. We'll give you anything you want. We are flying to the hospital in North Carolina. Everything is about to change.

When we stepped off the plane, the air felt like a skim coating of whipped cream applied to the skin. That's good; air is oxygen. We were all for oxygen.

We collected our stuff, rented a car, and drove to Alexan Farms, the condo complex we'd seen only online. Our sublet unit was much bigger than our place in Brooklyn but too near a busy road. I looked out the window at the cars whizzing past. They were about a hundred yards away, but only a quaint wood fence with wide-spaced slats separated us from them. I gestured with my head toward the road and said to Brian, "How would that be for an ironic twist?"

I went to the management office, Gracie in tow as evidence. She skipped ahead of me into the lobby where a tall bronze horse raked the air with its hooves. She ran her hands along its muscled legs, "What makes him so cold?" I rambled about the core temperature of metals, realizing that, on the inside, Gracie herself was essentially gilded.

"Are you chilly?" I pulled the cuffs of her pink shirt out from the sleeves of her darker pink sweater.

The woman at the desk stopped typing as soon as we walked in. This must be the South, I thought, if people pay attention to an opening door. I explained our plight. She gave me a rueful look. "I am so sorry," she said. "I hate to disappoint the transplant families. We try to accommodate y'all in every way we can, but we don't have any units left except that one by the road." Her obvious distress at not being able to help, the look on her face as she glanced from me to Gracie and quickly away, this was something new.

Gracie had always looked and seemed healthy enough to pass. We hadn't yet been subjected to the double-edged blade of pity and kindness most people display when encountering a visibly sick kid. I was at once piqued; this woman assumed my life circumstances were worse than her own (never mind that they likely were); and then grateful (she knew, she understood); and then flooded with a quick dose of potential power—the sick-kid trump card!

I tried to look somber. "Well, we really need the next unit that comes up. My son is only one and a half, and he'll be home with the babysitter while I'm at the hospital with my daughter, so I'd feel much easier if we were away from the road." She nodded and promised to relocate us if possible. Gracie said, "No! I don't want to move again!"

I didn't explain that she wasn't going to be living in the apartment long, that she would be in the hospital. I took her hand and led her back past the tidy line of mailboxes, the pristine blue pool, the petunias in neat rows, the long shiny bank of Camrys and Nissans, the border shrubs groomed into tight angular lines. Every living thing had bowed its head in submission to the landscaping team. It seemed like a movie set or Disneyland, where my little brother Dylan had once run up to each tree, placed his palms upon the bark, and asked, "Is it real?"

Surely living in such a controlled environment was a hedge against chaos or heartbreak. But I hated it. Every time I drove into the complex, the phrase "a less soulful life" would dart across my mind.

Back in the apartment Gabe was riding Brian around our new living room. For a man happiest discussing the nuanced differences between Henry James's late and early work, Brian was surprisingly willing to be a pony. He moved at an old-mare pace, afraid Gabe would fall off. Gabe flung his legs up and down. "Go, go!"

I looked around the room, flummoxed: there were no lamps and no dining room chairs. At the furniture rental place, a beleaguered woman answered the phone, probably juggling multiple disgruntled customers at once.

"Listen, if you can't get it together to deliver what we need, I'll come there," I said.

"I'm so sorry," she answered, "we don't disclose our location."

"You don't disclose your location? Really? You must be a very exciting, black ops furniture rental business." Lately, my public face had begun to warp.

She didn't say anything. Maybe she had a policy against responding to people who, within the first minute of a phone call, stooped to sarcasm and political innuendo.

I felt for her. But I also felt for me. I was exhausted and frightened, and she was the only one I could get on the phone. There were, to my knowledge, no customer service centers open for questions along the lines of *Why do innocents suffer?*

Ultimately, and not on the strength of my charm, we got our lamps and dining room chairs. Though it did not quell my larger anxieties, making the apartment functional gave me a delicious, illusory sense of control. Within twenty-four hours we had matching silverware, lemon-scented hand soap in every bathroom, sufficient paper towels and toilet paper to pass down through the generations, a utility room stocked with tinfoil, bug spray, laundry soap, and disinfecting wipes; we'd installed both Wi-Fi and a deluxe cable package, and stocked bottles of cabernet above a secret kitchen drawer that cooled multiple grades of dark chocolate. In our walk-in closet (another perk of southern living, I'd never before walked *into* a closet), my bras were folded (yes, they can be folded) into neat piles of ascending pink and ivory.

On Thanksgiving morning, Brian ran out to Whole Foods and returned with an entire meal. We heated, served, and ate it, laboring to feel thankful. Afterward I took the kids outside to fly a kite. There'd been an early snow, the lightest dusting over the open green space beside our unit. The kite lifted and dove, caught and lost wind. Against the snow, it formed a startling red diamond on white. Gracie ran to it, picked it up, and held it against her chest with care. "It's OK. Flying is hard."

32

WE'D BEEN TO DUKE ONCE BEFORE FOR A CONSULTATION, BUT walking in as the parents of a girl who would, for certain, receive a transplant in this building, we saw it as if for the first time. The ceiling rose four stories above us. On each floor an open balcony curved into the high lobby space. The balcony railings were rimmed with see-through rounds of glass, so that children could look down on doctors below in white coats, cut down to size. Finally, smaller than the children themselves! Hanging fifty feet overhead were gigantic mobiles made of colored feathers. They twisted in the ventilation breeze. Someone, probably many someones, had spent vast amounts of time and money designing a space that would put children at ease, delight them.

I tried not to think of Temple Grandin's humane redesign of slaughterhouse chutes with obfuscation. Don't let them see what's coming, how bad it is going to get. The cattle chutes, bending, dipping into water, bending again, but still, always, ending at the same silver blade.

Brian was making low-key jokes with the kids, pointing out the giant fish tank and fountain in the lobby. He took my hand and squeezed it in rapid pulses, an old code, *I'm here, you're here, I'm here.*

We rode the glass elevator to the Green Level, floor four, home of the Pediatric Blood and Marrow Transplant Clinic.

In the waiting area I looked around with dismay. Until now, we'd been in the minor leagues. Not only did these kids look terrible, but most of them looked terrible in the same uniform way. They'd been transmogrified. They were, for the most part, bald, bloated, sallow, and slightly hairy-faced. They'd traded in their healthy bodies for oddly shaped sacks. The life force, the spark, had been siphoned out of them.

An older, slightly overweight girl said to her mother, casually, "Maybe I won't have children."

A toddler at the train table in mismatched Crocs, one blue, one green, stumbled and leapt up again, "I'm OK!" he said. A little loud, a little overeager. An assertion to the world, get this, take note, *I* am OK.

A playful redheaded girl holding a Barbie by the hair said to her doctor, "Bye, Dr. Googley-Eyes." Her father, one hand on her shoulder, exchanged a look of despair with the doctor.

I felt an urgent wish to grab Gracie by the hand and run.

Look, I told myself, it's just a hospital. Don't be melodramatic. Take your cues from Brian, be calm. Take your cues from Gabe, get into the fish.

Across from us sat a boy some years older than Gracie. He was bald, with Groucho Marx eyebrows. His body looked overinflated and frail: a sack of vapors that might collapse under pressure. I might come to feel a certain affection for this look—the transplant bloat—but not today.

Gracie and the boy eyed each other, both a bit bored, investigating.

"Are you sick?" he said. She looked too good, out of place. He was questioning her credentials.

The mom looked up from her magazine. "Jake, that's not polite."

"I get blood," Gracie told him. This was good enough. She and Jake moved toward the balcony railing so they could look down to the lobby. Gabriel snatched a pair of reading glasses off Brian's head and trailed after them. That was his job description, trail after.

The mom gave me a look of apology, I mimed my understanding, and we started to chat. Jake had already had his transplant and since then had been stuck in an extended cycle of clinic visits for a litany of side effects. Here, we teetered, in silence. Should I ask more? Was that tantamount to making friends, our first Duke friends? We'd been cautioned against this: knowing, caring about, other families.

One transplant father I'd spoken to had said, "This will seem crazy, but don't make friends. You don't know which kids will make it and which ones won't. If you get too close to the family of a kid who doesn't pull through, it can send you off the rails. And you have to stay on the rails." I didn't tell him so, but I did think he sounded crazy. When I told Brian what he'd said, Brian didn't think it sounded crazy at all. "I think he's suggesting that it's best to save your energy for your own kid. That makes sense." Maybe, but what had always kept me steadiest in life was friends. On the other hand, what the hell could regular life teach you about transplant life? I'd never had to stand by while a friend's child suffered. Or died.

I knew Brian would preserve the core of his caring for Gracie. And that was beautiful. And for better or for worse, perhaps even selfishly, I knew I'd make friends.

"How often do you come to clinic?" I asked the mom, Cindy.

"Four times a week at least, and we are here for almost the whole day every time." I looked at her, hoping to appear more empathic than horrified. "We've been doing this for over two years," she said. "With no end in sight."

"Do you work?" I asked. "I mean besides this?"

"I was a nurse," she said, "but not now. It would be impossible."

I didn't ask her if her family was hurting without her salary, or if she missed working, or if she'd go back, or, if she wanted to go back, would they have her. I tried not to ask myself these questions either, because I was pretty sure the answers would depress me. Work, and a creative life, were things I would think about later. When Gracie was well. *When.* I reached into my purse and offered her some gum, Juicy Fruit, soother of all ills.

I looked around the room. Were all these families equally imprisoned? Coming to clinic all day, every day, for years on end? Stuck in a purgatory of half healing?

Gabe called down to the fish in the lobby tank, "Fishes! Look me!"

"Gabe, they can't *hear* you," Gracie said, as if their inability to hear was the primary reason they weren't answering.

Gracie and Jake stood at the railing, peering down at Lego-sized people moving across the lobby. They were pointing, laughing, talking.

Gabriel was trying to squeeze between his sister and Jake, to see over the edge. He couldn't get his eyes high enough, and so as a surrogate, he lifted up Brian's reading glasses. He pushed them up, over the railing, and let go.

"Daddy's glasses!" Gracie shouted out as they plummeted. Happily, fabulously, they did not peg anyone below. They landed beside the fish tank. Gracie said, "I can *get* them. Me and my friend."

And so they walked together to the elevators, one healthy-looking three-year-old girl, one toddler, and their leader, a boy of eight or nine, who appeared to have toured hell. I watched from the railing as the troupe emerged below. The glasses were, unbelievably, intact. When the kids arrived back, I showed them to Brian. "Unscathed," I said. "Good omen."

Finally, we were called back by a nursing assistant who said, "Hi, Gracie, I'm Nadia." She ignored Brian and me and offered Gracie her hand— patient as primary. Gracie must have sensed it was genuine; she took Nadia's hand instantly.

"Do you know where to go, Gracie? I forget." Gracie, good guesser, pointed left. Nadia beamed, and they headed that way. We tagged along behind. In the weigh-in room Nadia asked what Gracie would like to do first, temperature reading, blood pressure, or weight. Gracie took off her shoes but halfway to the scale lost momentum. She stood still and silent in the middle of the floor. Nadia said, "Gracie, you're in the alligator patch! Jump on the log, girlfriend!" and pointed at the scale. Gracie jumped on and gave her patented high-pitched giggle. Take note, I told myself: *Give the kid power, any way you can.*

Nadia hooked up the blood pressure cuff and told Gracie, "This machine is gonna squeeze your arm. Your job is to squeeze my hand as hard as it squeezes you." Gracie squeezed with her whole body. "Wow, Gracie," Nadia said, "you are strong. "

Gracie beamed. "Nadia," she said, "I think I know that."

In the corner of the room was a bulletin board covered with pictures of kids who'd been through the program. One was signed, in hot pink Sharpie with three hearts, "I love you, Nadia, cause you are the nicest one." The girl in the picture was rafting; the three hearts floated above the white river water. In another photo a girl jumped on a trampoline. Caught midair, her light brown hair flew around her head like an exploding star. There was a dark-eyed boy in a too-big fireman's hat, grinning mischievously at the wheel of a ladder rig, as if he intended to drive anywhere *but* the fire. And an uber-thin teenage boy blowing out a cake full of candles, in a black T-shirt that read "Fuk Nü." He looked so tired, as if he wanted to lay his head down on the cake and sleep.

One of these children, at least one, was gone. Pinned here, among the living.

"Gracie, are you going to put your picture up here too?" asked Nadia.

Gracie smiled at her, a full-wattage display. "Yes!"

No! I thought. *Fuk Nu.*

We were ushered into a private room to wait for Dr. Kurtzberg. To help quiet Gabe's restlessness, Brian began blowing up latex gloves into animals Gabe requested: a camel, a donkey, a sheep. Gabe was on a biblical roll.

After an hour or so, Dr. Kurtzberg arrived wearing what we'd come to know as her uniform: denim overalls, rainbow socks, a utilitarian haircut, and an air of confidence cut with curiosity. I felt like someone who, after only a first date, had agreed to marriage. I desperately wanted to like this woman to whom we were entrusting our child.

The dance between the doctor and parents of pediatric patients is an excruciatingly awkward love triangle, in which the three sides don't necessarily like one another initially (sometimes never), but all are devoted to supporting the one person between them.

Dr. Kurtzberg, using cord blood transplantation, was curing children who'd previously had no chance of a cure. She was a genius, undeniable genius. But her waiting room looked like hell's waiting room. Her sheer confidence, once so attractive, now made me nervous.

She chatted with us for a few beats about our move to Durham, recommended good Thai food near the hospital, asked how the kids were adjusting. "Feel free to call me Dr. K or Joanne, whatever is most comfortable for you," she said.

Then she looked over Gracie's latest labs and frowned. Even in overalls and rainbow socks, she was formidable. A tiny dynamo.

"Her iron is very high," she said. "The liver is compromised." Again *the* liver, not *her* liver. We were quiet, waiting for her to continue. "You've done her a real disservice by waiting this long to bring her to transplant."

Dr. K's comment struck me as an insurance policy against her own accountability. If, God forbid, things didn't go well, we were the ones responsible; we'd exhausted Gracie's liver with our dithering. I was furious. Blood-throbbing-in-the-temples, throw-furniture furious. I opened my mouth to say—Go take a look at the wrecked children sitting out front, someone has done *them* a disservice.

Many other docs had told us to wait, or not to come at all. Had warned us about the risks, the toxicity of chemo, the damage to a young child's developing nervous system. At least one had said that survival rates were better for older children. All of them had agreed that transplant was a long, nasty business not for the faint of heart. Which Gracie wasn't. But still, any rational person would think long and hard before buying a ticket for this train.

Beside me, I could feel Brian's anger too.

"This was the most important decision we've ever had to make," Brian said. "It took time."

Dr. K gave a curt nod. "I know you want what's best for her. I'm sorry if I offended you." She didn't argue; she had more class than that. She paused there, choosing her words. "Kids with weak livers have a hard time. You should just know that."

We knew. Kids with weak livers could develop VOD, or veno-occlusive disease, in which the liver fails. Full stop. Effective immediately.

Dr. K moved into problem-solving mode. "The best course of action at this point is to begin intense chelation. We can do it intravenously here in the clinic. Gracie will need to be here eight to ten hours a day, every day, from now to Christmas. After that, we will reevaluate her liver to see if she is ready. How does that sound?"

Um.

"Will intravenous chelation cause her any pain?" Brian asked.

"No, we will give her a port or a central line so that when she comes for chelation they literally just attach her line to the tubing. No need to stick her anymore. It would just mean an extra month or two here in Durham."

We weren't in any rush. There was nothing to get home to unless we were going home with her. We agreed, thanked Dr. K, and gathered our things.

As we stepped into the elevator, we passed a bald child in a wheelchair staring blankly ahead, emptied out. I couldn't discern the child's age or tell if it was a boy or a girl. Another wraith child.

I really, truly, deeply wanted to leave this place and not come back.

Gracie stood between Brian and me, holding each of our hands, subdued. The novelty of a new place had worn off. As the glass elevator descended, she looked through the wall as the cheerful colors, the bright feather mobiles, the enormous fish tank blurred past. She had an air of suspicion; she hadn't had to endure anything too painful today, but clearly this was a place filled with doctors and nurses.

"Are we coming here again?" she asked.

"Yes, sweetie, we'll be here tomorrow," Brian answered.

"What about the day after that?"

"Yes."

"And the day after that?"

"Yes"

"And the day after that?"

This was her favorite conversational move, keep the ball in play indefinitely. But she also needed to know. Should we tell her she'd be coming here every day for at least the next six weeks or for months, maybe for years? In the lobby we sat down on a couch with Gracie squeezed between us.

Brian said, "This place is where we are going to come for a lot of days. This place is where you will have a transplant so that you won't have to get blood anymore."

She thought about this for a while.

"Can I watch movies when I am getting my transplant?"

"Yes," I said. "You can watch as many movies as you want."

"Can I watch Dora?"

"Yes." Brian was stroking her hair. "Dora galore."

"I hate Dora," she said. Trick question, good sign.

"Can I eat candy?"

"Do you like candy?"

"Yes."

"Then you can eat candy."

"What if it is bad candy that I hate?"

"Then you don't have to eat it."

"You won't make me eat it?"

"No, sweetie, we won't make you eat bad candy that you hate."

"OK."

We didn't add that eventually, because of the effects of chemo, she'd be unable to eat. She wasn't interested in knowing that now.

Brian went to get the car while the kids and I stood in the cooling night air. It seemed like heaven out here, open sky, a cherry tree in the middle of the circular drive, a friendly valet captain who greeted each guest with "Hello, milady" or "Hello, my sir." There was neither irony nor servitude in his tone, just warmth and formality. Best of all, at this particular moment, there were no sick children in sight.

Gracie ran Gabriel's stroller in circles. They were a gleeful pair of released finches, flinging themselves in every direction. When we tried to load them into the car, it was open rebellion. Gracie kept shouting, "Wait, I'm not ready! I have to do my exercises!" This was reasonable, but I wanted to get home.

"Let's go, sweetie," I said.

Rather than get into her car seat, Gracie swung her legs in between the two front seats, resting her elbows on them for support, car gymnastics.

"I'm flying," she said.

"Great, lovey, now get buckled." I was trying to sound casual. If she sensed a demand, she'd be obliged to resist.

"No way," she said. "I'm doing my special tricks!"

I should be savoring her "special tricks" and everything else about her. But I wanted to get home, to get in bed, to maybe, if we were lucky, stay awake long enough to watch a crappy movie. "Gracie, in your car seat now. One . . . two . . ."

She ignored me and began to swing her legs so high she could kick the roof of the car. She looked at me from the corner of her eye. "These are *exercises*."

"Gracie," Brian said, "your exercises are so important. Let's get home where you have more room for exercising."

She wavered. "Will you exercise with me?"

"I will, my love. We'll exercise together till the cows come home."

She got into her seat and settled down.

"Stop showing off," I said to Brian. It drove me nuts how he made things with the kids look easy. How he made things with the kids *be* easy. He'd arrived late on the scene, but he was way out in front.

"I was here first, you know," I said.

"I know you were. And I'm not trying to make you look bad."

But he couldn't help himself; he had generally good impulses. When Gracie whined for more chips or another video, Brian would ask if she knew what the fairies did with children who whine.

"What do they do, Daddy?" she would ask, in her regular voice.

"Nothing actually. Fairies love whining."

Gracie would laugh, problem over.

Brian's creed was humor over force. I tried, but I wasn't good at it. I took the kids too seriously. I treated them as if they had as much, or more, power than I did. These were not world rulers, but I let them rule me. Which was nuts since one of them wore Dora pull-ups and the other insisted (nonverbally, but forcefully, successfully) on sleeping in his new bumblebee boots.

Brian's problem, I decided, was that he was not taking this entire situation seriously enough. That was hogwash, and I knew it was hogwash—he'd been up till 3 a.m., madly Googling bone marrow transplant survival rates every night this week—but that did not stop me.

"Did you not hear Dr. K say, less than an hour ago, 'Kids with weak livers have a hard time'?"

"You don't have a monopoly on fear, Heather. I'm scared. I'm just saying if we relax a little, it will be easier for everyone."

The surest way to enrage a tense person is to tell them to relax.

"Oh, you think you're so great? You think you're Mr. Kid Whisperer?"

"Only if you do," Brian said. And took my hand, which felt like the kindest thing anyone had ever done. I wanted to reciprocate, but I'd drifted so far from thinking about Brian's needs or wants that I couldn't conjure what he might like best. Something simple. Music soothed him; he was always putting on a song to take the piss out of a bad moment. I picked up the iPod and found David Gray, a songwriter we used to listen to in his studio. Before kids, before all this *mishegas*. Back when the best way to spend Saturday afternoon was together, in bed.

At home we shoveled the kids into their pajamas. As soon as they were settled, I climbed into bed with the remote. Brian slid in beside me. "Do you want to keep talking?"

"Maybe," I said. I knew we should turn the TV off and turn to one another. We were lucky, our kid was going to get a cure. We had two great-smelling people under our care. Neither of them was in immediate danger. We should celebrate the good.

But the wellspring of warm feeling for Brian that had flooded me in the car was gone. In its place was a jagged pile of unpleasant facts: in a few days he had to fly back to New York to teach at NYU and Sarah Lawrence because, even if we could have afforded for him to stop teaching (which we couldn't), it was essential that we maintain our health insurance. I knew that as hard as it would be for me without him, it would be harder still for Brian to leave Gracie. To worry about Gracie while forcing himself through the motions of pedestrian life. We should strategize—logistically, emotionally, maybe even spiritually—about how to get through this.

But talking, in Durham, felt like a pointless, Sisyphean task. Talking could not guarantee her survival.

So if not talk, then sex. We were on a lifesaving mission; why not fight death with the oldest trick in the book?

But sex, in Durham, felt self-indulgent. "Sex is a luxury vacation," I said. A remote, tropical location, which cost too much to reach.

"Sex?" Brian said, bemused, maybe hopeful.

"Brian," I said, "if I wanted to have sex with anyone, it would be with you."

To be together meaningfully invoked complete focus, devotion. Communion. Full, unified attention. Surrender. I didn't have that to give. I suspected Brian didn't either. The most crucial part of me was holding one end of a rope. The other end was attached to Gracie. That was my whole job: hold the rope. No matter what, hold on to the rope.

33

"THESE LOOK LIKE STEREO CABLES," BRIAN SAID. IN HIS HAND were tubes identical to those that would soon be protruding from Gracie's chest. Every transplant kid had venous catheters, or "central lines," surgically implanted into the subclavian veins leading directly to the heart—to deliver medications and TPN (fake food). Gracie was getting hers early to facilitate chelation.

To help prepare her, the hospital had sent us home with a little rag doll with stark white skin and primary-red hair. We cut a short slit in the doll's chest and gave it to Gracie with the tubes sprouting from the doll's heart.

"After tomorrow, sweetheart, you will have tubes just like the dolly has tubes."

She looked at us, amused. Lately, we said so many strange things.

She pulled the tubes from the dolly's chest, stuffed them in, pulled them out again.

"You have tubies," she told the doll. "You can get plugged in."

She humored us but did not believe, not for a minute, that we would do something so medieval to her.

The next morning she looked up from her elephant pancake. "How do they get the tubes inside you?"

I explained that they made a small cut in the chest. *The*, not *your*.

"I'm gonna have a hole in me?" she asked.

"No, lovey, they stitch it up."

"Sew me?" she said, aghast. "I will run so fast you will never catch me."

The hospital had given us a book for exactly this situation. In it, a little girl about to get a central line is comforted by her best friend, a bear named Teddy. At the very end of the book, Teddy points to the tubes snaking out of the girl's shirt and says, "See, I told you it was a good idea." At this line, Gracie looked at us in disgust. "Teddy is stupid," she said.

The day of the procedure, the surgeon came into the room to talk with us first. She asked if Gracie had any questions. Gracie nodded, yes, but was so shy that she asked me to have the doctor cover her ears, so that she could ask me her question and I could relay it to the doctor. The doctor covered her ears.

Gracie looked at me and said, "Ask her if it hurts."

"Will it hurt?" I asked the surgeon.

"Not during the operation," the surgeon said. "But afterward it might."

Might?

The surgeon showed Gracie the oxygen mask. "This will help you fall asleep while we operate."

Gracie, looking at the mask, gestured for the surgeon to cover her ears again. "Will I be able to really breathe in that?"

"You will, my love."

We were allowed to walk her into the operating room and stand beside her until she lost consciousness. I knew the difference between being dead and being unconscious. But they had too many things in common for my comfort: limp hands, the inability to answer when spoken to. I hated the whole deal.

Brian laid his arm across my shoulders with strong, steady pressure. "She'll be OK," he said.

An hour or so later, sitting in the waiting room, we heard screams. Little-girl screams, high-pitched and fierce. We followed the sound, at a run, to find Gracie sitting up in bed staring down at the tubes dangling from her body.

She pointed at the tubes and said to Brian, "Daddy, you need to call the doctor. She made a big mistake." She began to cry. If screaming was bad, crying was worse. Her screams possessed an overtone of fight. The tears were defeat.

Brian calmed Gracie down by telling her a story about a clan of anarchist ants. I hoped the sound of his voice could carry her away from the glare, the noise, the pain of the recovery room, and deep into the velvet pocket of her own imagination. I knew she would relish diminutive creatures toppling a king. In Brian's version, the ants began to eat away at the palace, brick by golden brick. By the end of the story Gracie was adding her own twist to the king's comeuppance, in a voice still hoarse from the breathing tube: ". . . and then they ate his feast food. And his hair. And his shoes. And then he was a bald, hungry, barefoot king, and nobody would be his friend."

In her worldview, to be friendless was the worst possible fate.

After a few hours, they let us go home.

The next morning she came into bed with us and held up her shirt to reveal the tubes.

"This hurting keeps moving around on me."

Gabe stared. "Gracie's tubies," he said.

Brian went to fetch her some pain medication.

"Gabe, you can touch them," Gracie said. But he did not want to touch. He didn't even want to look. Me either. I hoped she couldn't sense Gabe's revulsion. Or, pray God, mine.

Brian said, "Can I touch them, Gracie?"

"Sure, Daddy," she said. She handed him one tube. "Let's be puppets."

"Puppets?"

"Puppets!" and she began to make her tube speak to Brian's tube.

And like that, the tubes were part of the family. Tiny, animated presences enlivened by the life force of the girl who wore them.

We'd been instructed to examine the entry site daily for signs of infection. I'd call Gracie over, and she would happily lift her shirt. "Nothing is wrong with my tubies," she'd say. *My* tubies. Hers. Gracie would stand and wait for our worry to pass. She was patient, patting Brian on the head. "Good dog, Daddy," she'd say. The tubes entered her body under a clear patch of Tegaderm. We'd been warned that if they were ever pulled out, she would bleed profusely, and so we were incredibly careful with them. But she didn't fuss over them.

It was astonishing how willing she was to overlook the pain they'd caused, the ongoing annoyance, and the betrayal, on our part, that they represented. She accepted them: two white, soft, rubber straws, tucked beneath a mesh vest, pressed against her torso. They ran straight into the center of her chest and disappeared inside her.

The trope of kids' resilience was almost grotesquely true in Gracie's case. It felt as though, given enough time, she could adjust to, accommodate, stake imaginative ownership over anything. I worried that if we attached, say, the front end of an old Chevy to her midriff, she'd be driving herself around the living room within a week, shouting, "Look at me, I'm car girl!" I wanted her to complain, protect, resist. To assert her right to be a kid, without amendments to her person. But that wasn't her way. Her way was to make peace with the invading army, to claim it as her own.

34

GRACIE GOT INTO THE HABIT OF RUNNING INTO OUR BEDroom every morning to ask, "Is this another hospital day?" Typically, we'd say yes; so far, all we'd seen of North Carolina was the inside of pediatric hospital treatment rooms. Finally, after two weeks, we took a surprise day off.

"No hospital today!" Brian said.

Gracie was giddy with disbelief. "Really not?" she kept asking, as we got dressed, as we sat down to breakfast, as we got in the car. "Really not?"

"Not," we said. "Really not."

"Can we go swimming?" she asked. Then a second later, "Can we go to a forest?" And then as we'd begun to drive toward the park, "Wait, can we find ponies?" The pleasure of granting her small wishes was immense. We knew of a ranch nearby.

"We can find ponies and cows. Maybe even sheep or llamas," Brian answered.

"Can you ride llamas?" Gracie said.

"If anyone can ride a llama, Gracie, it would be you," Brian said, and she burst into squeaky laughter. We looked at each other, *soak it up*.

At the ranch Gracie went mute with excitement. We kept asking her, "Is this fun, do you like it?" but she wouldn't answer. She just looked from right to left, left to right, with her mouth slightly open.

"Horses!" she finally shouted as we walked between two pastures. On either side of us were sleek thoroughbreds, haughty fashion models tossing their glossy manes. Lustrous with good health, grazing their way through untroubled lives. I felt a bizarre surge of envy, even resentment. I wanted what they had, for Gracie.

We found the stable manager, who let Gracie pick between a high-spirited roan and a docile, sway-backed Palomino named Whispers. Gracie made the sympathy choice. She reminded me of my mom, who always took home the misshapen, orphan Christmas tree. The last tree on the lot.

"Do you want to feed Whispers before your ride?" the stable girl asked, and handed her an apple. I wished for some transfer of energy or identity to pass between them in that casual, exchange. I hoped the girl would confer on Gracie whatever it was that made her own ponytail so thick it could barely be contained by a rubber band. Be a girl like this someday, I willed. Be sixteen, be a barn rat. Be a girl with a crush on a horse and muscular shoulders and seven guys in love with you. Or just be sixteen, in any condition.

The girl fit a hard hat onto Gracie's head and patiently helped her up.

"Bye, Whispers," Brian said. "Have fun with Gracie. Don't ride her too hard."

Gabriel let us swing him up onto a very old, barely breathing brown mare. But the moment his butt touched the saddle he cried out, "Down. I off!" I walked him over to the arena's edge. Every time Gracie passed our spot, it was a celebrity sighting, "Sissy rides! Sissy! Sissy!" he shouted out for acknowledgment, a wave, anything.

As we watched Gracie, a cat came up to Gabe, sniffed him, then settled down in the grass at his feet. Gabriel, having discovered the pleasure of retroactive commands, said to the cat, "Fall down!" Then he offered his hand to the cat. "Help?" he said. This was a favorite game he had with Brian; he'd push Brian down and then help him up. He seemed baffled when the cat ignored his offer. "Kitty don't yike me," he said.

"Did the kitty say why?" Brian asked.

Gabe ignored the question and pointed to the grass, saying, "Down,

Daddy!" Brian obliged. Anytime Gabe found one of us at his level, he would scramble onto our backs. He pushed now at Brian's shoulders. "Be a pony, Tiger!" Brian moved mildly across the grass. "Be a *tiger*, Pony!"

On the drive home Gabe fell into a deep sleep, but Gracie was too excited to nap. "I rode Whispers for a long time," she said. "And she was a good one."

Brian and I looked at each other, triumphant; we'd made her happy. We could still do that. Her toes were dusty. She'd ridden an animal bigger than herself. She'd had joy. For that matter, so had Gabe. So had we.

Later that night, at dinner, we told Gracie that in a few weeks she'd go live in the hospital for a while. She looked at us.

"I guess Eden doesn't have to go to the hospital. My friends never get blood. I guess they are going to get big." We leapt to remind her she would get big too, and that most people spend time in the hospital at some point. At the same time, we wanted to acknowledge what she suddenly seemed to know—that she was an outlier.

After dinner we all climbed into bed to watch *Shrek*. The kids were not particular fans, but Brian and I loved Eddie Murphy's donkey. ("That's right, fool! Now I'm a *flying* talking donkey!") Lying in the king-size bed in Durham was a luxury after years of squeezing into beds too small for the four of us. We could sprawl out. Gabe got as close as possible to all in his proximity; Gracie was happy with an elbow touching one parent, a toe touching another. I felt the swell of well-being that comes from being in physical contact with everyone you love most.

"Today was good," Brian said. "We did good."

"We did do good," I said. And we both knew *good* encompassed more than the ranch.

This day was not a last-meal indulgence, I told myself. It was a happiness to store away—for when things got bad. Or went from bad to worse or from worse to unbearable. As we'd been promised they would.

A happiness to pull her forward, back to the small pleasures of life. I'll remind her of Whispers. Add it to the list of things she loved: ice cream, the geese in our backyard, the plum tree she tried to climb in Brooklyn, the Thanksgiving kite. Remember, I'll tell her, how you loved the red diamond in the blue sky, remember how, when it fell and landed in the snow, such unlikely North Carolina snow, you ran to it like it was a lost or injured friend.

35

On a night not long after the tubies went in, Gracie was playing with a pair of My Little Ponies in the kitchen. She interrupted her play to splay across the floor, eyes closed, silent and still. A pony dropped onto its side, near her head, unmoving.

"What are you doing?" I said.

"I'm being died," she said. "Can you hear me talk?"

"What do you mean?" I said.

She looked up at me. "Was I talking before when I be died?"

"You didn't be died, lovey."

"Yes, I did."

"Do you mean when you took the medicine that made you go to sleep when we put your tubes in?"

"When I be died, could you hear me talking?"

"You didn't be died," I said again, too sharp. Accusatory.

She gave me a look—*what's your problem*?—and took her ponies elsewhere.

Having sensed my discomfort with the concept, the kids spent the evening playing a resurrection game by commanding various objects "to be died" and springing them back to life. They practiced on each other. "You die," Gabe said to Gracie, matter-of-fact. She fell over. He chanted his magic phrase, "Flubby buzzy, flubby buzz!" Up she sat, reanimated. Oh, what fun.

That night at dinner, aiming for a little civilization, I put a flickering votive candle in the center of the table. Gabe was enthralled; he loved nothing more than to blow things out. I kept moving it away from him, and he kept blowing.

"Just put it away," Brian said.

"No," I said, "I like the light, it's pretty, and he can learn to leave it alone."

Gabe blew and blew until, from the other end of the table, he extinguished the flame. As it sputtered out he shouted, victorious, "It died!"

36

AT THE CLINIC, EVERY MORNING, THE KIDS RAN STRAIGHT
toward the fish tank. Brian stopped at the gift shop for the *Times*. I ordered
a latte from the old-timey pushcart vendor. Before going up to the fourth
floor, we'd watch the kids run in circles around the open lobby or play
the piano they were not supposed to touch. Any kind of life, if you live it
long enough, becomes routine.

One day, in our second or third week into this regime, a girl about
Gracie's age got onto the elevator with us, also headed to the fourth
floor. She had delicate bones beneath puffed skin, post-transplant. Her
parents stood very still, with their girl between them. When she coughed,
a sharp, deep bark, I looked at her with what I hoped was more concern
than fear. Her mother gathered her closer and turned the girl's head into
her own leg to cough again. It was a startling sound, deep and incongru-
ous from her small form.

As we swooshed upward, the kids watched the feather mobiles on
the ceiling twist and spin. Gracie asked Brian, "How does it move if no
one is touching it?"

"Magic," said Brian.

Gracie looked at him, a little disappointed, a little censorious. "Dad,
there is no magic."

Oh no, I thought, oh no no no.

We settled into the waiting area. The blond girl was on her father's lap, breathing with visible effort. The mom sat beside them with a baby boy over her shoulder, maybe fourteen months old. I hadn't noticed the baby in the elevator; I'd only seen the girl, the way her mother gathered her in. The baby, for all his adorableness, was an extra on set.

The mom was short and sinewy, with red-gold hair. The father was her match in the physical lottery, fit, handsome. When he stood up and carried the girl to the nurses' station, he moved with a fluid urgency, an athlete determined to make something happen.

When the mom spoke, she had a brogue. "Irish?" I asked a nurse. "I think so," she answered. Maybe Irish mom. I wanted to ask her questions; know their story. But the etiquette was simply to appear friendly and wait. I gave a little wave—a mom-with-a-sick-daughter-and-a-boy-on-my-hip wave. And she, mom-with-a-sick-daughter-and-a-boy-on-her-hip, gave a wave back.

The nurse quickly showed them back to a room and a while later came back for us. I noticed their curtain was pulled. They wanted privacy.

We waited. That was the majority of what you did in the clinic: wait. When Dr. K arrived, Gracie was watching the tail end of *Spirit*, in which the Mustang and his mate run through tall grasses. Dr. K said something about how strong they were, and did Gracie like—She stopped midsentence. An alarm had sounded. She looked up and took off in the direction of the Irish family's room. Nurses and doctors from all corners of the clinic streamed toward their room.

The curtain had been thrown open, and I could see the little girl, slack, on her mom's lap. It was hard to tell if she was breathing. The baby brother was passed hand to hand, out of the room. The little girl had, at some point, coughed up blood; it was across the mother's shirt. The doctors huddled, trying to stabilize the little girl.

The baby boy, who'd ended up in the arms of the art therapist, was flapping and struggling. I asked if I could take him. She gave him to me, and I walked with him up and down the hall, reading quotes from *The Little Prince* posters. *He escaped*, read one, *with the aid of wild, migrating birds*. I pointed at the flock of purple songbirds, trailing strings, lifting the compact, golden prince off his compact, golden planet. Chatting as I would chat with Gabriel. After a few minutes the baby quieted. I strained to hear what was happening in his sister's room.

Eventually, the dad came to look for his son. He thanked me, took him back, and said, "Our girl gave us a bad scare, but she's stable now." In their room the shallow arc of the little girl's ribcage rose and fell beneath a thin white blanket in time with her breath. Tiny sail of a boat on its side, capturing and losing the wind, over and over again.

The mom was talking with the doctors, frowning and listening, nodding her head. I imagined some part of her must be shaking, the way an animal who has escaped a predator continues to shake long beyond the immediate threat. I was about to excuse myself when the dad said, "We lost a son before we came here. We cannot lose another child."

I said nothing, just waited.

"He was a toddler, our son. It was sudden, from pneumonia, mishandled. Should have admitted him to hospital, and they didn't. A few months after he died our little girl is diagnosed with leukemia. Incurable, they say. 'Sorry, nothing more we can do.' Which was bullshit. Bullshit socialized medicine. They just wouldn't spend the money to send her here, where they *can* do more. We were in the papers; we raised over a million dollars. All of Ireland sent this girl to America to get her transplant. And it worked. She's cured. The leukemia's gone. But her lungs aren't quite right. Her breathing gives her a bit of trouble. She holds on to fluid; I think her kidneys need a wee squeeze. Then she'll be right again."

Though all this he'd been holding his boy, who continued to look around the room, calm and curious. I thought Gabe was operating with a handicap, but this sweet little guy . . .

I was terrified I might begin to cry, to usurp the father's grief.

"I am so sorry," I said.

"Every family goes through something, doesn't it?" he said, and thanked me for watching out for his boy. He told me all this in the hall, under the Little Prince lifting away from his planet.

This little girl. She'd ridden up on the elevator with us, and then, a couple of hours later, she'd almost died. The blood on her mother's shirt.

The blaring of the alarm. She'd had a brother once, whom she barely knew. Pneumonia. Fucking socialized medicine.

This was how we told each other our stories, in the margins, in the kitchen, over Styrofoam cups, while washing our hands at the decontamination trough, at the snack machine, without ceremony. Without self-dramatization. Without even the faintest nod to the horror of what was described because the assumption was everyone had horror.

The teller's job was to get the facts right, to preserve every detail, especially the little ones: How the ambulance driver had smelled of clove cigarettes, as if he'd taken his time. How the blood on the mom's shirt was shaped like a bird in upside-down flight. How their son, before he died, had greeted his parents each morning by saying, "Give me an eyelash kiss."

The listener's job was to hear the story. To record the use of particular phrases, exact adjectives, adverbs, unusual clauses, idioms, or truncated turns of phrase. To note the time of day, the weather, what the teller was wearing. To learn the story, as it poured into the room, as if it were a religious text, which it was.

Both teller and listener have one duty: to believe. No matter how bad. Believe. Believe and remember; remember and believe. Because remembering and believing were all we had to give.

People often said, "I don't know how you do it." As if we'd been given a choice.

When I returned to our room after talking with the father, Gracie was distraught. "Where *were* you?"

"I was holding a baby."

"We needed you," she said. "Gabey cried for you." Gabey looked happy enough; he had Luna Bar all over his face and hands.

"Here I am now," I said.

"We're done," Brian said. "Gracie got unhooked." The slight breeze of recrimination. I looked at her IV and realized it was capped and detached; they'd been waiting a long time.

"I'm sorry, it was important."

Brian gave me a questioning look.

"I can tell you everything later," I said.

"Only if you want to."

Brian had heeded the no-friends advice. He would elect to not be heartbroken at the exact point in time when his daughter needed him most. Gracie was the sole recipient of his caring, and that made perfect sense. But I was lonely; I wanted to tell him about the Irish family. How far they'd come, how much they'd lost. How they could not lose any more.

On the way home I sat in the back between the kids. I held one of their feet in each of my hands; I could feel a faint pulse at the ankles. The saphenous vein, that big wide conveyor of blood that had let us "get in" to Gracie many times as an infant. We were passing through a densely wooded area with tossing branches overhead.

"Trees don't yike me," Gabe said. This was his new refrain; he'd endowed the natural world with an amorphous antagonism.

"Those are trees growing, Gabe, not bad guys," Gracie said.

I wavered between wanting to assure Gabe that the trees adored him, would do him no harm, and agreeing. The trees don't yike me either, I wanted to say, the trees scare me too.

37

"Paradoxical reaction to the sedatives," the nurse said. "Try to keep her quiet till it wears off."

We were in a waiting room; Gracie had gone feral.

A few days before, Dr. K had scheduled an MRI to determine if Gracie's liver was finally strong enough for her to proceed to transplant. Looking at the machine, Gracie had said, "Can we tell them I don't want to go into the box?"

Nobody does, darling girl.

To calm her, they had given her a sedative, and she'd lain quiet, in a twilight state, as the metal tube whirled and clanged around her, peering into her liver. As soon as it was over, she sat up stiff, rigid; as if a switch had been thrown, as if she was possessed. She slid off the table and cross-stepped, a spooked horse dancing in erratic patterns, toward the waiting room. I ran after. But when I tried to pick her up, she writhed and kicked, twisted out of my arms. I managed to trap her body between my knees.

"What is happening?" I'd shouted at the closest nurse.

Gracie pulled free and dove forward onto polished concrete. Dove *into* concrete. A huge goose egg, bluish at the center, began to form. Most terrifying yet: she didn't cry.

I looked at my mom, who'd flown out to be with us for Christmas. "You get her legs. I'll get her body."

Captured, Gracie began to scream, "Let me do it! I can do it!"

Exactly what the *it* was, was unclear.

We carried Gracie across the main lobby and out to the parking lot strung between us like a live electrical wire. She was rolling her body to the left and right against our grasp and screaming, "I can do it!"

I loved her faith in her own powers.

On the drive home, she fell into a deep sleep, her head flopped to one side, rolling with the turns; a light sweat dampened the hair around her face.

I called Brian to tell him what had happened, and he said he was already boarding an earlier flight back to Durham. I carried her into the house and laid her in bed. She was limp and warm and pliable, and her breath smelled of saltwater taffy. I pulled the covers over her. When Brian arrived home, just a few hours later, she was still asleep. He sat beside her, patting her back while she breathed and he read.

Later, I lay down next to her to nap. We woke up at the same time, in a dark room. She put one of her hands on each side of my face and leaned close. Her eyes were two blurry, bright smudges in the dark. "I'm so happy you are back," she said. "I'm so happy it is you," and kissed me, very lightly, on the lips.

I walked out into the living room, "That was scary," I said. "She was like Jerry Lewis on cocaine and tranquilizers simultaneously." He gave me a wan smile. He was worried about the goose egg, about head trauma. As we sat there, deciding whether to fight or to cozy up to each other, my cell phone rang. It was Dr. K.

"MRI results are in. Her liver looks good," she said. "Really good. We'll admit you as planned, the day after Christmas."

When I got off the phone, Brian was mad. "Why didn't you ask her about the head injury?" he said.

"I was busy hearing the news that her liver is in good standing, and she can go to transplant. Sorry I forgot to ask about a bump on the head."

"Go look at her; she has a yellow, bruised lump the size of an enormous kumquat."

"Brian, you don't know what a kumquat is," I shouted. "You've never eaten one, and you never will. You couldn't recognize the most common-place kumquat, let alone an enormous one!" We laughed. But only a little.

38

Just before christmas, the *New York Post* called and asked to do a follow-up story on Gracie. I wanted to be packing for the hospital, gift wrapping, or cooking. But the *Post* had been incredibly kind to us when we needed to raise money. We wanted to accommodate the request as best we could.

The *Post* sent down a photographer, for whom Gracie was uncooperative in the extreme. Miserable in her purple velvety shift, she tugged at the neckline until it was so stretched out that she could easily climb out of the dress, which she did periodically during the photoshoot. The photographer laughed it off at first, but after about forty-five minutes of our shenanigans, with no passable photo, everyone's frustration level was rising, especially Gracie's. One last time I got her into position—the photographer wanted to capture her hanging an ornament that reflected her face. As she hung the ornament I said, "Okeydoke!" by which I meant, "For the love of God, take the fucking shot!"

The photographer got the shot, thanked us, and went on his way with a few Santa cookies. On Christmas morning Gracie was on the cover of the *Post,* hanging a shiny green ornament in hundreds of thousands of papers around New York City. Friends and acquaintances called to tell us they were looking at Gracie's face in their living room, on the subway, strolling down Seventh Avenue. Totally unbeknownst to her, she was having her fifteen minutes of fame. Kathy called, elated, and promised to buy a bundle of papers. My mom cried, saying that even though she couldn't see the paper, she could feel the caring it was generating.

Gracie meanwhile was oblivious. Her amazement was reserved for Santa.

Christmas Eve we ate a quiet dinner. Gracie asked, "How is Santa going to get back up the chimney after he gets down?" She had a beautifully pragmatic streak. It wasn't that he delivered presents to billions of homes in twenty-four hours; it was that he did it all without ringing a single doorbell.

Earlier, when we'd reminded her that we were leaving for the hospital the next day, she'd said, "Eden is going to be so happy that my scratchies are gone."

Somewhere along the way, she'd come to believe that the point of transplant was to alleviate the itchy rash she had from the chelating agent. It was true that after transplant she wouldn't, if all went well, have the rash. But that was sort of like thinking the point of chemo was to stop having to fuss over your hair.

Brian said, "Eden will be so happy for you."

Gracie didn't ask, "How long will I be in there?" or "How can I get out?" She asked, "Can I bring my ponies?"

I'd lit a pair of candles for the dinner table. Gabriel did his job and blew them out. I lit them again, and the game continued. The flame would erupt at the tip of the match, pass its orange-blue light to the wick, then instantly disappear. A beautiful, little ephemery.

We had Bûche de Noël for dessert. I explained that it was made to look like a log used in the ancient fire-festivals celebrating winter solstice. "Is there chocolate on the inside too?" Gracie asked, picking up a soup spoon and preparing to lop off a branch. Gabriel started flapping his hands. We were going to eat a *tree*! At last the trees were at our mercy!

When we put them both to bed, Gabriel flopped around in his crib, talking to himself, "Yacie loves me."

I lay beside Gracie. "Sweetie, we're going to be in the hospital for a long time." We'd told her this so many times, but I wasn't sure she knew.

"Why?"

"So your body can get healthy."

"OK."

In bed Brian and I lay side by side, wired and anxious. Neither of us could sleep. Everything would change tomorrow. We were astride the nebulous line that divides before from after. I wanted to stay here forever.

"Next year," Brian said, "we'll be back in Brooklyn with two healthy kids."

I tried to visualize us next Christmas, in Brooklyn, kids bickering beneath a lopsided tree. It was a faint, diaphanous vision. Not a mirage, I told myself, a vision.

It is impossibly hard to take a child who looks more or less healthy and place her into the medical mill of transplant, but we did it. We held our breath and stepped off the edge of the known world. Whatever the odds were, they were ours. We had this boy, this girl, this bag of cells; one chance for a cure, and we took it.

39

GRACIE PACKED EVERY SINGLE MY LITTLE PONY SHE OWNED, and a few of Gabe's. I packed her pajamas, her toothbrush, a hairbrush, her favorite snacks. Soon she would not be able to eat or brush her teeth. She would have no hair to comb. But we packed for the present.

We'd woken up early. On the slope behind our house, dozens of wild geese waddled in agitated circles, a shifting gray carpet honking their anxieties into the morning air. I wanted to wade out and join them.

Gracie had appeared in our bedroom, wearing her Dora pajamas. Gabe had trailed in after, in his T-shirt, diaper, and bee boots.

"Can I go pet the geese?" Gracie asked.

"Those are wild geese, love, not for petting," Brian said. "When you come home from the hospital, we will go to a petting zoo and find some tame geese."

"How long will that be?" Gracie asked.

We stared at her, searching for a number that would sound acceptable. "Some few weeks," Brian said.

Gracie never asked us *What am I doing here?* Or *Why would you do this to me?* She was not philosophical about her suffering. She didn't want to know *Why me?* She only wanted to know how long it would last.

She asked us, over and over, "When will I see my friends again?" and "Does Eden miss me?"

The power of her feelings—for Eden, for Gabriel, for the boy we'd met on our first day, Jake, whom she hadn't seen in weeks but still talked about with great animation—was startling. As we packed she sang to herself, "And I just love you, Eden. And I just miss you, Eden."

"Me," Gabe cut in. "Miss me, Yacie."

"Gabriel, you are here. I can't miss you."

"Miss me!" Gabe said again. Gabe, who was always missing at least one of us, wanted to be missed.

Brian carried Gabe to the car; Gracie loped along beside us, trusting, willing. We had said she had to live in the hospital for "some weeks," and she accepted it. She buckled herself into her car seat. As we backed down the driveway, Gracie said, "Bye, house, I won't see you for a couple of days. I have to catch up to the *Nemo* bus."

Often I had no idea what she was talking about, much less thinking; she had an ongoing inner life of quiet and powerful sympathies for various imaginary characters. But the bus we understood. She had a dream of chasing the cast of the Ice Capades show *Nemo on Ice*. She and her friends, she'd explained, would "jump on that bus and take it for our own. No grown-ups can come with us; just me and Eden and our *Nemo* friends are gonna have that bus." Her idea of perfect happiness hinged on a world run by, and for, kids alone.

Fair enough. Considering what adults did to her.

As we passed Gabriel's menacing trees, I prayed a wordless, half-faithless prayer: *Let the same four people pass these trees from the opposite direction.*

At the hospital entrance we piled Gracie's bags onto a cart. Gabriel wanted to ride on top. Having him with us added a layer of complication and unpredictability, but he deserved to see where his sister was going. We set him atop the bags: " I uppy!" he shouted, from the top of the luggage, at anyone and everyone, "I uppy!" The boy in bee boots, sending salutations to each passing soul in the lobby. And so began Gabe's reign as a hospital celebrity.

"Be careful, Gabey," Gracie said. She was, at heart, a grandma, a mensch. She kept on chatting with Brian and me, exuding an air of merry anticipation. To her, this was more or less like checking into a hotel. She skipped along in front of us, past the lobby fountain with its glimmering layer of coins, each one an underwater wish.

On the fifth floor we turned down the long corridor toward our unit, 5200. Before you can enter the transplant unit, you have to first pass through the scrub room, a large antechamber with a trough sink. This sobered us up. The room is designed for decontamination. To keep the children of 5200 safe from outside germs and viruses, every visitor completes the protocol of scrubbing arms up to the elbows with disinfectant soap, donning shoe covers, and wearing a protective gown.

Gracie didn't want to put on the shoe covers. Gabriel didn't like the smell of the soap; he shrieked as Brian scrubbed him down.

"This is important, sweethearts," Brian said. "It keeps the kids here safe."

"They are not safe?" Gracie said.

We faltered. The children on this unit were so fragile, any renegade germ or garden variety virus could fell them.

"Washing keeps the germs out," Brian said, "so the kids can stay healthy."

Gracie nodded, a hero accepting the mantle of responsibility, and pulled the stiff blue paper covers over her shoes.

The unit was shaped like an L: two long corridors connected at the elbow by a nurses' station. I looked in every room we passed. Each had a large window onto the hall, but all the shades were down.

As we approached our room, an adjacent door opened and a young mother emerged, a pretty brunette. Her hair was done in a retro upflip, Marlo Thomas–esque. Her makeup was smooth, evenly applied, appropriately subtle under the harsh hospital light. I was in awe of her coping mechanism: under duress, look nice. She smiled at us with both warmth and distance. A don't-talk-to me smile, a welcome-to-hell smile.

Brian was bent down, listening to something Gracie was asking, but I smiled back. I wanted to stop her, to ask her everything, but she walked past us toward the communal kitchen holding an ominous plastic bag that looked like it held something wet and heavy at the bottom.

Brian took my hand, squeezed, a gentle reprimand, *Get your head here, now.* Our room was nearly at the end of the hall, second to last. I took this as a good omen—end of the hall, out of the way. Don't tempt fate. We stepped into our room, and Gracie immediately scrambled on top of the bed. She reached out for Gabe, who was standing beside the bed, with his arms up. He believed she could lift him. She believed it too. She might pull his arms out of the socket trying, but she would get the job done. Brian put his foot under Gabe's butt and hoisted him upward onto the bed. Gabe said, "Yacie uppied me." Matter-of-fact, not at all surprised by her powers.

The room was a small, strange shape, maybe a trapezoid. I tried to remember my geometry. There was space enough for the hospital bed, a big chair that pulled out into a cot, and a wall-mounted TV. In one corner a tall, skinny window looked out on a single tree.

"That better be a good tree," I said.

"What?" Brian was putting a few of Gracie's pajamas in a drawer.

"Nothing."

I was taking stock of all the daunting, gleaming, ominous, ever-present equipment. Monitors, IV stand, oxygen outlet built into the wall. And much more. This was a room designed to sustain life. Or, if necessary, restore it.

A nurse had told us, "All the rooms are under negative pressure. The air flows out, exclusively. No germs can enter, so your daughter will be safe." I certainly felt as if I was under negative pressure, whatever that might be. But I also felt supremely unreassured.

We had signed all the papers put before us—describing, in cryptic terms, the many possible "negative outcomes" of transplant, up to and including the most negative outcome of all—disbelieving each page. We were at the beginning, when good things still felt possible.

A line from Mike Tyson came back to me, something Brian said once: *Everyone's got a plan, until they get hit.*

"She'll be OK," Brian said.

And I loved him for saying that, whether he knew it or not.

40

Our "primary nurse" was named bobbie. "hi you gracie," she said in a North Carolina drawl. "I'm the one you're gonna ask for anything you want in this hospital. And I'm gonna help you." Bobbie was delicately built, though tall and wiry. She had cat-eye glasses, a short bob with blunt bangs, which expressed an earnestness, playfulness, and readiness; the hairstyle equivalent of rolling up your sleeves. She wore a pink cardigan with pearl buttons over scrubs and an air of complete competence.

Gracie watched Bobbie with interest. On principle, she disliked everyone in scrubs, but Bobbie made it hard. Under her prim presentation there was obvious power. She bopped around the room with a fluttery, restless energy. When she left I said to Brian, "She's the one to stand next to in a street fight. Warrior-librarians are the best!"

Eventually, we would learn that Bobbie worked with refugees all around the world, that she was married to an Irish doctor, that they had four sons together. We'd know she was someone who did not give ground when ground had to be held. We'd know that her oldest son was a gifted musician, and her youngest a natural comedian. But that first day we only knew that she made Gracie laugh.

As soon as we were settled, Bobbie rolled a large IV pole into the room. "Okeydoke, Gracie, time to hook you up." The pole held multiple pumps, programmed to dispense medications round the clock. Each med flowed through tubing that would be attached to one of Gracie's three central-line catheters. Bobbie hooked them up, med by med. As she attached each tube to the catheter and screwed it in, she'd introduce the two ends to each other: "Mr. Red, meet Mr. White; you two are gonna be good friends." Gracie laughed at this little skit, each time, and asked if she could attach them too. Bobbie said sure, as long as she cleaned her hands with alcohol wipes first. I knew Bobbie was guarding against bacteria. Bacteria in the blood is a bullet. You don't want it near the heart.

When Bobbie finished, Gracie and the IV pole were tethered together, inseparable.

"How long will she be hooked up?" I asked.

"Pretty much all the time," Bobbie said, with an apologetic look. Nurses were so often the bearer of the bad news that docs neglected to mention.

"But how will she get around?" I said, wishing I'd put it less starkly in front of Gracie. Bobbie motioned me out into the hall.

"She likely won't feel like getting out of bed much anyway, but for the days when she feels good, she can get unhooked for about an hour. Total."

As soon as she was hooked up, Gracie wanted down. "Ask Bobbie if I can get off from this!" she commanded, pointing at the pole. She had anointed Bobbie the ultimate authority. Brian and I had been demoted to ancillary underlings. "Ask Bobbie!" Gracie said again. These were phrases that we'd come to hear dozens, maybe hundreds of times a day. "Ask Bobbie" and "Get unhooked."

Gracie's IV pole was about six feet tall, made of steel, with a round tri-wheel base wide enough to stand on. The pole was her traveling companion, her straight man. All day, every day, he towered over her, silent, forbearing, doing his duty. And like anyone under the constant eye of a protector, she often wanted to give him the slip.

My mom, who'd stayed for our admission day, had diversionary ideas.

She pulled a bottle of nail polish out of her purse, glittery gold. It was the most cheerful thing in the room by miles.

"Gracie," she said, "would you please do my nails?"

Gracie painted my mom's nails carefully, slowly, with her full attention. If my mom had offered to do Gracie's nails, it wouldn't have worked, but to ask for Gracie's help was perfect.

When she got gold polish more on finger than nail, she said, "Sorry for that, Didi."

My mom kissed the crown of her head, "I don't mind, sweet Gracie girl."

When she fell asleep, my mom said, "Go home, you two. Or go out to dinner. Pamper each other for a few hours; we're fine here." Brian and I looked at each other.

"It's OK. She's gonna sleep for a long time," Bobbie said, as if reading our minds. "The first day really takes it out of them."

And so we left. Only for a few hours. In our bedroom, getting out of my slacks felt heavenly. My dress-up-for-doctors habit (to emanate a little dignity, a little litigious power) was getting old quick. Hospital life is pretty much the reason sweats were invented. I got into pajamas, washed my face, brushed my teeth.

I slid into bed beside Brian, who was looking at online menus of local places.

"What would you like, of all the many foods of Durham?"

"I'm not sure. What sounds good to you?"

This was a game we sometimes played: What do you want? No, what do you want? A dance of deferring desires.

"No, you," he said.

I gave him a blank stare. "Whatever sounds good to you."

I pictured Gracie tied to her pole, all kinds of odious drugs flowing into her body via the catheters. I had nothing left with which to make a decision.

And I didn't want to communicate with anyone, not even Brian. I wanted to stop picturing the moment Gabriel had dropped Brian's glasses from the balcony, and we'd watched them fall, four stories down.

I wanted an isolation tank. I wanted to bob in the blackness and silence of body-temperature water. Gravity suspended, I wanted to be a beautifully blank slate. To forget for an hour. To be breath and black, and black and breath; skin and bones, empty and alone.

Skin and bones, empty and alone—I was turning into a country music song.

"Any mind-obliterating drugs on those menus?"

"Not at first glance, but I can keep looking."

I knew he meant it. Though we didn't do drugs, never really had, if I asked him now to help me go numb, I was pretty sure Brian would. He'd be concerned, he'd ask if there wasn't a better way of dealing with one's anxieties, but he'd probably help me score. I felt a rush of affection for him. But I still didn't want to talk. Or think.

"Listen," I said. "I know this makes no sense, but I want to go back to the hospital."

"We just left the hospital."

"I know."

"Sweetheart," Brian said. "Pace yourself. The hardest parts are still ahead."

"I know," I said again. But I wouldn't relax until I climbed into bed beside Gracie. Even if this was a pointlessly melodramatic gesture, even if she was not in any immediate danger, and we were exhausted and hungry, I wanted to be there.

"I'll go back with you."

"That's OK," I said, as if I was letting him off the hook.

In fact, he wanted to come, I could hear it in his voice. And he could come. Our Durham babysitter, Denise, was living with us for exactly this reason: to be home with Gabe when one, or both, of us needed to be at the hospital. Or, in Brian's case, working in New York. So Gabe was covered; we could both return. But I wanted to be alone. I wanted to drive through a perfectly quiet North Carolina night, with the windows down, letting the snowy air pour through the car.

In Gracie's room my mom was in the sleeper chair. I climbed in beside Gracie. Her hair—her silky thin toddler hair that curled, gently, at the nape of her neck—smelled like plastic ponies. I breathed in the whole of her, the faint medical sourness, the high note of plastic, and beneath everything, my girl, earthy, ordinary.

My mom stirred. "Why are you here?"

"How's she been?"

"Fine, good."

"Did she eat?"

"Mac and cheese. Did you guys eat?"

"Not really."

"Sweetie . . ."

"We were so tired, and food is . . . so foody."

"Does Brian also think food is too foody?"

"I'm not sure."

"You know, if you want to talk about how things are, I will listen. Just listen, no opinions."

"We're fine."

"Because it is totally natural to be stressed when you have a sick kid. Both you and Brian are going through something monumental."

"OK, Mom. I'm not one of your clients." I'd been saying this to her, in more or less the same tone of annoyance, since I was ten.

Then again, I was no longer ten. I didn't want to hurt her feelings. "Sorry, I'm not up for talking."

My mom reached across the minuscule space from the chair to the bed and grabbed my wrist. "Gracie is going to be fine. And you're my girl; I'm worried about you."

"Thanks." There were tears in my voice. I felt a surge of relief to feel something, anything. At the same time, I felt as if I was betraying Brian. Here were actual feelings, rushing to the surface, but not with him.

41

THE NEXT DAY, GRACIE'S FIRST WORDS WERE, "CAN I GET unhooked? Go ask Bobbie!"

Brian was reading; Tolstoy open on his lap. He gave me a short, sympathetic smile. "You look like a person who slept."

"When did you get here?"

"A while ago."

Brian kissed Gracie and me, both on the forehead, and went in search of Bobbie who we were pretty sure had the day off. We hadn't yet told Gracie that Bobbie wasn't on duty every day. When Brian returned, he punted on the Bobbie question.

"Lovey," he said, "you can get down and go for a walk, but you have to take this guy with you." He gestured toward the pole.

"He wants to stay inside my room," Gracie said. "The hall is too cold for him."

"We could put a hat on him."

Gracie didn't exactly smile, but she climbed down from the bed, on the same side as the pole, and gave him a pat, "He's a tough guy, he doesn't need a hat." And with that, the pole was domesticated, named. Turned into her pet.

She suited up for the hall: gown, mask, shoe covers. Out in the hall she was the only kid. Sixteen beds on the unit; one patient walking. Most of the others were farther along in their treatment and too sick to get up. Gracie said, "Mama, I wanna see who's inside. Open their windows." I explained that the shades were controlled from the inside, the people in each room had to choose to open them. "Why don't they choose?" she said.

In the room beside ours was a girl Gracie's age, Mia. Her mom was the pretty brunette with the updo. We hadn't yet met Mia, but Bobbie had given Gracie some details, which Gracie recited, like a commentator providing color, as we passed Mia's room: Mia comes from California, Mia loves dogs, Mia has brown curly hair, Mia has a sister but *no brother*. The way she said, "no brother," as though it were a terrible fate, touched me.

Gracie walked past Mia's door several times, hoping for a sighting. No luck. She'd given up and seemed ready to climb back into bed, when an idea dawned on her: "I can ride him." She pointed at Tough Guy.

She planted her feet on his wheeled base, clutched the center pole, and commanded, "Run!" I pushed, tentatively. Brian stood behind her, ready to catch, fretting. "Faster," she shouted, until I broke into a jog.

"More faster!" We got several raised eyebrows, and some pursed lips at the nurses' station, but sped up. It felt impossible to deny her any stumbled-upon happiness.

At the end of the hall, a new thought occurred to her: self-volition. She dropped one foot and propelled Tough Guy forward with a quick thrust. Then she leapt off, as if to race him. I dashed after the two of them. The lines connecting girl to pole could pull taut, pull loose. If she moved too fast, the lines could dislodge from her chest. Catastrophe. Brian was right there. Ready if she needed him, but not interfering. Helping pace her. He placed a hand on her shoulder. "Sweetie," he said. "Slow down. Mommy and Tough Guy have to keep up with you."

Gracie looked back with annoyance. "Then keep up."

Farther down the hall was an open door. A mother stood with her infant son against her chest in the doorway. IV lines and monitor cords ran from the bottom of his blanket back into their room, their pole. The mother had a quiet, serious aspect. She said nothing at first, but carefully watched Gracie ride Tough Guy. I paused to chat with her.

She introduced herself, "I'm Ramya." Her baby son, who'd had his transplant before we arrived, was Varun. "He's doing very well," she said in the elegant, elongated syllables of a British education. She'd grown up in India but emigrated to the United States with her husband years ago. Their home was in New Hampshire; like us they'd relocated for the transplant. Varun had been born with a lethal autoimmune disease for which transplant was the only cure.

Varun stirred on Ramya's shoulder and looked at me, evaluating a new face. His eyes were outsized and luminous. Large, brown eyes that met mine in a steady line of attention. He couldn't yet talk, but it felt as if we were conversing. "Varun," I said. "Hi."

I pointed to Gracie, "That is my daughter."

"I know," Ramya said. "Only the new kids have so much energy."

"Have you been here long?"

"Day three. But we've been here almost two weeks."

Two weeks but day three, whatever that meant.

I was totally disoriented in time. Clocks had become irrelevant. Time was a wisp of air when the door opened; a brush against the ankles. A whisper, half overheard, out in the hall. Hospitals reminded me of casinos, sealed worlds devoid of time. Fall wouldn't come sweeping down the hall, nor spring, nor summer, nor winter. The hospital was evenly heated, brightly lit, austerely colored, 365 days a year, 24 hours a day. Without a single sign of outside life. Which seemed odd for a place whose primary purpose was restoring life.

Day became night, became day. It didn't matter what hour you ate breakfast or brushed your teeth or combed your hair or watched *America's Funniest Home Videos*. It barely mattered *if* you did these things. Time was something we had to slog through to reach the other side.

I didn't ask Ramya what she meant, *day three*. I figured we'd find out soon enough.

42

As soon as we meet another family, the first question is, "What Day are you on?" Transplant, we find out, does have a clock. A very particular clock.

Each transplant day is assigned a number. The countdown begins with Day −10 and continues to Day 100, a mythical day. On Day 100 you're "done." Every day prior to transplant is expressed negatively. Every day after transplant, positively. Days −10 to −1 are spent ingesting the chemo drugs. This is time before time. Day 0 is Transplant Day, ground zero, when patients reset their clock. Are made new. After transplant, time is expressed once more in positive numbers because each day forward is a gift. A bonus. These are days your child might not have been allotted. Days received as grace.

Days 1 to 10, we are told, are when patients typically begin to feel the effects of the chemo. And Days 10 to 20, when the drugs hit the liver hardest, are the most dangerous period. Especially for Gracie.

By Day 40 the hope is to be discharged from the hospital and to be treated as an outpatient in Duke's clinic until ready to return home—on Day 100. It's a blueprint, a plan. There is no guarantee that any patient will follow it precisely or even loosely, but I'm happy to have goals, markers toward which we load our bow.

In a spiral-bound notebook I make a vertical list in my smallest, neatest print beginning with Day −10, traveling past Day 0 (Transplant Day) and ending with Day 100. One hundred and eleven days. Doable. Beside each day I intend to take notes.

Once, before I had kids, let alone a sick kid, I read the Lorrie Moore story "People Like That Are the Only People Here," in which a husband advises his writer wife to "take notes" on their son's treatment for cancer. How could you take notes, I'd thought. At a time like that. Now I think, what the hell else can you do?

DAY −10

They give her the first dose of chemo. Brian holds my hand as they load it into the dispenser on Tough Guy. We can't undo this now. I try not to think about that, how time only blows in one direction.

We have a window, outside of which is one tree. Leafless. In the distance there is ice and snowy goings-on, the occasional slice of blue sky. None of it feels pertinent.

DAY −9

Gracie smiles every time Bobbie comes in, "Bobbie, you wear glasses!" As if Bobbie should be made aware of this astonishing fact. Last night she woke out of a deep sleep, saw Bobbie's glasses glinting in the darkness, and opened her arms to hug her. I think that is the first spontaneous gesture of affection I've seen her extend to a medical person.

DAY −8

Chemo continues.

Busulfan and soon its equally poisonous cousin, ATG. Chemo, as it's used in transplant medicine, has been described as "carpet bombing" the body. An assault, from the inside out: massive doses, given over a short time, designed to empty the bones of their own marrow. Gracie's drug regime will last eight days. Several of the drugs come only in oral form.

Oral chemo—a nonintuitive phrase. The dose arrives every four hours. The drug looks like sludge cut with metal flakes, thick and foul. To administer it, we must wear protective rubber gloves. Gracie—who up to this point has done almost everything we've asked—is distraught when we request that she eat poison. Today, at the midnight dose, a drop landed on my pants. Bobbie looked at me with alarm and said, "Ya'll better change!"

Every four hours we place the syringe on her lip. "Swallow, please."

"I will take it," Gracie says, "when Daddy gets back with my drink. When Bobbie comes in tomorrow. I will take it when it snows . . . *inside* this room." We stand firm.

"It's her job to fight us," Brian says, "and our job to win."

The alternative to her willingly swallowing the drug is to feed it to her forcibly through a tube pushed through her nose into her stomach. Each time she swallows, I am flooded with relief; she has exercised agency. She *chooses* to do the awful thing, rather than have it done to her.

DAY −7

I watch a spelling bee documentary as Gracie sleeps. She wakes and watches high school students struggle to spell words like *fatigue* and *ennui* for an hour without demanding, as she usually would, to put on a "kids' show." When I ask her, "Sweetie, do you want a kids' show?" she makes no answer.

Later she turns on her side to face me and says, "If I do all this stuff, will it get rid of my itchies?"

"Yes," I say, "no more itchies." If she is going to lose her hair, feel sick, and be stuck in a hospital bed, she wants a reason. For her, that reason is the eradication of itchies. She looks at me, sensing a beat of equivocation.

"OK," she says, "I'll do it."

DAY −6

I leave the hospital and return to the apartment complex in the late afternoons. It's a split-screen existence. Spending time with Gabe is a ripple of joy. If my fear is a plane hurtling toward the earth, Gabriel is a hit of oxygen on the way down.

While Brian stays with Gracie at the hospital I play with Gabe, feed him dinner, play with him some more, change him into pajamas and bee boots, give him a bottle of milk, and pray he will fall asleep on the drive back. If he doesn't, he has to watch me disappear once more in the big mouth of the revolving glass doors when Brian and I trade places. Mostly he does sleep; he is tired, it is dark, and I sing to him as we drive.

But after a few nights of this routine, it dawns on Gabe that if he doesn't fall asleep, maybe he won't wake up to find me gone. All through the drive he struggles to keep himself awake with an unbroken stream of chatter: "Truck. Big trucks. Daddy. Daddy's tiger. Daddy's pony. Hospital. Yacie sick."

I pull into the semicircle of the hospital driveway and call Brian to let him know we've arrived. I say, "Gabriel, yes, you have a truck and a daddy, and Gracie is in the hospital." I stroke his cheek humming, *Please fall asleep, love.*

But he's wide awake. When I lean down to kiss him he grabs hold of my hair. "No leaving!" he says.

The week before, I gave him a coin to toss into the lobby fountain and asked, "What do you wish for?" "You," he said.

I kiss him again. "I have to leave, lovey boy. But I'll see you tomorrow."

He still has hold of my hair. "No leaving!"

I don't know how to respond. "I *have* to go," I say. "I have to take care of Gracie."

He is quiet for a moment, taking this in. And then very deliberately, very slowly, he says, "Take . . ." Big pause as he works to remember my word, "care," he continues. Another pause . . . "Gabey."

Take care Gabey. A fine, fine idea if ever there was one.

Brian arrives and—in pursuit of a Coke for the drive home—runs into the lobby gift shop with Gabe, hospital celebrity. The guard smiles at him and says, "Baby Gabe! Wearing your boots tonight?" The gift shop woman offers him a fat Tootsie pop on the house. And two complete strangers stop to admire his cheeks (so round, so dimpled) and his general joie de vivre.

I kiss Gabe one more time before going upstairs, drawing out the good-bye. Never good. Back go his hands into my hair. "You'll have fun with Daddy!" I say. Brian hates being touted as the consolation prize. He and Gabriel have a fantastic relationship; he doesn't need a propaganda campaign. But I can't help trying to deflect Gabe's sadness. Though it's a doomed effort; he is, all day, bobbing in the thrashing tide of our collective anxiety.

DAY −5

New Year's Eve around midday Gracie falls asleep for an hour or so and wakes up in a mysteriously good mood, singing the Barney song, "I love you, you love me, we're a happy family."

She goes on eating Doritos and playing with her ponies and asking to walk Tough Guy in the hall, even as the drugs rise to therapeutic levels. We know the side effects of chemo are delayed, but still . . . Will she skip over the pain entirely? Only her mouth is peeling in huge, dry rinds of skin. This is far beyond chapped lips, more like a snake sloughing skin. Not a condition conducive to taking oral meds.

Bobbie comes on at 8 p.m. She has the overnight shift. Just like her to take overnight on New Year's. She arrives with bubbly apple juice and three plastic champagne flutes. Around midnight she and I and Gracie toast each other. Gracie seems unclear what makes this a new year. She keeps asking, "*How* is it a different one?" I can see her point.

Brian calls from the apartment, so we can toast each other. Gabe is asleep on his chest. Gracie's nodded off on my shoulder. We are a nuclear family of four, divided into two twos. Separated by six miles. I feel eons apart.

"Cheers to you, darling," he says. "Cheers to everything you are doing for her every day." "Cheers to you too," I say, "for getting on and off planes. And teaching when you're worried sick. And, most of all, for being a tiger, Pony."

"Cheers to a better year," Brian says.

We both let that idea drift out there.

Tomorrow Gracie begins ATG. We've been told to expect the possibility of high fevers, chills, nausea and vomiting, seizures, burning and bleeding of the bladder, terrible rashes, or more serious allergic reactions. I do not ask for a definition of *more serious.*

I look up ATG online. "Anti-thymocyte globulin is an infusion of horse- or rabbit-derived antibodies against human T cells, used in the prevention and treatment of acute rejection in organ transplantation." Dr. K has to choose whether to give Gracie ATG serum derived from horse or rabbit cells. Would Gracie's love for horses make her body more or less inclined to accept a horse-based drug?

DAY −4

I want to ask Ramya which ATG drug Varun had, rabbit or horse, and if he reacted against it. But I don't; we're still getting to know each other. Varun is some weeks ahead of Gracie and recovering well. He benefits from the undivided attention of his mom. She does not leave his side. Ever. She's there every minute of every day without interruption. I never see her in the parents' kitchen. I never see her without Varun on her shoulder. As many minutes as Varun's dad, Deepak, can be there, he is. This is the most loved baby, I think, of all time.

He gurgles, he coos, he smiles; he flings his huge-eyed calmness around the room. He does not cry. He has myriad reasons to cry, every day, but I have no idea what his cry sounds like. Only his laugh, his soft whoop of surprise or curiosity. Or his sigh, as he settles into his mom's shoulder. Gracie considers herself an honorary aunt. She calls him, as though she were decades older, "Baby Varun."

DAY −3

It is late afternoon when we find out that a child has died on our unit. I don't know the family, don't know the child, but feel stricken. How has this been allowed to happen?

Bobbie is off duty. An unfamiliar nurse comes into our room. "It is OK," she says, "the family was prepared; they knew it was going to happen." She wears heavy blue eye shadow and smells of Jean Naté perfume. She looks too young, too naive to realize what she's just said.

"Do you have children?" I ask.

You can't prepare to have your heart pulled up your throat, plucked from your mouth, and hurled into space.

When Gracie falls asleep I walk down the hall, to what I believe is the door of the room where, hours before, a child has died. It's closed. The blinds are drawn. There is no sound from within.

The door is identical to the fifteen other doors on this floor. Thick wood, steel industrial knob. Window, with curtain drawn. I linger there for as long as I can without seeming to be lingering.

I wonder if the parents are still inside. How long will they be permitted to stay? I would not leave. I would refuse to go. This is self-deluding. But it comforts me to believe I would never leave that room.

Why am I standing here? Am I looking the way you look at an accident? The parents, should they open the door, won't want to see a stranger. But I want to look into their faces, to occupy them, for a sliver of second. To know if such loss is survivable.

Losing a child makes time reverse direction, flow backward. To survive loss on that scale, I imagine, you have to become someone you make up, whole cloth, to impersonate you, for the rest of your life.

On the way back to our room I pause at the nurses' station. There is a subdued vibe, but everyone continues to work. I want to gather information. Of course, this is impossible; I cannot ask; they cannot answer. But I want to know. Give me a map. Tell me where not to go.

When I get back to the room Gracie is awake and anxious.

"Where did you go?" she asks. I'd been gone ten minutes, maybe fifteen.

"I went for a walk in the hall, lovey. I was right outside."

"You weren't here when I woke up."

I climb back into bed with her even though I want to get on the phone with my mom, Cassie, Suzi, Kathy. I want to tell someone about the door, how it looked like any door. Like our door.

It isn't a big bed, but it is big enough for the two of us. I keep as much physical contact with her as possible. I want her to know I have the rope.

DAY −2

The child was a boy. Six years old. Sam. He loved horses. A picture of him in his cowboy hat appears in the parents' lounge. Under the photo is a quote from John Wayne, "Courage is being scared to death and saddling up anyway." There's an address to send condolences. In the photo his right hand holds the reins, a slender length of leather connecting him to the mouth of a huge brown horse.

It's OK. The parents were prepared.

After this, I don't believe anyone else will die. I tell myself a loss so large won't be followed by another. This belief is childlike, willed blindness. Children die here. But I believe it.

When Bobbie comes to work I say, "Did you know Sam?" She nods. She wells up. I have the sense that even when she is at home, mothering her own four sons, she is thinking of her patients. Occasionally, she calls the ward on her days off to see how Gracie is doing, how the other kids are.

Many of the nurses on our unit respond to the loss with an understandable steeliness. Bobbie, by contrast, transmutes her grief into a reservoir of caring. Instead of being inured to the suffering of the children, she is wholly present. For them. With them. Into every mundane interaction, she brings to bear all her skill, all her experience, all her heart.

DAY −1

Rabbit was the right choice. No fever, rash, vomiting, chills, burning bladder, or "more serious" allergic reactions. Probably this can't last. It's cognitive dissonance—bone-marrow-transplant girl feels terrific or at least no worse for wear. Probably we are in a liminal space, a calmed threshold before the storm. But I prefer to believe transplant is nothing worse than a bored girl eating bag after bag of Cool Ranch Doritos, hoping Nemo finds his father.

Her crankiness and fatigue are probably as much from the bad food and confinement as anything else.

Tomorrow is the actual transplant.

Just before dawn, she sits up and says, "I don't want this shirt," then topples back asleep. Brian says Gabriel woke up around the same time at the apartment and said, "Bad pony!" They are having a conversation, from across town, dreamer to dreamer.

I don't want this shirt.

Bad pony!

They are connected and will soon be more so.

We haven't emphasized that her donor is Gabriel, but it seems worth saying, "Gracie, tomorrow you're going to get Gabe's blood, and then your body will get well."

She looks puzzled and annoyed. "You are giving me Gabe's blood for my blood?"

"Yes, sweetie, but once it is in your body, it will be yours."

"OK," she says, as if to say, *not my first choice.*

Maybe she doesn't like the idea of getting Gabe's blood because he's a boy or her brother, or maybe because it is inherently icky to allow someone else's blood to circulate through you. We don't tell that her bones have been emptied, that without an infusion of new cells she's made of straw, a scarecrow girl.

DAY 0

Transplant Day. All day our people send emails from California and New York, wishing Gracie well, asking for updates. The word *transplant* has everyone hyperactivated. It sounds like the violent rearrangement of delicate interior spaces. In reality, it is shockingly simple.

Last week Gabriel's cord blood was FedExed from Oakland to Durham. I'd said to Dr. K, eyebrows up, "FedEx?" Life on dry ice, life with a tracking number. But the bag arrives unscathed. Ready for its big debut.

My mom and Gabriel and Brian are all present. Bobbie is on duty, great luck. Around noon she walks in the room with a plastic bag of scarlet fluid. Life force harvested from one child, conserved, frozen, and flown cross-country to be thawed and poured into a second child. It is odd to imagine the biology of our two children mixing in this way. It seems like a garage science experiment concocted out of boredom on a summer afternoon: *OK, we've got this Barbie and this Ken. Let's pull limbs off one and attach them to the other and see what we get!*

Another nurse follows Bobbie in; together they read the numbers on the bag aloud to each other, back and forth, several times to affirm that it is the right bag, for the right recipient. The wrong bag, with incompatible cells, is a lethal mistake. But this is the same bag Brian helped the doctors fill in the moments after Gabriel was born, the same one that waited for us so patiently.

Gabriel's gift. A glorified Ziploc stuffed with stem cells from the day of his birth.

Now Gabriel is two; he has opinions and verbs and aversions. He has an incredibly complicated cocktail of feelings about his sister: love and anxiety and jealousy and admiration. But the bag is more or less invisible to him. He looks up at it, in Bobbie's hand, without seeing it. It is another piece of hospital paraphernalia, another thing of mystery.

Bobbie says it will take Gabe's cells about four hours to flow into Gracie's bloodstream. She plans to "run it slow" so that the blood won't give Gracie a chill.

While Bobbie hooks up the bag, Gracie gallops a turquoise My Little Pony up the length of Tough Guy to one of the pumps, where the pony lies down. Bobbie primes some tubing with Gabe's blood and threads it through the pump with the pony on top, to regulate the speed. Then Bobbie attaches the other end of the tubing to Gracie's central line catheter, which leads directly to her heart. Girl and bag are now attached. Bobbie programs the pump with a series of fast, syncopated bleats.

"Bobbie, your machine's too loud for my pony," Gracie says. "She likes to sleep in dust puddles." The pony lies motionless, a tiny plastic horse corpse.

"Bobbie's doing her work, sweetie," I say.

Brian touches Gracie's arm and says, "Do you want to watch *Spirit*?" I stroke her hair; he strokes her arm.

Gracie says yes to *Spirit*, and we put it on. Bobbie releases the clamp on the central line, and the stem cells begin to exit the bag and enter the girl. This is the big *tah dah*. Gracie is oblivious to the momentousness of the moment. Her eyes are glued to the opening credit sequence, in which a Mustang herd gallops across a western landscape, leaping gorge after gorge. "They chase!" she shouts, as she shouts each time. "They chase!"

Brian and I are on opposite sides of her bed, both of us watching the pump and the bag. We do not look at each other. Brian pats her. "They do, sweetheart," he says, "they do chase."

I say nothing. I want us to exchange a look, an affirmation. But I am afraid that if I look at Brian, I won't see confidence. We watch the numbers on the pump tick forward as the blood streams through the tubing and travels toward her.

For lunch, Gracie wants rainbow sherbet. Brian volunteers to run out to a place nearby. Good, let him be the sherbet hero. I want to be alone with Gracie. I want to put good juju around her, though I've no idea how.

When Brian leaves I say, "Gracie? Sweetie?" She doesn't look away from the screen. "Can you hear me, love?" She nods slightly. "Good things are happening, lovey. You are getting Gabey's blood, and it's going to cure you." I am lying beside her in the bed. She rests her head against my shoulder. Brian doesn't like it when I superimpose my adult anxieties on her child's reality. *Let her watch her video*, he'd say. Let her have this experience as a three-year-old. But I want her to hold on to this idea: she will be cured.

Brian arrives with sherbet, and with graham crackers for Gabe. My mom returns with pulled pork sandwiches for everyone, including Bobbie, who drifts in and out, monitoring Gracie's vital signs. We eat lunch while Gabe's blood drips into Gracie's veins slowly. The nursing notes for change of shift read "no distress signals."

After lunch, Gracie falls asleep in her typical pose—head tossed back, as if listening hard for the answer to a question. Her chin pointed toward the ceiling, her neck arched into a sharp C-curve, body limp, eyelids twitching in time with her dreams.

When she wakes, she wants to watch another movie. Brian goes to the family room for a selection of videos; he presses DVDs, one by one, against the glass, from outside her room, so she can give each movie a thumbs-up or thumbs-down. This becomes a new game. He could just as easily walk into the room and ask, but the silent ritual thrills her.

When the bag is nearly empty, Brian notices that the room has begun to smell strange. "Is that from the sandwiches?" he asks, wrinkling his vegetarian nose. I sniff around, trying to find the source, and keep coming back to the girl herself. I lift her arm, sniff. Smell the back of her neck, under her chin. It's her. A sickly sweet scent, like candy left too long in a hot car.

Waking up to find me sniffing at her, Gracie asks, "Am I the smelly part?"

I walk down to the nurses' station. How to phrase this? "Um, why does my daughter smell like decomposing candy corn?"

The nurse is cheerful. "Oh, you mean the creamed corn smell?"

"Do I mean the creamed corn smell?"

"All the kids smell like that when they get their new cells. It's the preservative the cells are packed in, DMSO; it's used in canned vegetables."

"OK," I say. "Thanks?"

When every drop of fluid is drained, Bobbie unhooks the empty bag and tosses it into the bio waste receptacle out in the hall. Gracie is now sleeping facedown, with two pillows under her stomach so that she forms a little hillock in the bed. My mom gets ready to take Gabe home and put him to sleep.

At the door I lean down to hold Gabe. "I love you," I say, and kiss his head.

He looks at me, panicky; he's come to associate "I love you" with me leaving or with being taken away. For him, every kiss is a good-bye kiss.

"No leaving," he cries, "no leaving."

"Gabey, love," I say, "I'll see you tomorrow." But Gabe has no solid concept of time. Tomorrow might as well be the year 2050. All he knows is that he's once again being whisked offstage before the play's climactic end.

My mom picks him up. "Gabe, I have a plan," she says.

"What, Didi?" Gabe looks at her, sensing there's a treat in store, maybe ice cream. Maybe cows, which he newly loves.

As they walk past the nurses' station, Gabe waves to each nurse, mayoring it up. Two of them stand up to see if he's got the bee boots on. He does. They blow him kisses that he catches. In a sealed ward of half-broken bodies, his exuberance, his shiny health, his unpained giggle is a form of nutrition we all devour.

The transplant is complete.

Brian and I stay up watching stupid television. We are too washed out for talk, for food, for anything. We've done nothing but sit all day; we are exhausted by our inertia, our inability to affect how things turn out. Exhausted by the strain of projecting calm optimism. Exhausted by avoiding each other. If we look closely at the other, we'll see our own fear. I should go sit with him in the sleeper chair, but I stay where I am.

I can't manage even the mildest intimacy, and Brian seems to feel the same. I lift Gracie's hair off her forehead, blow to cool her down, and close my eyes. *They chase!* No other girl would say precisely this. I hope this means our world can't do without her.

Her body relaxes against mine. Her breathing grows deep and regular.

Once the stem cells enter the bloodstream, they are self-aware. They *know* they are stem cells. They survey the body, perceive where they are most needed, and collectively, as a flock of birds bends and turns, they go there. I find the intelligence embedded into cellular biology, at the microscopic level, so touching. En masse they bore out of the vein wall, burrow through muscle, through fascia and bone, to reach their destination. They do this of their own accord. Without any medical inducement or coercion.

They do this just to be nice.

DAY 1

This is the first day; time begins now. As if she were brand-new. In a way, she is.

There is no going back. She's had the drugs that will change the rate at which her cells replicate, turn her bald, and sick, ripple her nail beds, compromise her liver function, and cause the lining of her entire digestive track—mouth to bum—to slough off. Drugs that will seep into the quietest pockets of her body. Every part of her is littered with toxins; there is no way to create a no-fly zone. Even the recess where her eggs are stored—her future, her potential little people—is awash in the chemo tide. No way to protect them. It took nine months to grow her and only a few minutes to meddle with her future.

At the same time, we've obliterated what was malfunctioning. Her defective marrow is razed. She is between bone marrows. And now she must grow new marrow. We have no guarantee that this will happen.

In every other kind of transplant, you take out an organ and put in a new one. You aren't biting your nails waiting for a new heart to grow back, or a new set of lungs to show up. But that's just what you do with bone marrow: you wipe out the old and pray that the new appears. Because without bone marrow, which produces red cells, platelets, and white cells, you are nowheresville. For a while, medicine can pinch-hit. But only for a short time. Ultimately, engraftment is everything.

When we signed up for this, it was explained with charts and graphs, in blocks of time, with numbered days. The doctors had said, "We will ablate her marrow, transplant the donor cells, and then she'll engraft." And we'd nodded our heads, as if affirming an itinerary in which every connection would be made, on time and without drama. Taxi to train to boat to plane to car to home. I never considered that we might stall out, alone in a strange city, where the trains refuse to run.

There are a million tiny trap doors: she can fail to engraft; the liver can falter or sputter to a stop; a virus or germ can invade her. I am vigilant, hyperalert. If I relax for a minute, a sliver of a second, the black dog might trot down the hall, rest against our door.

DAY 2

She's still eating, which everyone told us not to expect. She's hungry, even though the drugs act like Drano poured through the digestive tract, causing everything from mouth sores to stomach ulcers to sores on the bum. But she still wants Doritos.

DAY 3

She's hurting. It came on last night.

She kept waking up, clutching her knees against her stomach, as if she was trying to squeeze the pain out of herself. Or squeeze herself out of the pain.

DAY 4

More abdominal pain, now accompanied by high fevers. She's sweaty and lethargic, twisting around on the bed, making whimpering sounds. If we sit beside her, she pushes our hands away, "Get off." If we get up, she's anxious, "Where are you going?"

When we ask her, "Are you hurting?" she shakes her head. This "no" is a blanket rejection, it's as if she's saying no to existing.

I ask, "Do you want a cool washcloth?"

No.

"Shall I tell you a story?"

No.

"Should I stop talking and be quiet?"

No.

"Shall I keep talking?"

No.

"Do you want me to rub your back?"

No.

"Are you sure?"

No.

"Do you want the TV on?"

No.

"Do you want the TV off?"

No.

"Should I get down from the bed?"

No.

"Shall I stay next to you here?"

No.

"Are you hurting?"

No.

"Are you sure?"

No.

Her world is contracting to its component parts: the blanket's plush edge, a mouthful of water, Brian's voice at a whisper telling the anty story, again. Small mercies. Stimulation of any kind, even light, seems to pain her.

Still, I hesitate to start the morphine pump that has been standing beside Gracie's bed for the last many days. When Bobbie arrives late in the night, Gracie is curled up in a ball, not sleeping, but not moving. Bobbie says, "Come chat with me in the hall."

"She's hurting," Bobbie says.

I tell her about the boy we played dominoes with in the common room, whose hands shook. His small face shook. His entire torso shook and shook. His mother had whispered, "Too much morphine—nerve damage—don't do it." Another mother told me her child required surgery for the complications caused by constipation from the morphine.

"She's hurting," Bobbie says again.

I am afraid that morphine is a gateway drug to the place where children turn into old people, where they bend and shake and rail against their will. After morphine, I'm afraid they can be patched together but never made whole.

"She says she's not in pain," I tell Bobbie.

I am also afraid to acknowledge that Gracie is in pain so severe only opiates can extinguish it.

Bobbie looks at me, half empathy, half horror. "Look at her," she says. Gracie is limp and unsmiling. An inert mound of girl.

Bobbie knows what suffering looks like; she's witnessed people suffer on at least three continents. She will not collude in denial. She is waiting for my answer; she doesn't look away from my face.

I hesitate. The domino boy shook and shook.

Bobbie says, "Listen, just try it. If she responds well, then you'll know you did the right thing."

Maybe I'll call Brian to ask his opinion but probably not. He is already angry with me for not starting morphine sooner. He thinks I'm imposing my California drug-averse paranoia on a child in pain. But he didn't hear the mother say, *Nerve damage—don't do it.*

"OK," I tell Bobbie. "But just a single bolus dose, not the continuous drip."

"You got it," Bobbie says.

Finally, Gracie sleeps. A true, sound sleep. She does not whimper or roll from side to side. She makes no sound or motion for five full hours. When she wakes up she is not only refreshed but vaguely excited. She demands the bed controls, she motors the head and foot up and down until she finds a configuration that pleases her: a U-shaped bed. She scrambles to the top of one side and slides down into the valley in the middle. Sliding down, she says with pride, "Look what I *made*."

Bobbie has left for the night. I can't call her at home to say, "Thank you." But I ask the new nurse to start the continuous drip. It has a bright red self-administration button that Gracie can push any time she hurts.

She won't have to say she hurts; she won't have to admit defeat; she can just push the button.

DAY 5

When Bobbie comes in, Gracie beams. "Bobbie!" she says. "I feel like I'm gonna have a bath." Bobbie looks at me with delight, not an ounce of I-told-you-so.

In the bath Gracie plays with her plastic horses and croaks out their stories in her newly raspy voice: "I'm falling. Catch me. He got up!" I wash her hair, which has begun to fall out. When I run my fingers along her wet head, dozens of strands cling to my palms in dark lacy patterns.

I call Brian into the bathroom; should we talk with her about going bald? He sits down on the toilet. Gracie is happily drowning her ponies, one by one.

Brian says, "Sweetie, can you listen to me? Do you remember how Mommy and I told you your hair would fall out? That's happening now. In a while your hair will be gone. Then, later, it will grow back, maybe curly."

"Daddy," she says. "I don't want curly hair." Brian looks at her. A resurrected pony is swimming, by her hand, the length of the bathtub underwater. She lifts it up. "This guy has a flag on him butt!" He's the patriotic My Little Pony, stars and stripes cover his haunches.

"Wow, he's lucky," Brian says. "I wish I had a flag on my butt." She doesn't laugh but gives him a charity smile.

I give him a pointed look. *Press on. Tell her she is going to lose her hair. All of it.* "She's as prepared as a three-year-old can be," he says later. "She heard us."

I nurse a flame of annoyance. His way may be better, but I can't stop myself from wanting to explain things or from wanting the reassurance of hearing her responses.

She's only three, Brian says in my head. Three. She's three. Soon to be four.

The most important thing is for her to feel we are united in loving her, protecting her. Brian is still sitting on the toilet, chatting with the red, white, and blue patriotic pony.

"And you, sir," he says to the pony, "what are you going to be when you grow up? You can't stay a pony with a flag on your butt forever, you know." Gracie finally laughs.

I want to touch Brian, hand to knee or chin to head. But I don't. The most I can do is be in the room. The two of us and her. Mostly her.

My field of vision is narrowing; I see Gracie huge, each tooth as large as a farmhouse, each eye as wide as Lake Tahoe. Everyone else is vaporous, grayed out, barely visible.

Later, when Gracie falls asleep, Brian (ever sensitive to unspoken thoughts) says, "We don't have to disappear each other to get through this, you know. We can do this shoulder to shoulder. Maybe even face to face."

"Or," I say, "we can just see each other on the other side."

DAY 6

Her first words on waking are "Get this hair off me." It is everywhere. Coating the sheets and pillows, all over her clothes. "It itches," she says, as if there were no worse fate.

We offer her a buzz cut; she accepts. It's a classic you-can't-fire-me-I-quit solution.

After we are done with the clippers, she turns to me and says, "Now I'll do you." I am prepared to do it though I hope not to. I like my hair and already had a buzz cut once in the wake of a disastrous dye job. If I'd been thinner, I might have looked tragic or mysterious or hiply countercultural. As it was, I'd just looked like a military reject or a confused spiritual recruit. Buzz cuts do not become anyone, except the young Sinéad O'Connor and the old Georgia O'Keeffe. Otherwise, not to be attempted.

Thankfully, Gracie seizes instead upon two of her favorite ponies, both of whom are happy to make the sacrifice. She hacks off their plasticized manes and tails with a silver nail scissors, humming to herself. "It's just hair," she tells them, "you don't need it."

Later she perches a single rider on top of a horse's head and makes the rider jump into the ocean below. In her play, peril is the driving force. Figures are perpetually falling and being saved, drowning and springing back to life.

Before she falls asleep, in one of her soft, pre-dream moods of float-ing affection, she turns to face me. "Mommy," she says, "it's all love from me to you."

DAY 7

We can once more see the pale strawberry birthmark at the nape of her neck. I'd forgotten it was there. How is it possible to forget something intrinsic to your child?

Gracie doesn't mind being bald. She is delighted to be done with the hair in her bed, on her pillow, down her shirt, in her ears—itching her. Rubbing her bald head reminds me of the tenderness I felt for her five-pound infant body. Touching her scalp is oddly comforting; it is as if she's imminently reachable, right there, living on the surface of her skin.

She loves this. "Do my head," she'll say, and tuck her skull into the palm of our hands.

For us, it's weird. Her baldness triggers a series of chain reactions in the brain. It's not only that she looks like someone on chemotherapy—which reads *cancer*, which reads *death*. And not only that in myth the loss of hair signifies diminishment of vigor, life force, and defensive power. What's most disturbing is that she's beginning to look like them, every other child on this ward. It feels like the beginning of an unstop-pable slide taking her farther and farther from us.

We knew; we watched the other kids transmogrify. In the before photos taped to doors, bright-eyed, glossy-haired children lean back in swings and stretch their legs toward the horizon. They lean out of their lawn chair, arms reaching upward, as if to capture a cloud. But the children inside the rooms are swollen, bent, and bald. They look broken. It is as if, one by one, each child has been forced into the decrepit body of an old person.

I know she's Gracie, and she knows she's Gracie, but she looks very little like our daughter. The incremental changes, the hair loss, the swelling around her eyes, the puffy, overinflated quality to her extremi-ties, have accumulated. It is bizarre to look down at your child and not recognize her.

Suzi writes from India, "Thank God she is on the inside looking out."

DAY 8

She has two kinds of recurring pain: acute cramps right before she vomits and chronic pain from the sores we assume are in her stomach and intestines. She's spiking fevers and is hypertensive. Bobbie comes in and out; she whispers to Gracie and rubs her feet. The doctors round through, all saying the same thing: her misery is "normal." The morphine's ability to abate pain is diminishing. She doesn't motor her bed up and down anymore. She smiles very little, only as a kind of gift to us.

Still, her refusal to see herself as sick or deprived is dazzling and a little scary. One minute she is vomiting up stomach bile. The next, she wipes her mouth and picks up her ponies. Back to playing. She has no inner narrator, lamenting her situation, saying, "Oh, I'm sick. I can't believe I'm sick." To her, throwing up is sick. The second that is over, there's no reason not to play. And nothing to be said about it.

As much as I admire her, I wish she were less stoic and more able to talk about what she is experiencing.

"Gracie, you can say you hurt," I tell her.

Brian scowls. "Let her coping mechanisms work the way they work. If she knows anything better than us, it's how to cope." I know he is right, and I resent him for it.

I begin to pray with her at night. I only do it when we're alone. When she has enough energy, she's game. One night, when our single tree rubs its single branch against the window, she says, "That's the God." When we pray, she is very casual with God, very offhand. She likes to end her prayers with "Tah Dah!" Sometimes she signs off with "Have a nice night!"

I imagine her God as a mashup hybrid of Jimmy Stewart, the Wizard of Oz, and the three good fairies of *Sleeping Beauty*, Flora, Fauna, and Merryweather.

I also pray. I'm not so casual. I am respectful, subservient. A blatant suck-up. I don't believe that what—or who—God might be is involved in micromanaging children's illness or recovery. But neither can I stop from groveling. From doing anything that might give her relief.

DAY 9

Tomorrow begins the most critical period, Days 10 through 20, when she is at risk for developing veno-occlusive disease. VOD. Dr. K told us repeatedly that Gracie's VOD risk was high, given the condition of her liver and the force with which the chemo drugs will hit her system. I keep reminding myself of the many ancient alcoholics in the world—the liver is resilient; it can take tremendous battering and remain functional. Still, every organ has its breaking point.

VOD shuts the liver down immediately. When the liver is unable to perform its filtering functions, fluids back up in the abdomen and then, ultimately, in the lungs. Patients with severe VOD essentially drown from within. We were told this. And we listened, but we didn't hear. It was so far in the future, Day 10 through Day 20. Now it is Day 9, and there is no way to get out from under tomorrow.

DAY 10

Gracie does not know that the next ten days matter in a way no other days have. She does not know what VOD is. Or double-blind studies or percentages or morbidity rates.

She knows that Tough Guy never leaves her side, and that she will fall asleep with one parent or another stroking her bald head. She knows that her mouth is sore, her lips are cracked, the pink skin lifting away in thick rinds. She knows that her fevers come in waves. That when her stomach cramps, she can push the red button. She knows that when Bobbie leaves, she will be back. She knows she's stopped eating. She knows she misses Eden. She knows she is up all night, awake while it is dark, asleep while it is light.

She's flipped her days and nights, which is common for kids uncoupled from time; from sunlight, from weather, from family meals, from trips to the pool, the farm, from a walk around the block. All the ordinary signposts that locate us in the day don't exist here. She knows she wants to go home. And, that she can't.

DAY 11

Gracie and I watch an awards show; the actresses slink across the stage and speak in baby doll voices. *Plant your fucking feet*, I want to tell them. *Talk in your true register.* But they are oblivious to this hospital room. Even to Gracie, who looks at them with awe and says, "Their hair has sparkles."

Gracie picks up a piece of my hair and begins to suck on the ends. This should charm me; she wants connection. Instead, somehow it bothers me; it seems like a babyish act, a crutch, at the exact moment when I want her to be strong. "Please don't do that, sweetie!" I say. She shoots me a look out of the corner of her eye, confirming what she suspected, that I'm not where she needs me to be.

True. Half of me is watching the show, while the other half catalogs signs and symptoms of VOD: rapid water weight gain, distended belly, painful enlargement of the liver, elevated bilirubin, renal failure, jaundice. And the list goes on. The definitive test is a sonogram that, if the liver were shutting down, would show a "reversal of flow" in the main arteries. Essentially fluid running backward through the system, filling the abdominal cavity, filling the lungs.

We do not want reversal of flow. No one does. We want all the fluids of the body to run in one direction—through the liver, the urinary tract, and out, with ease and flow. Ease and flow.

DAY 12

I watch her stomach for an hour before she wakes up. Is it more swollen than yesterday? Hard to tell. Her breathing is labored; her whole body shudders slightly on each out-breath.

A nurse, not Bobbie, arrives about noon with a measuring tape, as through she is ready to do something as innocuous as take up a hem. Instead, she wraps it around Gracie's belly, back to front, just below the belly button, and records the number on the chart.

"Is it better or worse?" I say.

"This is our baseline," she says. "Now we've got a number against which we can measure growth."

"Why didn't they take the baseline before Day 10?"

"I'm not sure about that," she says, sounding defensive. I look at the number she records on the chart. Our world expressed in two digits.

On the floor, here to visit us, are the Pedersons. This is the family we met on the day Gabriel threw Brian's glasses over the edge of the balcony, when they dropped four floors without breaking. The day the mom, Cindy, and I made friends by exchanging gum.

Jake is still going to clinic almost daily, and they've made the short trip from clinic to our unit to say "Hi."

"She's feeling pretty awful," I tell Cindy at the door.

"We won't stay. Jake just wants to give her something." I look at Jake; he's dyed his hair blue. She'll like that.

"Come in." I want Gracie to see this boy who's traversing the rigors of transplant with a genuinely blithe spirit intact. With a blue head.

Jake walks into our room with a giant bottle of Sponge Bob bubbles. "These are for you, Gracie. When you get bored of TV you can blow them into the doctors' faces." He sits on the edge of Gracie's bed and looks up at her monitors with intent, as though he might have an opinion about her oxygen saturation or blood pressure. He looks at the lunch tray, untouched. "Gracie," he says, "you don't have to stop eating as soon as your mouth hurts, you know. Chew with your back teeth and swallow fast." The seasoned con passing advice to the newbie—here's how to adjust to life in the joint. I don't tell him, and neither does Gracie, that it's already been many days since she's eaten.

Gracie takes the bubbles from Jake and holds them against her chest as she watches the TV, impassive. I stroke her head. Jake's mom and I exchange information in coded whispers and glances. We run through the transplant people we know in common—who is doing well, who isn't. We dart our eyes upward to indicate when a child has gone "upstairs," to the PICU. To intensive care. To the ventilator.

The PICU is the place we all most don't want to go. We've seen children transferred upstairs for respiratory failure, but we've yet to see a child come back down.

In the middle of our talk, Gracie gets sick. There is nothing in her stomach to vomit; she convulses in heaves, throwing up something that looks like algae. Green. Vibrant green. Jake looks at her small, shuddering body. He doesn't look away. The Pedersons get ready to leave. Gracie turns away from the TV for the first time that day and says, "Bye, Jake." Just two words, and the only ones she's said to him, but a rare acknowledgment. The energy to speak costs her, her vocal cords are stripped raw, but she says it again, "Bye, Jake."

DAY 13

Her stomach is growing. She's gained two centimeters in diameter since yesterday.

Am I transmitting fear to her in a thousand plucks at her blanket, a hundred rubbing motions to her head? I order myself to hold still. Don't smooth, fix, tidy, wipe, brush, arrange—anything. Sit next to her. Quietly. Try that. It is excruciating to do nothing precisely because there is nothing I can do.

DAY 14

Another three centimeters. There is a great deal of fluid in the abdomen, and the liver is enlarged, both bad signs. Dr. K orders a sonogram to determine whether there is also "reversal of flow."

The sonographer arrives at 10 a.m., the middle of the night for Gracie. I am determined that the woman do her job without waking Gracie. It is crucial she get all the rest she can.

The sonographer is in her midfifties with an accent I can't quite place. She is plump and gentle and perfectly happy to go along with my plan to keep Gracie asleep.

Under Gracie's nightshirt the skin stretches across her distended stomach, so taut it's nearly translucent. The sonographer pours warm gel onto the roller ball of an imaging wand. Gracie stirs when the wand touches her body, but doesn't wake. The wand rolls left and right as the woman gives her full attention to the grainy lunar landscape on the screen. I try to read her face. She looks calm and focused. She reaches all the way over Gracie's body to get a better view of the other side. I slip both hands under Gracie's back and press lightly to remind her, in her dream, that she's with me.

The woman finishes her work, puts the wand away. I wipe the gel off Gracie's stomach with a tissue and pull her nightshirt down. It is dark in the room; we've left the lights off. I look at this stranger, who has peered inside my daughter's body. She knows the true condition of Gracie's liver. The liver is everything, all of everything. If the liver is not working, there is no way to get another. If the liver shows reversal of flow, if this is VOD, we are in a free fall.

I have to know, I have to ask. And I cannot know, I cannot ask.

Brian is in New York. My mom is in California. Gabriel is with Denise at the apartment. All our lives hang in the balance—yes or no to reversal of flow.

The sonographer knows. She says, "Your doctor will deliver the results as soon as possible." A stock line, but delivered with tenderness.

Three hours pass before the doctor appears. It's afternoon. Gracie is still asleep. Brian has arrived back from New York. We stand up when the doctor walks in, shoulder to shoulder.

Dr. K is not on duty. Instead it's Dr. P, whom we like. He's calm, he's responsive. He seems like the kind of doctor who promises himself, daily, to be a human first. But today he stands as far from us as is possible in this tiny space. He's near the door, as if poised to leave. We wait for him to speak. He opens his mouth, pauses, and then states the following without fanfare: the liver shows no reversal of flow. I feel Brian's body relax against mine.

"Thank you," I say. Jubilation. I want to kiss Dr. P.

"Wait," he says. "We are still concerned by the volume of fluid accumulating in her abdominal cavity." His speech picks up speed and efficiency. "Though there is no reversal of flow, her other symptoms would indicate that Gracie does have an early iteration of VOD. There is a fifty percent chance it will progress. If it does progress, she has a fifty percent chance of surviving." As he speaks, his hands hang limp on either side of his body. He moves neither closer to us nor toward the door.

I hate Dr. P.

I stand very still, trying to mirror the stillness of his stance. Maybe if I can stand as calmly as he stands, he'll blink, flinch, take it back. If not, I will drive him from this room.

A 50 percent chance the VOD will progress.

And if it does, a 50 percent chance she will not survive.

These numbers, applied to Gracie, are malicious. They are personal.

I reject the numbers, en masse, and also one by one. Fuck the percentages given to every patient in this hospital and every other hospital, worldwide. Fuck their arrogant, razored corners, their cleaved sums. Their little stick-fingered hands, rubbing out your odds. Fuck their precise tallies, in neat lines, to the last decimal. *Lucky to the left, remainder to the right.*

The numbers are rigid, void, inflexible; all they can do is breathe on you with their viciously clean breath and wait for you to make them correct. The numbers don't love or know or care to listen.

They can't express the central facts of her person. The numbers might know what time of day she was born, but not what the sky looked like, how it was an incandescent indigo. Numbers can't stroke her head, whisper songs in her ear, fall asleep with the pulse of her breath breaking warm on one cheek. The numbers don't know how she hums when she eats, that she favors feta cheese and olives, any savory food, over sweets. How, then, can the numbers predict what might become of her?

Fuck them, one and all.

She belongs to me and to Brian. She belongs to Gabriel and to herself. She belongs to my mom, whose smile flares every time she says Gracie's name, and to Brian's mom, who will still get down on the floor to play with her, at eighty-three. To her dead grandfather, who ran a union and never set eyes on her, and her living grandfather, who reads her *The Hobbit* over the phone. She belongs to Eden and the friends she hasn't met yet. She belongs to the person who will love her most as an adult. Her true love, and the smaller loves in between, she belongs to them. She is ours. She belongs to us, with us, with me. She is mine. I will not hand her over.

I know other parents in this hospital, on this ward, in this room, have despised the numbers. Have tried to lash their child, psychically, to their own body with the twine of love, righteous anger, magical thinking, with anything, everything, they had. I know my sense of possession, of power, is as frail, as flawed, as theirs. But I use it all. I will mow the fuck-ing numbers down, numeral by numeral, until we boomerang back. To zero. Zero. Where there is no chance that she can be taken. None at all.

I call Cassie, whom I have always called. I tell her I'm terrified. I explain the numbers.

She does not sound calm, and I love her for this.

DAY 15

A day worse than yesterday. She's in misery. She's spent the day vomiting blood in increasingly bright and large volumes. While she was napping, a pool of blood collected in her mouth. When she sat up, it dripped down her chin onto her pajama shirt, settling into the shape of a deformed red elephant, hind legs bent, as if in some odd elephant prayer.

"Why am I bleeding in my mouth?" she asks. "What is wrong with me?"

Later she spikes a fever, and her blood pressure refuses to come down.

Brian and I pass worry back and forth, a toxic, contagious vapor we share.

When she falls asleep, Brian says, "Let's imagine today as her low point. Tomorrow she is going to feel better, and every day after, she'll gain more ground."

That's one possibility. The other breathes under the door, stretches out beneath the bed, a dog with a midnight coat we refuse to recognize.

DAY 16

We have less Gracie than we arrived with. Less hair, less breath, less appe-tite, fewer heartbeats per minute. Less of her voice making the ponies talk, fewer jokes, fewer demands, less of her hands forming shapes in the air as she speaks. The law of diminishing returns, whatever that means, keeps coming to me.

I've begun to do grotesque emotional calculations in the abstract.

By day I wonder—if one (not me!) were to lose one's child—is there a best-case scenario? Is it better to lose your child in increments, to a pro-tracted illness so that you have time to encapsulate them in your love, to say everything? Or better to lose your child mysteriously, without confirmation of death, so that hope resides, co-occupant, with grief?

By night I picture scenarios in which I might be able to save her. She's been taken, for reasons not made clear. The kidnapper's demands are bizarre: I must walk without stopping, in the heat, in the snow, carrying weight in the form of grocery bags, metal bars, sacks of sand. If I stop, even hesitate, the kidnapper will harm her or refuse to return her. I must keep walking. I will keep walking. How long can I walk? Three days, four? I think I could walk indefinitely. Without food or water, or in extreme heat, extreme cold, eventually I would drop. But I don't see that happening. I see myself lifting foot after foot. I worship a false god, the idol of parental love.

DAY 18

The ultrasound woman returns each morning. She's gentle, she's quiet. Gracie sleeps through it. Every morning I am standing on the edge of a very high cliff. Prepared for the sick feeling of dirt sliding, the rocks soft, then loose, then gone. But every morning the ultrasound woman repeats her phrase, "Your doctor will deliver the results as soon as possible." She's said this for five days in a row. Each day when the doctor arrives in the afternoon, he confirms that the sonogram shows no reversal of flow. Two days remain in our window of risk. Today he will say the same.

DAY 19

Brian comes in while we are asleep. He has brought me a stack of trashy magazines and a bar of dark chocolate. He's brought nothing for Gracie because she isn't able to enjoy anything. I read my magazines. He reads E. L. Doctorow's new novel. Gracie breathes in, breathes out, breathes in. Beautiful sound. I'm not sure if I'm breathing, or if Brian is. How long since we drew a deep breath, eight days? Nine? We don't talk. I'm aware that, sometime over the last weeks, my feelings for Brian have radically rearranged.

Glancing at him used to bring me joy. Or a sense of well-being. Now, watching him turn pages, I feel nothing. He's the same man. Same long, studious face, which can break into an immense smile at any invitation. But

Brian no longer looks entirely real to me. He cannot affect the outcome of Gracie's sonograms. He cannot prescribe lifesaving medicine. He cannot ensure she lives; he doesn't have that power. So he can't help me. He's one of the nonessentials, receding, half ghosted.

He looks up and catches my eyes. I look back down at my magazine, afraid he'll see what I'm thinking. Afraid he already has.

Later in the day, Dr. P comes to see us.

"So her mortality risk is over?" Brian asks.

Dr. P looks at us carefully. "Her risk of mortality from VOD specifically is over. As you know, transplant is a dangerous process. She still needs to engraft, and until she engrafts she's vulnerable to infection or virus."

I block out the second half of the sentence and focus on the first. "Can you repeat what you said about VOD, please."

"We can say for certain that her mild case of VOD failed to progress." I love this phrase *failed to progress*.

I feel light. Like when you force your arms against a door jamb, and when you step out, they float upward, of their own accord, weightless.

Dr. P is handsome. Extremely handsome. How have I not noticed before? Dark, wide-set eyes, an aquiline nose. I actually squeeze his arm a little. Dr. P, kind but reserved, recoils toward the door. "I'm very glad to give you good news," he says, and steps out.

I turn to Brian, who is also suddenly, acutely handsome. I want to make a joke, "Where have you been all my life?" As if I hadn't noticed him until now. But think better of it. Too close to home. I put my arms around him; he puts his arms around me. "Her VOD failed to progress," I say. "I'm so happy and proud to be the parent of a failure."

It feels as if everything that matters has already happened: she's walked to the edge of the abyss, looked down, peered over her shoulder at us, as if to ask, "Should I stay or go?" And, beautifully, mercifully, chosen to stay.

Brian and I walk around wearing the insipid, blissed-out smiles of recent religious converts. Even though we know nothing is settled. Even though the abyss still surrounds her bed, and she's still a patient on 5200, a transplant unit, with the ricketiest of immune systems, still between bone marrows, unengrafted, unable to produce sufficient red cells on her own. Even though she's blank and bored, and awash in the malaise of living in a box, her liver works. Her liver works!

DAY 20

Time shears in half: before and after. After is better and faster; the days lift their heels out of the sticky tar of anxiety and fear and speed past us in flip-flops, spewing sand. We're allowed to be happy again or to relax, space out. Singular moments leap into focus.

Gabriel and Brian are at home, where I can finally spend a night. Gabriel pats the bed beside him and says, "Sleep, Mommy" and "Sleep, Daddy." He wants our company, even when unconscious. We hope to lie down just for a minute, but he entangles a hand in my hair, pegs a foot on Brian's arm; two sleepy-time paperweights to make sure we stay.

Brian and I both swear that, just before falling sleep, Gabriel mumbles "bone marrow transplant." It is the end of a long day, and he is babbling a lot of stuff. We ask him to repeat it, and he does. He isn't enunciating with perfect elocution, but he says the same thing several times, and the thing he says sounds like *bone marrow transplant*. He's two years old, almost.

When he's asleep I say, "Your cells are doing a great job." I bend to kiss his feet. "They are helping Gracie." This idea might be as arbitrary, as anthropomorphizing, as trees who don't like him, but I believe it's true.

I keep wishing Gracie could see him. He would be a Tasmanian devil in a jar, in her tiny room, and he is too germy for the unit, but he would cheer her up. Once or twice they talk on the phone.

"Hi, Gabriel."

"Yacie!"

"Hi, Gabriel."

"You sick?"

DAY 24

Engraftment is our new everything.

"She needs to engraft," Dr. K says, "so we don't have to keep dumping blood in her. We need to see that the marrow works, that Gabriel's cells can do their job."

"Do your job," I say as she sleeps, speaking to the soles of her feet, to the palms of her hands, to the cells of her interior spaces.

Engraftment is defined as three consecutive days of an ANC (white cell) count above 500. If the body is making that many white cells, theory has it, then the stem cells have transformed into bone marrow cells. Her ANC count bobs erratically; it hits 500 then dips below, hits it again and dips once more. Our spirits are tied to this value; our happiness rises and falls in direct correlation.

DAY 25

It's the coldest day we've had in Durham yet when Gracie, at last, engrafts. Outside our window, a thin layer of ice coats every surface. Inside Gracie's bones, Gabriel's stem cells fuse to the walls, divide and multiply, replicating his healthy matrix in their new ecosystem.

I take a walk after we get the news. The gardens of Duke are crystallized beneath a suspended veil of white branches; lace shot with sunlight. I envision her engraftment like this, as a stunning architecturally intelligent design writ in miniature and encased inside her. I walk and pray, let it work, let it work, let it work.

When I get back to the room, my face is cold and red.

"Poor Mama," Gracie says. "I will warm you up!" She presses her cheek against mine. She's happy to share whatever she's got, even body warmth. I can feel her heat, her inner engine. I hug her back, too tight. She pulls away. "Look what I learned to do while you were out!" She motors the head of her bed all the way up and the foot of the bed all the way up, to make the U shape. She has already learned this trick and shown me, but if it feels new to her, I rejoice in the discovery. She climbs to the top of the head of the bed and flings herself off, into the valley, like a cliff diver. Brian and I stand and applaud. Inflationary approval; we can't help ourselves.

Later Brian says, "It seems strange to say you admire a child who's three years old, but I do."

I know exactly what he means. She finds the speck of gold amid all this dross.

DAYS 30–33

One morning I realize her belly has lost its distended, malnourished look. Even her peeled lips are almost normal. She looks more like herself. She is still bald but in a delicate, lovely way. The only physical marker now of what she's been through are her nails, which are rippled with pale crescent rims halfway up, where the growing cells were interrupted by the chemo. They look like stumps of old-growth trees that show the year of fire.

Her appetite returns.

The first thing she asks to eat is a Luna Bar, then Doritos. I think we should push for some nutrition.

Brian says, "Are you crazy? Give her what she wants. Eating is life affirming."

There are, anyway, restrictions—she's on a neutropenic diet. She can't be exposed to any form of bacteria or fungus. No eating things that can harbor a living organism. No raw fruits or vegetables. No feta cheese, her favorite. No blue cheese. Basically, nothing healthy. She either doesn't care about these new rules or pretends not to.

She says, "It's OK they won't let me have blue cheese dressing for my croutons. It's OK I can't have cream cheese on my bagel." It strikes me as a mantra of self-consolation. I think what she means is: I'm so sad I can't have the things I want that I won't want them.

Or maybe her sympathies just don't revolve around herself. A day or so later, as she's about to eat a bare cracker, she whispers to it, "I'm sorry I can't eat your friend feta."

* * *

Soon after Gracie can eat again, Cassie comes to visit. At the apartment she cooks for us, veggie soup for Brian, miso salmon for me, mac and cheese for Gabe; she vacuums and folds our clothes. At the hospital she makes Gracie laugh by turning a pair of chopsticks into battling brothers. She creates a fierce character, Edith the Avenging Cook. Edith is abrupt; she orders people around; she shouts every sentence. She threatens bodily harm if you don't do her bidding. "You don't like my soup?" Edith tells

Gracie, "Fine. I will cut off your favorite finger. Which one is your favorite? Show me!" Gracie, sick child, coddled, catered to, and pitied, is thrilled by Edith's intensity, her bullying. "This one," she says, and holds up her left thumb.

By the time Cassie leaves, Gracie is revived. Gracie asks, "Where's Auntie Cassie?" When I tell her Cass had to fly on a plane back to New York, she throws her hands into the air. "Oh no!" she says, as if Cassie has suffered a calamity. Does she think Cassie was coerced onto the plane? I often forget how little she is, how literal. I'm surprised and happy that she can track the comings and goings of other people again; she can notice, she can care.

She is coming back to life in stages. Look! Here's my sense of humor, my food preferences, my powers of empathy, of gossip, of concern. Her world is dilating. It now includes Cassie. And Edith. Her imagination is reinflating.

DAY 34

We wake up to a flyer in the kitchen: a simple memorial service will be held for the four children who've died on the ward over the last eight weeks.

Ramya and I sit next to each other during the service. Varun, who cannot understand what the chaplain is saying, sits on Ramya's lap, looking around the room with interest. He's well enough to be out a bit. We are in the common playroom known as "the Connection." Gracie is in our room, probably missing me, watching a video. I feel guilty, but I stay. I want to be here with people who knew the children who are gone.

Varun gurgles. He's also growing stronger each day. He'll go home soon. He is grasping at the gold bangles on Ramya's wrist, clinking them together and singing out elongated, airy vowels. Part of what makes his eyes so big, I notice, are his lashes; they've begun to grow back long and thick. A good sign. I want to touch his cheek, but that's not done. We don't touch each other's children. Transmission of infection is everyone's greatest fear.

As the chaplain says her ending prayer, "And reside beside Him, in His house," a computerized voice bleats out a fire drill, "Code one five seven one," punctuated with piercing beeps. Ramya and I exchange a look. Life on the unit, typical mix of the holy and the institutional. But I know she feels like I do, grateful for this service, grateful for the chance to sit together and grieve.

They played in this room, each of the four children. They touched the crayons in that box by the door. They handled the videos. They took out the games. We are surrounded by things they picked up and put down, but with no way to call them back.

I drive home from the hospital crying. I'm not sure if I'm crying with grief for the four children who died beside us, whom we did not know. Or with relief that my child has lived. Or with lingering fear. I wipe my face and turn up the music and try to get ready to mother Gabe.

At home I try to strap Gabe into the kid seat on our blue Schwinn. He arches his back and yells, "Oolie ba ba!" His latest creed.

"Gabey, let me put you in!"

"I do it!"

If you try to help him do anything, say, put his bee boots on, he's indignant and demands to do it himself. If he can't do it, he's outraged that you have let him struggle. Being two years old is an ongoing schizophrenia; the wild vacillations between *I can* and *I can't*.

Finally, he's in. We coast downhill in the cooling air of early evening. At the edge of the forest we pass through the fertile scent of wet upturned earth. "Yummy air," Gabe calls it. I pedal like mad to make it back up our little hill. "Again!" Gabriel cries every time we crest the hill. I sing to him, snippets of Joni Mitchell, snippets of Van Morrison. But mostly we ride in silence, listening to the trees sigh out at the end of the day, to the multiple squawks and squeaks and chirps and khaas that are the lingua franca of the lush woods around our complex.

Gabe loves this. I love this.

A flock of wild geese flies in a ragged V along the horizon line, gray specks against an orange sky, calling to each other. *This way, this way, this way, follow me.*

"Gabe, do you see the geese?"

"Geese mine," Gabe says.

"Gabey, next week is your birthday. Are you ready to be two?"

Gabe says, "Go faster!"

Four children in eight weeks. Three boys and a girl. Three of these children died before we arrived, one after. Sam, the cowboy.

It feels wrong to be happy, to be riding through dusk with Gabe, in his bumblebee boots, while children who once lived on our unit cannot see the sky, the geese, cannot smell the wet ground permeating the air. But I keep pedaling.

The art therapist, Mary Margaret, arrived at the service with art made by two of the boys, Sam and Ramone. Sam's piece was a collage of shredded magazine pages, strips woven together, in the blue hues of the ocean, which his mother loved. Ramone's was a velvet stencil of a large cross, intricately and delicately hand-colored, like stained glass, made for his deeply religious grandmother who sat beside his bed for eleven months. Small marks of self-expression that pulsed with vibrancy, with their maker's particular sensibilities. Intention remains even when the children are gone.

There was a collective hope at the service that the children were in heaven. Riding ponies, playing bingo, exploring the sea. But I don't think heaven is so much like earth. If heaven exists, I hope it is far beyond what we conjure with our gravity-soaked imaginations.

To my mind, it is OK if there is no heaven. It is miraculous enough that Sam and Ramone lived. They were here, on earth, as themselves. The spontaneous eruption of an individual consciousness out of nothingness. I know this is too easy for me to say—I have one child healing, and the other murmuring self-soothing songs on the back of a blue bike. It is too easy. But still, it's what I hold against my chest. They died, but, before that, they lived.

DAY 35

Gracie is allowed, for the first time, to take a walk off the unit. She suits up in the yellow gown, the mask, the shoe covers. When we reach the imposing electric double-doors that have held her in the ultrasterile environment of 5200 for almost two months, she hesitates. She peers through the door's window to the hall beyond and asks, "Am I safe there?"

Stepping outside the unit feels as alien, as adulterous, as a moon walk. When she takes off down the hall, her gait is lopsided, a bow-legged half waddle with the toes of her left foot turned in. The result of lying in bed for weeks. She stops at a handrail and tries to pull her feet up, to hang upside down, something she did routinely before being admitted. She doesn't have the strength; her feet dangle a few inches off the ground.

I say, "It might take a while for your body to remember how to run and jump and play."

"It's OK," she says, "my body didn't forget how to run." She limps past me, saying, very matter-of-fact, "You know why my ankles isn't working right? Because I was in the bed so much."

She is overcome with happiness at being in a new corridor, even if it's the same beige hospital corridor with the same generic seaside art as ours. For me, the thrill of watching her "run" is cut with the knowledge that she could be reduced to a ventilator by an unseen germ coughed out by any well-meaning passerby. Or a virus on a handrail. I run in front of her with a tub of antibacterial wipes, imploring her not to touch anything until I have wiped it down. She is a good sport about this; she points to whatever she wants to touch, so that I can wipe it first, saying, "Clean, please."

DAY 38

Gabriel turns two.

My dad and his wife fly out for the party. They buy dinner for eight at Chai's Noodle Bar and Bistro and bring it to the hospital. Gabriel refers to them as a single entity, Baba-Nana. "Baba-Nana come!" he says to us. On this trip my dad—renowned for being domestically inept (he used to keep a single, perpetually unwashed pot on the back of the stove, and whenever it got low, he'd simply add a new can of food)—does all our laundry, folds my shirts with care, hangs Brian's dress slacks.

My mom flies out too, and I revel in the sight of my mom and my dad on either side of Gracie's bed, each with a hand on her. A complete genetic circle. They have been divorced for thirty-six years, but they both want what is best for the girl between them.

Gabe spends the whole day saying, to one grandparent or another, "Is mine birthday!" It's Lincoln's birthday too, for that matter, and Darwin's.

But they answer, "Gabriel, it is your birthday!"

We hold our party in the Connection, all clad in the canary yellow gowns of contamination containment. Gabriel is habituated to these papery gowns, the smallest of which billows around him as he walks, a diaphanous cloud.

Gabe pings from gift to gift like a drunk, ripping, tearing, shaking, dropping, tossing, ripping some more. A yellow blur of manic happiness, high on the surplus of ambient anxiety and spirit of celebration.

I try to collar him.

Brian says, "He's OK. He's opening presents Gabe style."

I feel, once more, corrected. "Wow, Brian. Where are you getting all this incredible parental insight? Books? Meditation? A secret life coach you call in California?"

My mom looks up, startled by my tone. How mad can I be? Gracie is better, Gabriel is two. I'm eating a delicious Vietnamese salad. The bite in my voice surprises even me.

Later, as we stuff shredded gift wrap into a trash bag, my mom offers to stay with Gracie in the hospital that night so Brian and I can spend the night together at home. A total rarity. It's February 12, a few days shy of Valentine's.

We take the back way home, through the country roads. I'm glad Gabe is not here to lament the trees' dislike of him. As we turn a corner, a crescent moon lies on the horizon line. A rind of new moon, slim and ghostly and seemingly self-lit. It is a cradle, reclining on the land, close enough to walk to. We could climb in and fall asleep. I think of suggesting to Brian that we stop the car and stroll to the moon. But as soon as I have the thought, I remember a time in California when I'd said, "Look, a full moon!" And he'd replied, "Not yet, it's only almost full."

We drive along in silence; neither of us mentions the extraordinary moon touching the ground. Nor do we talk about Gabriel being two or Gracie having engrafted. We don't talk about how scared we were during the VOD days. We don't talk about the children's memorial service or about the latest child to go upstairs to the vent, a little boy with light blue liquid eyes that seemed never to blink. We don't talk about how much we miss each other or how stressful it's been to have our parents visiting, even when it's been helpful. We don't even talk about Jack Bauer.

When we get home we change Gabriel into his pajamas and lay him down in his crib to dream birthday dreams. Soon he'll be sharing this room with Gracie. We hope. We say nothing about this either.

We brush our teeth, climb under the covers, in silence. It is obvious what should happen; it has been weeks. Maybe months. I've lost track. But it is equally obvious this is not going to happen. I turn away, but let my foot drift over to touch Brian, the smallest of conciliatory gestures. He doesn't move away or toward me; just lets my foot rest against his. Toes to toes, the best we can do. Brian turns to face me. "Alone is one way to get through adversity, but is it the best way?" This formulation is a joke, something we say, *That's one way to . . .* whatever the thing is *. . . but is it the best way?* No response from me. No giggle, no touch. Silence.

"In hard times," Brian says, "people typically do better when they huddle together for warmth."

"Who are you, Shackleton? I know how to cope with adversity, Brian, but thanks for the lesson."

This silences us both. I have no idea why I'm lashing out. Gracie is OK, she's sleeping not six miles away. But I am bizarrely furious. Fury in search of an object.

We've been dangled by our ankles while children dropped around us; children fell. Surely there is someone to blame.

DAY 40

I spend Valentine's Day reading to Gracie under a string of diffuse heart lights, a gift from Bobbie, who'd noticed Gracie's growing light sensitivity. Yet another side effect. We hang the hearts above her bed, and they soften and rosy the room into twilight.

Dr. K comes in the next morning, "Her numbers look great," she says. "She's ready."

"For what?" I ask. I'm afraid she means some new treatment.

Dr. K looks amused. "To go home," she says. "She's ready to go home."

I start to cry. Dr. K, who knows the rhetic count and the hemoglobin and the liver function numbers of every kid under her care, does not know how to respond.

"This is good news," she says.

"I know," I say, and cry a little more. For once, I don't apologize for crying.

Gracie says, "Mama, why are you sad?"

"I'm so happy I'm crying," I say.

"Mama," she says, and leaves it at that. There is nothing, apparently, one can say to someone as daft as I am.

I walk out to the parents' lounge to call Brian. "We're being discharged."

"That is beautiful news," he says, and I can hear the catch in his voice too. This news means more to us two than to anyone else on earth.

Gracie spends the day before discharge watching, for the umpteenth time, the *Wizard of Oz*. Dorothy goes on an arduous journey populated with allies and terrifying enemies. Dorothy collapses in a poppy field and gives up. Dorothy makes it home, where she's told it's all been a dream. Gracie calls the cowardly lion "the courage lion." He's her favorite. At the end she turns to us with excitement and says, "The courage lion's not afraid of *anything*!"

Well . . .

She arches her eyebrows and turns her hands palm up. "Are they living? Actually?"

"If they are real," I say, "what do you think the courage lion is doing right this second?"

She gives me a withering look. "Brushing him teeth."

Can a kid who can't get her possessive pronouns straight be employing irony?

"He could be brushing him teeth," I say. "He could be brushing them *scientifically*." A phrase Brian uses to get Gabe to brush.

"I don't know because I can't see him," Gracie says. I love her pragmatic, dogged streak. Just tell me, damn it—is he or isn't he real?

DAY 44 (DISCHARGE DAY)

Gracie wakes up nervous, her first sentence, "Is Bobbie gonna be at my good-bye?" Leaving Bobbie is terrifying. Bobbie keeps her safe. Bobbie knows how to handle things. Bobbie has bubbles and juice and secret ways to make the pain stop. We strip the room in anticipation. All the cards and toys and accumulated clutter are gone. We leave the string of heart lights in place until the last. "Can I bring the hearts home?" Gracie asks. "Will they work there?"

Bobbie arrives with her air of mischief, her cat-eye glasses, her calm, her humor. How are we going to keep recovering without her?

"OK, Gracie girl, get ready to say good-bye to Tough Guy," Bobbie says.

Gracie shoots us a smile. "Bobbie came."

"Of course I came," Bobbie says. "I have to make sure you don't steal my machines!"

Gracie giggles, her lilting, air-burst giggle.

"Gracie, this is gonna be the last time I unhook you from Tough Guy. After this, you'll be off leash forever. Are you ready?"

Gracie gives a solemn nod.

Bobbie unscrews the plastic IV tubes that lead from Tough Guy to Gracie's chest catheter. She rubs down the catheter ends with alcohol, flushes the lines with saline and heparin, and recaps them. I watch intently; this will be my job at home, and keeping bacteria out of the lines is crucial. Any bacteria that make it into the line have direct access to Gracie's heart.

Gracie looks up at Bobbie. "Good job," she says, and this phrase seems to encompass everything Bobbie has done for her over the last fifty-four days. The gum she made appear out of thin air, the bubbly apple juice and plastic champagne flutes on New Year's Eve, the morphine drip with its magic red button, the heart lights. Bobbie, the mother of four sons, has made Gracie feel like the most important young person in her life.

Bobbie wheels Tough Guy, now an independent operator, to the door. Before she pushes him outside, she pauses and asks, "Gracie, do you have any last words for your friend?"

Gracie looks Tough Guy up and down. "Be good to the next girl," she says.

I expect leaving the unit to be anticlimactic, the way big change sometimes streams by in a slew of undifferentiated details. But I've forgotten about the "confetti parade." When a family leaves the unit, staff and any patients well enough to stand line the halls and cheer and throw confetti.

This strikes me as a form of heroism. Patients and their families celebrating someone leaving, as they stay behind. We bow our heads under the tiny colored disks of paper that fly toward us as we walk, as the other patients clap and cheer. Gracie grins and grins and grins, and waves her regal wave, devouring the moment.

Ramya stands in the doorway of their corner room. She tosses her handful of confetti gently toward Gracie's knees and leans down to say good-bye. "Have fun at home, Gracie. We will meet you there." She stands up, and we hug.

Behind her, as we embrace, I see baby Varun asleep on his bed. He is hooked up to all the standard stuff, wires and cords and IVs. And at the center of the equipment, the boy. Dark headed, huge-eyed Varun, dreaming his one-year-old's dream. I imagine he's dreaming of his mother's neck and hair, the nest in which he spends each day, Ramya's hand cupping the back of his head.

I don't want to say good-bye to Ramya, and at the same time, I can't wait to get the hell out of there.

In the scrub room I examine Gracie, free of Tough Guy, free to move around unfettered in her pink sneakers and street clothes. I look at her closely. She is almost normal. Not too swollen, not too hairy, not yet. That would come later, with the steroids. Now, she looks pleasingly like herself, except bald. But bald in a nice way; her exposed skin is a delicate, translucent pink over a skull that is perfectly round. A few pastel pieces of confetti cling to the crown of her head, the ridge of her ears. She is a human cupcake of a girl.

The moment we step outside the ward she is disoriented, a recent parolee, dazed by the sunlight. She usually had a great sense of direction, but she's been on the inside almost two months. She has no memory of which way the elevator lies. And she won't let us guide her.

As much as Brian and I are dying to get out of here—quick before someone changes their mind!—we try to be patient as she leads us from one random hallway to another. When we make it down to the lobby at last, she asks where the Christmas tree went and why there is no snow outside. She's an incredulous Rip Van Winkle. At the fish tank she searches for a misshapen goldfish she'd once claimed as her own. When he, or a passable substitute, appears she shouts, "Look! My orange fish remembers me!"

She moves to the lobby fountain, a massive structure of cascading tiers. She points to a piece of bark in a nearby planter. "Can I touch it?" Can you wipe bark with an antibacterial wipe? "If you put a glove on, lovey," I say. She puts the glove on without complaint and picks up the piece of bark, studying the fountain. She throws the bark into the top tier and watches it swirl down to her level, then she throws it to the top again and waits for it to return to her, over and over.

Finally we get her outside; she looks up and around. "I'm out," she says, and shivers. I try to get her to put on her sweater, but she doesn't want anything weighing her down. As Brian gets the car, I squeeze her hand in a quick rhythmic pattern. She squeezes back, but barely. She's distracted by all the cars, the sounds of traffic, of birds, the dozens of conversations taking place around us. Her world was so small for so long. And now it is tantalizingly big again. A bus pulls up across the street. She pulls me, leaning her full weight against the anchor of my hand, "Come on, Mom," she says, "let's take the bus."

It scares me how possible this seems—heading off for a new life together, just us two. Though there were many people around us, Gracie and I had done this—get well—together. Brian was there; of course he was there. But in some fundamental way, pulling her through illness had felt like a two-person dance, or I'd made it one.

The mom/daughter blueprint of my childhood was reexerting itself, flexing its muscle. Meanwhile Brian was coming around with the car.

Gabriel was at the apartment waiting for us, excited and nervous to see his sister again.

Time to shake off the old architecture. Time to reconstitute ourselves into a four-person tribe. Crooked as we might be.

Time, too, to stop counting. There will be more days until we can go truly home, to New York. There will be days and days. The chance that we'll be released home on Day 100, as the doctors implied if not promised, is microscopic. That's just a carrot the doctors dangle to keep you moving. And that's fine by us; we're in no rush. This day is gift enough.

43

Gabriel looked Gracie up and down, "Yacie?" During her stay in the hospital, he'd watched her transform physically. But this was home; here she should look like herself, but didn't. "Will Yacie sleep in my room?" He sounded half pleased, half spooked at the prospect. "Gabe," Gracie said, "you're sleeping in *my* room." Brian leaned into me. "It's like when the mafia boss gets out of prison and takes over his turf again, and the second in command doesn't want to give it back."

But the hierarchy of birth order was quickly restored: on the way to their room Gabe stepped into all the places she stepped, touched every object she touched.

While they played, Brian and I set up a mini–staging area for the multiple medications we needed to infuse via her pump, at precise times throughout the day. The protocol was so complex we'd bought a white board to track dosage, time, and temperature. We placed each medicine on a separate tray with its attendant tubing and directions. Some of the meds had to be refrigerated, then brought to room temperature so they wouldn't chill her heart during infusion. One of the medications could only be disposed of, legally, in a Hazmat container.

I was the designated med-giver. Every morning and night as I hooked her up, I would pray in earnest, *Please God, let me not fuck it up.*

That first night, they took a bath together, Gracie's tubes taped to her shoulder so they wouldn't get wet. Post-bath, in their pajamas, they smelled like French-milled soap and sourdough bread, almost too good to bear. Side by side, they brushed their teeth, which Gabriel hated. Brian coaxed him by saying, "Let's just brush a select few of your teeth, scientifically."

"Scien-tif-ically?" Gabe said.

"So very scientifically," Brian said. Gabe brushed.

I cleaned Gracie's lines with alcohol, attached the pump, and started her infusion. Gabe, flaunting his scientifically fresh teeth, climbed in beside her in the double bed they would share. We told them a story as they drifted off, reveling in the way we could lift a plump hand and lay it on a plump cheek without waking them. Reveling in the way their leaven bodies rose and fell in tandem. Two kids breathing side by side; ordinary and miraculous.

A few hours later, Gracie appeared in our room, clutching her pump under one arm. We'd disconnected it as she slept but she hadn't noticed. She carried it carefully; her little sidekick. Seeing her attend to the pump, even when it was not connected to her, moved me. It was a friend she wouldn't leave behind. I reached for it; she passed it to me carefully with two hands. "We unhooked you already," I said. She gave a wriggle of freedom. "I'm a girl with no pump!"

* * *

Gracie was safe here, five miles from Duke, but we were afraid to travel farther than that. Her marrow still wasn't yet making sufficient white cells to fight off an infection or a virus. Until her immune system rematerialized, we were tethered to Durham. And, most crucially, we weren't allowed anywhere people congregated, anyplace germs could ride the current of a central ventilation system into her vulnerable lungs.

But, if we lived within our limits, we could impersonate a normal family: stroll around the apartment complex, visit the local outdoor mall to throw coins in the fountain, sit beside the nearby lake at dusk, when all the germy kids were inside eating dinner.

If our grazing lands were limited, at least we were together. Sometimes

Gabe was so overcome with feeling for Gracie that he'd throw his arms around her from behind and squeeze, "My sissy." When Gracie's infusion finished and the pump clicked off, she'd often slip out of her bed and into ours where she'd burrow between Brian and me, touching my face with the back of one hand, touching Brian's chest with a toe. Body as bridge; this had always been her way. When I'd nursed her as an infant, if Brian sat down near us, she would stretch her legs and feet to make contact with him.

Gabe would usually follow her into our room and clamber on top of us three, spread-eagle. This was classic Gabe: pin your loved ones in place. Protest was useless, Gabe's capacity for bliss was irresistible. We'd sleep like this, in Gabe's lumpy puppy pile, for hours.

One night, when the kids failed to crash our room, Brian got up to check on them near dawn. He woke me with a whisper and waved me into their doorway, "Come see this." She was curved around a pillow; he was tangled in a sheet. She was in feety pajamas; he was in his diaper and his bee boots. And, they were holding hands. An outlandish, family movie gesture; her fingers curled around his thumb. They didn't hear us, didn't stir. They were busy doing the covert work children do at night: the multiplication of cells, the silent, unstoppable growth, the hatching of private plans.

44

At the end of our first week "home," Gracie sat at the dining room table playing with shells Suzi and David had sent her from a beach in Thailand. It was an improvised, high-stakes opera.

A pink shell sang, with gravitas, "We give you our babies."

A dark shell gasped, incredulous, "You give us your babies?!"

The pink replied, "Yes sir, yes sir."

A third shell—a dull, humble clam—cried out, "Oh no, my babies. Please not my babies!"

I was in deep ideological alignment with the clam, *anyone but my babies.*

Time for some air; I suggested we picnic for lunch. Brian said, "Why don't we eat indoors and then go for a walk after." I shot him a murderous look.

"What?" he said. "I'm a spoilsport? Outdoors-averse New Yorker?"

"We three will go," I said. "You can stay here." We would picnic or know the reason why. Gabe went to the front door and opened it. "Let's take a walk," he said. Then, "Let's take a walk in the world."

I packed peanut butter and jelly sandwiches, probably forgot to bring water or bug spray, and led both kids outside. We found a spot near the man-made pond to sit and eat. At the water's edge a disgruntled group of geese waddled in circles, disoriented clowns in search of a homeland.

Gracie studied them. "Would a goose eat a Dorito that fell on the ground?"

"I'm not sure, love."

They did seem interested in Gabe's sandwich.

One or two of the geese flapped into our path. I waved my arms and made some grunting noises. A few of their friends hopped over. Was I inadvertently attracting them? I flapped again and made higher-pitched sounds. Another five or six joined the group. Suddenly we were at the epicenter of an angry, honking goose mob focused on Gabe's peanut buttery fingers. Dozens of goose heads bobbed aggressively; dozens of goose necks craned our way. The crowd honked and hissed and advanced.

I began kicking the air in their general goose direction. They didn't budge.

Geese, in Europe, guard sensitive military installations. Still, these were not trained ninja geese. These geese were Canadian for God's sake; how dangerous could they be? But they were alarmingly organized. They closed in, forming an unbroken circle around the three of us. *Finally, a threat I can see, touch, kick, strangle.*

I would grab their palm-sized heads and swing them through the air, hurl them hundreds of miles. I'd take them out, goose by goose.

The kids didn't quite see this as the opportunity I did.

Gracie pulled on my hand. "Let's GO!" She kept pulling. "Mommy!"

I ripped the crust off Gabe's sandwich and threw it outside the goose flank. Their many gray heads turned in unison. We broke for home.

I was hoping the kids wouldn't mention the geese to Brian; I didn't want to affirm his picnic paranoia. But Gabe was nothing if not a sharer of news, and this was an enthralling headline.

"Daddy!" he said. "The gooses eat me." His outrage, his indignation, made his face shine with excitement.

Gracie added, "Mommy tried to kick the geese. She wanted to fight them. But she missed." She seemed amused by this: Mommy tried, Mommy missed. The story of Mommy.

"Mommy tried to kick the geese?" Brian said. The kids nodded.

Brian looked at me, half appalled, half admiring, "That's the thing about Mommy; she never backs away from a good fight."

That night in bed I said, "Sorry about the goose debacle." I braced myself for an "I told you so," an investigation of my motives. I expected Brian to ask why I complicated things; took the kids past their comfort zone to satisfy my own needs. Plus, geese were water fowl rife with germs, something that had not occurred to me until that moment.

Instead he took my hand under the covers. "No apology necessary. Picnicking always involves a certain level of risk. And those geese never stood a chance; you're a fierce defender."

I was grateful for the generosity of this description. It might not be accurate, but it was sincere. I nuzzled into him, an unusual gesture for Durham, outside our everyday lexicon. He looked at me, "You're not against me?"

"When was I against you?"

"Ever since we got here."

"I haven't been against you, per se. I've just been holding the rope."

"Oh the rope," Brian said. "That explains everything."

And we left it, exhausted as we were, at that.

45

NEARLY EVERY EVENING WE'D WALK TO THE DESERTED PLAY-
ground that was part of the complex. At first Gracie seemed cowed and
disoriented by the swings, the slide, the climbing apparatus. Gabe, in def-
erence, hung back. Waited for her to figure things out. Over time, she grew
more confident and imaginative on the equipment.

One day she pulled herself the entire length of the tunnel slide. Only
a week before her feet couldn't find purchase on the slick metal; she'd
been a cartoon character running in place, going nowhere at a frantic
pace. And now, having achieved the top, she stood chest out, flush with
pride. "Look, Mama, I'm up!"

Gabriel, forever the caboose, pulled and slid and scuffled to the top.
Together they surveyed the scene: the wood chips, the empty swings,
a darkening sky. They sat side by side on the plastic platform singing
Barney songs until the slimmest sliver of moon appeared, a translucent
slice. "Gracie," Gabe said, "it's an onion moon."

I had a rush of gratitude. Of all the many possible people who might
have sprung into existence, we got these two, friendly with the moon.

Except, riding beside my joy was the thought that this moment
might not have taken place. She might not have struggled up the slide;
he might not have followed. She might not have seen this particular

moon, nor any other. The future, the long line of days and nights stretching out before us, might have turned and dipped and disappeared.

* * *

When we'd been back in the apartment about a month, Gracie paused on her way to bed one night and said, casually, a thought tossed over the shoulder, "I have to go back where I belong."

"Where do you belong?" I peered across the dark room, trying to read her expression. She didn't answer. I asked again, "Where do you belong?"

"In the dreamy land you can't get to when you are awake," she said.

"What's the dreamy land like?" Brian asked.

"It has a forest. I ran through the forest with my sister. We lost our shoes. We had to run in our bare feet. And then I lost my sister. I have to get back with her, where I belong."

Brian gave me a look. *Don't overthink this. She's free-associating.*

Gracie looked up at me, relaxed, but sensing my anxiety. "Don't worry Mama, I will still love you even when I leave you."

You have got it so wrong, kid. I will leave you. When I'm a brittle husk, a bent wire.

I gathered her up and squeezed. She squirmed down and pulled me by the hand toward her room. I tucked her into bed. She was not in the woods, shoeless, running toward a sister. She was not lost.

I opened the closet. Inside, their shoes lay in a jumbled pile, Gracie's thin-soled leather sandals with the orange heel straps, Gabe's bee boots. I wanted to hold the sandals up to her face. *These are yours. You are ours.*

When she was asleep Brian and I sat on the couch sharing a glass of wine; he thought she was retelling *The Wizard of Oz.* "Think about it," he said, "returning home requires the right shoes."

"Or," I said, "she could be trying to mentally organize all the scary things she's endured that she doesn't understand, creating a sister who died to exorcise the deaths hovering overhead."

"Maybe," Brian said.

The dreamy land you can't get to when you're awake.

"Or maybe she's prescient," I said. "Maybe she senses something coming."

He looked at me. *Calm down.* I knew he felt our job was to start seeing her as a regular kid again, to try not to confound our fears with hers. Probably he was right, but when I looked at her, I saw a kid trailing a wake of needles, tubes, midnight drives to the hospital. I saw a child who had lived beside other children, not fifteen feet away, as they died. She never saw their faces but their pain, their parents' grief, saturated the air she breathed.

We moved to the bed, without talking. When Brian fell asleep, I turned on my side to watch him; his wide forehead erased of all the grooves of the day was once a sight I'd wait for. Now, I wanted him awake and worrying with me.

Brian always had an uncanny way of knowing when I was thinking about him, or us, with any special intensity.

He woke up and looked at me. "Are we OK?"

"I'm not sure," I said.

"Well, take a guess," Brian said. It was a peace offering, a chance to laugh. But I didn't laugh.

"Brian," I said. "I don't have the energy for this."

I wanted to explain, but what I had to say would sound too strange: *I want your ear pressed against the glass wall of Gracie's unconscious. Listening for signs. I want you vigilant.*

If I listed my multiplying fears, pointed to the spore of alienation that grew from them, between us, he'd likely say something reassuring, something to set the record straight.

I didn't want the record set straight. I wanted his internal landscape to look like mine—a grassy field where a little stick man ran in frantic circles, hands up, eyes wide orbs of panic, clutching his corncob pipe. I didn't know what Brian's inner landscape looked like—I hadn't asked in a long time—but I felt sure that if he had a little corncob pipe man, his man was calm, leaning against a fence.

"Yes you do," Brian said. "You have the energy of ten thousand suns for the things that matter to you. Talk."

"Your corncob man is too calm."

"I see, my corncob man. And is he also holding the rope?"

"I want you to be as worried as I am, about everything. That is what I want."

"I take your worries seriously, I share them. But I don't think we have to be in the same psychic state to be connected. And I don't feel like you give much thought to what I want. Or even to what I can give you. It's like you've turned me into some genial uncle who you smile at politely and push out the door before pie."

I laughed, finally. But Brian grew serious and sad.

"It feels, lately, like you're pretending to be in this relationship when you're not. Like our being together is more a matter of geography than desire. If you could go back to the West Coast and I could still see the kids, we might do that."

I was stunned. Beyond stunned; slapped awake in cold, open ocean. To say such a thing, he must be very lonely. Which I could understand. I was lonely too. But it was more than that.

If I understood him, Brian was saying anything could happen, even the unthinkable. And that included the dissolution of us.

A person you cherished could pass right through you, atom by atom. Vanish into the mystery. We'd seen that happen. Children loved to the farthest star and back again had disappeared from the discernible world.

"Brian," I said. "I love you. I want to be with you."

It was true; I could feel its truth as I said it. But I also felt rigid and breakable, encased in a veneer of ice.

Our very first Valentine's together, I'd written Fiona Apple lyrics into a card: *And all my armour falling down, in a pile at my feet. And my winter giving way to warm, as I'm singing him to sleep.*

That felt like a hundred thousand years ago.

He was right; I'd given virtually nothing to our relationship since we'd arrived in Durham. I'd assumed Brian had shared my sense that there would be time for each other later. *After.*

"I just thought we'd see each other on the other side. And this isn't the other side yet."

"Let me know when we get there."

46

A FEW DAYS LATER THE KIDS WERE OUTSIDE, PLAYING ON THE porch, when Gracie screamed, "Get back! Get away!" I thought she was hassling Gabe over a toy and ignored them. Brian went out to see what was actually going on and found Gracie bent double, clutching Gabe's diaper to keep him away from a bag of birdseed. Gabe, in defiance, was struggling to plunge his hands into the bag. Floating above them both was a fat black spider with a red hourglass on its belly. Black widow. Brian scooped them up and carried them inside. "That's not the spider for us, kiddies."

They clung to his neck. "Don't put us down!" He didn't.

"Gracie, you did good," Brian said. "You kept your brother safe."

"I know that," Gracie said. "I saved his Gabey lives."

"And Gabe saved yours with his cells," I said, trying make their efforts at lifesaving sound even.

Brian gave me a look, *might be better if we didn't keep score.*

Later, in bed, he said, "We have to get back to civilization. It's the savage wild out there. The geese, the rude insects keeping us awake, and now lethal fucking spiders."

Outside, the tame, manicured lawns of Alexan Farms were hemmed with box hedges; the trees were pruned into sleek, obedient obelisks. I rolled my eyes.

"Eye rolling is a sign of disdain," Brian said. "Very bad on the Gottman scale."

We'd been reading a book, *Why Marriages Succeed or Fail*, by this guy, Gottman.

"I take it back," I said. And rolled my eyes in the opposite direction. I nested into him.

Brian kissed me. I kissed him back, quickly. Any moment, the great veil of exhaustion would drop. Or my mood would shift against my will.

"Thanks for the reversal," Brian said.

He picked up the remote. "Should we?"

We watched *The Wire*. Watching *The Wire* is not the same as making love, but it's something.

47

To celebrate gracie's fourth birthday, we planned a visit from Kathy and Steve and Eden and Chloe, our Brooklyn tribe. In advance of their visit, Gracie and Eden talked on the phone.

"Eden, do you think I am still three years old?" Gracie said. "I am not. I am four!"

A few days before they arrived, Gracie woke up bearing a striking resemblance to Ernest Borgnine. This was the rampant, random hair growth of cyclosporine, one of the drugs that prevented her body from rejecting Gabe's marrow. The hair was very dark and downy and grew in a sort of Uncle Fester pattern, a thick fringe along the hairline and forehead and then down across the eyebrows and cheeks. Brian said she looked like Lon Chaney Jr. as the Wolfman.

When she saw the hair on her face, she said, "Mommy, there is something horrible that we have never noticed. This!" She pointed to the darkening mustache above her lip. She'd been standing on a table to see into the mirror; she jumped down shouting, "Now presenting the most Gracie-est of jumpers." Problem dismissed. But at bedtime she said, as if working out the solution to an intractable problem, "I know! I'll go deep, deep inside the forest, where they can't find me."

What would Eden make of her friend, as wolfman?

When they arrived late on Thursday night, exhausted from the drive, Eden dashed into Gracie's room and shouted, "Hi Bracie!" The adults stood silent, eavesdropping: long pause, in which (we assumed) Eden was taking account of the many changes in her friend's appearance. Finally, "Are you a girl or a boy?"

"I'm a girl," Gracie said, unruffled. Stating the facts. And they both seemed satisfied that everyone was who they said they were.

On the last day of their visit, we took the kids to the Museum of Life and Science, to its legendary butterfly tent. When we got there I realized how stupid I'd been. Of course it was not made of netting. It was an enclosed plastic dome, which Gracie couldn't enter. She couldn't be sealed into a crowd, period. Not in a store, a movie theater, a mall. Not even in a butterfly tent. Gracie saw this as ludicrous. What harm could butterflies do her?

She begged to go in. When I told her there were too many people and thus too many germs, she said, "I won't breathe the whole time, Mom, I promise."

Eden, in solidarity, waited outside with her. It had rained hard earlier, and they ran in circles through the puddles, playing nothing. Just running, two girls glad to be getting their heads damp and their feet wet. "Remember," Kathy said, "when they got drenched at Coney Island and thought it was the best thing that ever happened to them?"

That is what a friend is, I guess: someone who sees the potential in you, even when you can't go in the fun place; someone who, given a second, accepts you as either a girl or a boy. These two people couldn't yet recite their address or fry an egg, but they enjoyed a complex relationship. They could accommodate foundational changes, hurt each other's feelings, forgive, reminisce, crack each other up. Run for it.

Later, we bade good-bye to Kathy and Steve and Eden and Chloe on our driveway.

The kids played in the yard, procrastinating. Kathy and I leaned against their van, procrastinating. All of us trying to squeeze more out of the last few minutes. The grown-ups had spent three days talking, but we'd also been bathing and feeding four kids; we'd barely said anything.

"Are you guys happy?" I asked, pointing my chin toward Steve.

"Mostly. Mainly on the weekends and after ten p.m. You?"

"Is there a category between *sort of* and *mostly*?"

She slung an arm around my shoulder, I slung one back. More to say, no time to say it.

"Are you writing?"

"I'm writing," Kathy said. "If you count writing in my head, in the five minutes before I fall asleep."

We laughed but we were sad. It was astonishing how little time there was to make sense of the world.

Their gang climbed into the van and drove away. Our gang stood on the driveway waving. Gracie said, "I hope Eden knows me when I get back to Brooklyn." Gabriel watched Gracie's face fall as the van pulled out of sight.

"Gracie," he said, "are you sad when *I* leave you?"

"I don't know, Gabe," she said. "Will you be sad when I leave *you*?"

Let's not find out. Let's all stay where we are.

48

Day 100 arrived; we did not go home.

We'd known we wouldn't. Day 100 was always a pretty mirage to trudge past. Instead, we made bubbles. The humid, still-cool evening was perfect bubble-making weather. Spring drew an ad hoc community of transplant families onto the common lawns at twilight. We stood in clusters, reciting our kids' strange side effects as incantations to stave off worse: hair loss, hirsutism, muscle weakness, deformed toenails, fungal infections, gooey eyes, bacterial invasion of the central line, loss of appetite, ravenous appetite, hearing loss, neuropathy of the feet, fingers, and knees, light sensitivity. We could go on.

We began to do this every night: talk about how long it might be until we could return home; discuss families we knew in common; list our rational and irrational fears. If a child was readmitted to the ward, or transferred to the PICU, we talked about it. With agony for the other family. With guilty relief that it was not us.

We talked and made bubbles.

The pursuit of the perfect bubble became an obsession. The bigger, the better. We bought special soaps, glycerin, a designated bucket, and complicated bubble wand gizmos, which could also, incidentally, be used as a lasso, a jump rope, or a stick with which to poke your sibling. The kids held their breath each time we dipped the bubble wand into the bucket of suds, lifted it out, and slid the loop open. Mostly what we made were filmy circles of iridescent wavering would-be bubbles, which never quite graduated into spheres. They would quaver and ripple, inflate for an instant. Then pop.

One night when I opened the loop, a huge shimmering lima bean sprang into the air. It floated briefly upward then descended to hang inches above a dormant rose bush. The kids nearest gave an audible gasp. The bubble was beautiful and unexpected; tremulous but whole. "She made it," Gracie said, to no one in particular. We held our collective breath; the bubble's surface swam with swirled color. In a moment it might pop, it *would* pop, but for this instant, it was our glory.

* * *

One night, walking home from bubbles, we ran into baby Varun, recently discharged from the ward. His eyes were full of curiosity and energy, but his body was calm. He had the deeply relaxed affect of a baby whose every need has been fully met, continuously, since the moment of birth. No need to fuss, to fidget. During his first year, Ramya had probably not been away from him for two waking hours, total. And Deepak radiated happiness, like the man from my poster emitting pastels, when he spoke of his son.

Ramya, Deepak, and I stood and chatted while Varun pounded his chubby fists on the plastic tray of his stroller, pleased and proud of his sounds. We exchanged drug levels and lab results and info about other transplant families. I told them about the bubble spot. "Go there tomorrow," I said. "It's nice. We just hang out."

"We will come then," Ramya said.

The kids were restless. "Let's gooooooooo," Gracie said. "The bugs sound scary."

The woods that surrounded the complex on three sides teemed with uproarious insect life, a chorus of chirps and buzzing that scared and thrilled the kids. There was the sense that, just past the edge of the asphalt, was a wild, unruly place where anything might happen. The kids wanted to go into the woods. And also, they didn't. We walked on toward home.

When the kids were in bed, Brian and I sat out on the porch. He turned to me. "Your point about her working out her fears through her play," he said, "is taken. Her poor dolls are the most beleaguered, plague-riddled people I know."

"Thank you," I said. "I take your points, too."

"Which points?"

"Just, you know, the genial-uncle-denied-pie thing."

He laughed. "Go on," he said. "Say more about this underappreciated uncle."

You could never vaguely apologize to Brian. You had to be specific, be real, bring your A game. Which was infuriating. And wonderful.

* * *

A week or so later, on another evening walk around the complex, we ran into Ramya and Varun again. Varun was dozing, his enormous dark eyes closed. "He has a low fever," Ramya said. "I am going to take him in as soon as Deepak arrives home."

Later Ramya called. "They have admitted us again." And the next day there was a message, "We're in the PICU."

I dreaded going to visit the PICU. Its waiting room was the most unloved zone in the hospital and the most hard used. Parents were not allowed to sleep at their children's bedside in the PICU, so they would stumble out for an hour or two of rest in the waiting room. There were stains on the backs of the recliners from fretting heads tossing left, tossing right. Chairs were pushed together to form sleepless beds. There was always at least one chair askew, angled toward the door, as though someone had leapt out of it, into a sprint.

The first day I went to visit, Ramya came out to meet me in the waiting room. We chatted, she told me how Varun was doing. It was very up and down. His lungs were in trouble, the ventilator settings were high. They were praying they'd be able to reduce the settings soon. I asked if I could see him. Ramya said, "Please, let's wait until next time."

I could understand, or thought I could. If my child were on a ventilator, I would want to protect their image in other people's minds. I wouldn't want anyone to see them unrecognizable. And so I held on to the image of Varun from our last visit, chubby fists pounding his stroller tray, brown eyes sweeping Ramya's face; glancing at Gracie, glancing at Gabe, but returning, always, to Ramya, his lodestar.

The next time I visited, Ramya invited me into the room. Varun's body was obscured by the machines, the tubes. He was a small form beneath the sheet, softly vibrating with the pulse of the vent. His eyes were closed, but the lids moved every so often.

Deepak was also there. I watched them move around the room, brush against each other, lean over Varun to kiss him or smooth his cheek with their fingers. Deepak laid his palm on Ramya's back, a casual touch, but conscious. A transmission of support, of tenderness. I was amazed he had the inner resources to give anything to his wife while giving everything to his son. Mother and father in hell, but in hell together. When Deepak put his hand on Ramya's back, she looked up at him with a recognition of their pain, not feral blame, but understanding. If the gravitational pull of their love was this strong, it would hold Varun in place. It can be done like this, I told myself.

When, days later, Varun came off the vent, it felt miraculous. We'd yet to witness a child who'd come off the vent. He was sent down from the PICU back to the transplant ward. He was healing. He was free of the horrible, oscillating machine. He smiled and spoke gibberish to his parents. He was still in the hospital, not out of danger, but better.

49

WE WERE ALWAYS AT CLINIC, CHECKING ONE DRUG LEVEL OR another, having Gracie examined, stern to stem. One afternoon, Sue, the nurse practitioner, leaned down to listen to Gracie's lungs. We'd come to clinic worried; Gracie had a cough. Sue wrinkled her brow, dipped the sides of her mouth, and held up one finger to quiet Gabe, who was pretending my scarf was a parachute, complete with sound effects.

"Stop that," I said, pulling the scarf too forcefully out of his hands. And to Sue, "What do you hear?"

"Just a few crackles. On the left side."

Sue ran an RSB test; it came back positive for a common respiratory virus. OK, I thought, this is how it begins, with a few crackles on the left side. A common cold, with uncommon powers. Gracie's body, unassisted, could not fight off a cold. The one thing all our frantic cleaning and germ avoidance had been designed to protect her from, and she had it.

Every post-transplant parent worries about the lungs. Anything but the lungs. I called Brian. "She has crackles in one lung."

"Which one?" he said.

"The left."

"What are they doing?"

"An immunity-booster infusion, and Sue said they'd watch it closely."

"OK, will they keep you or send you home?"

"They're not sure yet."

Brian met us at the clinic to take Gabe home. Leaving, Brian gave Gracie a kiss on her head, "Make sure to ask Mom to buy you some treats from the machines." He and Gabe left for the night. I wanted to go with them—home to dinner, bath, bed, plus red wine, dark chocolate, and mindless television—but Gracie's med still had another couple of hours to go.

Gracie was relaxed and placid, watching TV. Every so often she'd emit a sharp bark of a cough. I kept thinking of the family we met on one of our first visits to the clinic, before the transplant. The little girl from Ireland who'd coughed up blood onto her mother's shirt, whose baby brother I'd held while the doctors and nurses huddled around her. I must have given Gracie a dark look in response to a cough, because she said, "Mama, are you mad?"

"I'm not mad, sweet girl."

Close to midnight, her infusion finally finished. As we passed through the lobby, Gracie asked to ride in a wheelchair she spotted languishing in a corner. I didn't like the idea of her playing sick. But she'd had a crummy day, and I wanted to make her happy. "Fine."

She hoisted herself onto the seat with a little wheeze. Come on left lung, keep it together.

It was late, she'd had no real dinner, she'd spent all day hooked up to a machine doling out medicine, but she was in a purely sweet mood. As we pushed through the double doors into the parking lot, I took in a huge breath of damp, warm, living air, soaked in oxygen by the million exhalations of the countless green things of this Durham spring. Surely this had to be better for her than canned hospital air. Hospitals, what a bad idea. Except when you need them. Above us, a single star struck a pinprick of light in the dark dome of sky. I stopped pushing her wheelchair to say a prayer for her, and for Varun.

Gracie noticed that we had stopped and wanted to know why. I said

I was praying for a boy who was sick and had to spend tonight in the hospital.

Gracie said, "Who is sick?"

"A boy," I said, not wanting to tell her, hoping she'd let it go.

"Why is he sick?"

I said there is no real reason, he is just sick, it happens. She wasn't satisfied.

"Say why."

I reinforced how she, Gracie, was well enough to go home, and we didn't always know why.

"That little thing followed us here," she said, pointing up to the star.

As we drove home, she said, "Guess what?! It's magic. That little thing is still following us." And then later, "Mom, guess what? It was behind a cloud, and then it came out. Isn't that magic?" I didn't know what was magic and what wasn't. I didn't know why we got to drive home, chatting about stars, while Varun didn't. I didn't know what to count on, whether Gracie's cough might progress or disappear by morning.

I tried to live with these cohabiting facts: Varun was off the vent but not yet back at home; Gracie had the beginnings of a cough that could worsen; the night sky was as indifferent, as beautiful, as ever.

The next morning it was, suddenly, spring. The geese, in their elegant dark gray hoods, their sleek feathers, clustered on our porch cooing into each other's ears like lovesick teenagers. And Gracie was better. She might have gotten worse, that could have happened, but instead she was better. Thank God, thank each and every god.

* * *

Varun had been healing, and then all at once he worsened. He was transferred back upstairs to the PICU, placed back on the vent. And then he grew sicker still. I was driving to the hospital to visit him with Gracie in the car when Bobbie called; our plan had been for Bobbie to watch Gracie while I went upstairs to see Ramya. When I saw it was Bobbie calling, I pulled over and parked along the edge of Duke's forest. Cars sped past.

Bruce Springsteen was playing on the radio. In her car seat Gracie was doing hip-hop arm jerks and shoulder drops.

"Don't come," Bobbie said, "go on home."

I understood her without wanting to. I knew she was telling me that Varun was gone.

Which was impossible. But also maybe true.

"Is Deepak with Ramya?"

"Yes, they are here together."

I could feel a sob rising. Bobbie had likely heard more grief than anyone I knew; and was the most willing to listen.

But not Gracie.

"Thank you for telling me, Bobbie," I said. I hung up.

"What's wrong?" Gracie said. "What did they say?"

I knew it would be wrong to turn around. I knew she would see grief or terror on my face. At the same time, I didn't want to know this alone. I didn't want to know it.

"What's wrong?" she said again.

I unbuckled my seat belt. "Please stay in the car, love. I will be right back, I promise. You will be able to see me." I got out of the car, walked a short ways away, turned around to wave at her. She waved back, unsure of what this was. A game? I walked a few more feet away. Wave, wave. I stepped into the woods.

I was surrounded by the obscene explosion of life that is southern spring—glossy, nascent, waxy leaves, blooming lilac, the yellow-green lace of weeping willows, the white innocence of opened dogwood. Wisteria in warm filtered light. Veil upon veil of silvery green branches, split by an astringent blue sky.

This crescendo of life could not contain death.

I rejected that possibility with every atom; rejected it out of hand.

Sentinel of trees: pitch pine, scarlet oak, sweet birch, Virginia pine, bald cypress. Every one silent. Agnostic.

Say why.

I was far enough from the car that Gracie could not hear me, and far enough that she was worried. I could see her squinting, frowning, in my direction. I kicked the nearest tree. *Fuck you*. My foot felt strangely liberated from my body. I kicked and kicked. The thwack was dull, unsatisfying. My ankle began to throb. I kept kicking.

Overhead, a pair of woodpeckers, unperturbed, drilled in and out of the trunk. Two heads bobbed in unison, each with a bright racing cap of red feathers. *Get out of here*. I waved my arms. They kept on boring their holes. *Go!* They stayed.

When my foot was numb, I limped back to the car.

"What's wrong?" Gracie asked. "Are you sad or mad?"

"I am sad and mad."

"Why?" She looked at me, a level, direct stare. "Tell me."

She was four. There was no way to tell her without pointing to the same possibility for her. She could sense vital information being kept from her.

"Tell me now."

"I will, sweetheart," I said. "Someday I will tell you."

But I wouldn't. I would tell Brian, my mom. I would tell Kathy, Cassie. I would tell Suzi, who, every time we talked long-distance, said, "Tell me everything." I would tell her how, the last time I saw him, Varun's body shook with the oscillator's vibrations, how I felt his pulse throbbing in his right thumb, about the goo they put in his eyes to keep them moist, the bruises. I would tell her how Deepak touched Ramya's back.

I would tell anyone willing to listen how beautiful Varun was, how beaten up by the machines, how loved he was. Is. I would tell everyone, anyone. Except Gracie.

I felt the inverse of what I'd felt the day the first child, Sam, had died on our ward. Then I'd wanted to understand, to know. With Varun, I wanted to unknow.

At home Gracie ran to Brian. "We're not hospital people, we are home people."

He picked her up and snuggled her. "You're home people!"

"Yes, but Mama was sad and mad."

He set Gracie down, and she scampered off to wake up Gabe. He looked at me. I walked into his arms.

"Varun died," I said into his ear.

"My god," he said. "Sweetheart, I am so sorry."

"Me too." We stood there for a while, and then I pulled away and went into our bedroom.

I closed the door and lay down on the bed. Brian followed me in and lay down beside me. He took my hand. I rolled onto my side, away from him. He rolled onto his side, to cradle me. I scooted away, and he did the same, to close the space.

"I can't," I said. I wasn't sure what it was that I couldn't do. Be a parent whose child had survived when other children had died. Be a parent who would never trust that her child was safe. Let myself feel this much pain. Block this much out.

"I can't," I said again.

"My love," Brian said. "I beg to differ. I think you can. You already have."

I turned around. He was crying. I was crying. The kids were in the living room watching midnight TV. He put both hands on either side of my face.

I felt there was nowhere I could go that Brian would not follow.

"The world is upside down," I said. "They are the kindest people I've ever met."

"They are."

"This is not God's will. Who would will that?"

"No one, my love."

"God has leaves and rivers, molecular structures, whatever the fuck, fields of barley. Half Dome and puffy clouds pretty enough to slice you open. But *not* will. I don't believe that."

"You don't."

"Humans have will. We can be any kind of way to one another."

"We can."

I believed in Deepak's hand upon Ramya's back in the PICU. In the sanctity, the sanctuary, of chosen tenderness.

I believed in Brian. Whose love for us was immense, without end or border. My love for him, for the kids, felt the same. All of it was invoked inside our two-person sphere—hand to face, face to thigh, arm to leg, lip to ear, eye to eye—for however long it takes to be reminded of who you are, of who someone is to you. To be recalled to home. *Hey, remember me, I'm yours, you're mine.*

* * *

The day before they left I visited Ramya and Deepak at their apartment. They were packing to return home. Ramya told me about Varun's services, how meaningful the rituals had been to them. Deepak kept repeating, with wonder and gratitude, how the funeral director had waived their fees. That Ramya and Deepak had noticed this gesture was the astonishing thing. Grieving my child, I could only imagine being bent on hurting the world. But that wasn't their way. They were making piles of medical supplies and canned foods to leave for other transplant families. They were casting their eyes around the room, asking me what we could use.

Most of all, they continued to ask after the other children, after Gracie. How was she? Ramya wanted to know. If anything, Ramya's concern for Gracie had sharpened.

"She's fine," I said. Ramya smiled. I smiled. And then we cried.

As I was leaving, Deepak told me that his cousin was coming to accompany them on the ride home. "We were three coming down here," he said. "And we would be only two going home."

If what you've been is a mother or a father and your child is now gone, there is no word for who you are. If you lose a spouse, you're a widow or a widower. But if you lose a child, you go on being a mother or a father. There is no word because we refuse to cede that much authority to the possibility. It is literally the indescribable pain. If we can't call its name, it can't come. Only it can.

50

Near the end of our time in Durham, brian's mom, Tasha, came for a visit. On the last night of her stay, we took her and the kids to a local place with a row of picnic tables set into a pretty little garden. Behind a curtain of wisteria, the children found a patch of dandelions.

"Gabe, these flowers are wishes," Gracie said.

"Let's eat wishes!"

"No, they are for blowing."

Gracie gripped a stem and blew its wispy white crown. "I wish to be a pony, never anything but a pony."

They began to romp around on all fours, pawing at the earth, tossing their heads in the air, touching their lips to the grass, nibbling. Their bowed necks, in the darkening light, formed twin pale bridges.

Tasha looked at them, then at us. "So she's OK?"

"She's OK," Brian said.

"Then what the hell are you still doing here?"

Classic Tasha, straight to the point.

"We're scared to leave," Brian said. It was true; as scared as we'd been to come, we were almost as scared to leave. Duke was our security blanket.

"But she's OK?" Tasha said again.

"Yeah, she's OK."

"So then," Tasha said, "you two did good."

* * *

In truth, the moment we knew Gracie was out of danger was invisible. We passed through it many times, without recognition. Transplant is like that. There are few clean borders. Your child is puffy and bald and in lots of pain, but the doctors send you home from the hospital anyway, with an injunction to *avoid crowds*. Your child regrows her hair, can tolerate a chat with more than two people at once, but a bad cold could still be her undoing.

Parents of perilously sick kids never stop being afraid, not even when their kid swims the English Channel or dances ballet with Baryshnikov or has twenty-three kids of their own. The other shoe is always above our heads, just out of reach, about to drop.

Likewise, returning to an intimate understanding with your partner after a long, fraying time doesn't happen in a single instant. For Brian and me, it happened slowly, painfully, often imperceptibly over many days. Few of them in a row.

I do remember that Brian came home from a trip to New York with an unexpected gift. A necklace. A beautiful pearl-studded choker, unlike anything he'd ever bought me. Silver that looked and felt like lace, from the Metropolitan Museum of Art gift shop. Very precious, apropos of nothing. Apropos of everything.

Brian, who would beg me to tell him what I wanted on birthdays, at Christmas. Brian—who made notes in a little black book on food preferences the kids expressed or I did—took a risk.

He bought me something that said, *I see you this way.*

The necklace came with a note: *You are my alpha and omega.*

I cried as I put the necklace on. Wearing it, I felt elegant, of another time and place. Somewhere Old World and civilized, maybe Prague.

Definitely not Durham. We went out to dinner at an intimate French place downtown, Vin Rouge.

"A man who buys a necklace like this for his mate probably believes they are held together by more than geography," I said.

Brian touched my cheek with two fingertips, ran them lightly down my throat to the pearls. "Probably."

We held on to one another's legs under the table. *I am yours, you are mine.*

Between us was the first time we ever sat in a room together and I couldn't look Brian in the eye, just smiled, hugely, stupidly, into my own lap; between us was the first time he kissed me on Twelfth Street, leaning in, shockingly, thrillingly confident, "I'm going to kiss you now," the kiss of recognition, *Oh, hello*; between us was my walk, alone, in the hills behind the house where I grew up, with Brian's tennis shoe in one hand and, in the other, the pregnancy stick announcing Gracie's presence; between us was the moment he snatched the twenty-dollar bill out of my hand in the Cuban-Chinese restaurant, but also the moment he said on the phone, while I was in labor, "I love you," as though five months of alienation could disappear, a tissue devoured by flame; between us was the first time he saw his daughter, at four months old, in her rosebud sack and cried, quietly, so as not to disturb her; between us was every one of Gracie's screams, at every IV insertion, when he wasn't there, and the one in her jugular vein when he was; between us was Brian's forbearance with my lingering rage when we first reconciled and his joy in discovering I was pregnant with Gabe; Gabe in his bee boots, *be a pony, tiger*; Gabe, on our first day in Durham, standing beside the wide rail fence as cars whizzed past; Gabe's yell of anarchy and self-invention, *oolie ba aa!*; between us was our terror that Gracie would never be fully well, and the willed belief that she already was. Between us was the grief for children we'd known who had died, who could never return, nor ever be forgotten. Between us was the future, who we would become as we grew older, as the kids left home, and also the future of the two small people we loved most, our aspirations for who they might become, the revelation of who they already were.

All of this reverberated inside the gaze we held for a long quiet time.

Brian lifted his wine, we clinked and pressed glass against glass, globe against globe. "To the end," Brian said, "and the beginning."

HOME

CODA

Not long after our transplant experience was over, totally over, or as over as it ever will be, Brian and I stayed at a lodge with a deck that cantilevers over Mt. Tamalpais, in Marin. Where I grew up. Where each of our children was born. Standing on the deck, alone in the dark and the fog that wraps Mt. Tam on summer nights, we kneeled. Him first, then me. We asked each other if we'd like to be married. The answer was, is, always, yes.

A year later, when the kids were five and three, respectively, we married at that same lodge, overlooking the ocean. Gracie was the ring bearer; Gabriel was the flower boy. At the crucial, aisle-walking moment, Gracie cried under pressure. Gabriel needed to be picked up midceremony. It was not nearly as orchestrated or as elegant as I'd envisioned, but it was beautiful.

We left Durham eleven years ago. And in all this time Gracie has been, and is, well. Cured. Which is the gift of our life: we can dream and wake and eat breakfast because our child lived. She lived.

Unlike many, many other children, she lived.

A truth I live with but don't like to think about: I can name a child who died in every one of the sixteen rooms on our transplant unit.

I have no idea, still, how to make sense of this, except to pray, in repertory and for perpetuity, *Thank you, I'm sorry, I'm sorry. Thank you. Thank you.*

Gracie is fourteen. She has long, long auburn hair. Rapunzel hair, shiny and glossy. It hangs past her waist. She has a waist! Though you wouldn't know it; she wears camo cargo pants and baggy plaid shirts. She has a sly sense of humor and an all-consuming crush on Captain Picard. She is a bookworm, who, at school, goes by her given name of Amelia. She is our late sleeper, our deep dreamer, our secret writer. Working, forever, on the best first sentence of a book she hopes to finish. "I want to be a writer," she says, "if I'm good enough."

Gabriel is twelve, he wears his hair in the same shag fringe bangs that the Beatles wore as they stepped off the plane in America in 1964. He adores John Lennon and Frank Gehry. His interest in the world knows no bounds. He is the same at twelve as he was at two; our exuberant boy, spinning his million questions. *If you could edit one song, change a line or a word or a tune, what would it be? If you could relive one minute of your life over and over again, which minute would you pick? If you could be the maker of something that is already made, what would you be the maker of?*

Um, you.

We have accepted our luck. Our daughter and son. We could not earn them, we'll never know if we deserve them, but we hold on with both hands. And still, we understand that nothing given is permanent. Not wealth or well-being, not sweet dreams or morning coffee. Not a daughter or a son, a husband, lover, friend, mother. Anything, everything, is up for grabs, can fly back from whence it came.

In 2012 Hurricane Sandy felled a tree in our yard. As the tree went down, a branch broke off, the wind lifted the branch and rotated it, midair, so that it struck the largest window in our house jagged end first, like a javelin. Glass shards flew through our bedroom; invisible splinters of glass slid into the drapes, the drawers, the deep recesses of the carpet, the soft soil of our potted plants. We cowered, all four of us, under a thick comforter on our bed. We were OK, but we were also reminded that what is whole can be made unwhole in the space of a breath.

A few months ago Gracie—dreamy girl, consummate reader—

looked up from her book at the breakfast table and asked, "Would you really die to save me from dying?"

Gabriel paused his stream-of-consciousness chatter to make sure he was included. "Yeah, would you eat bullets?" Gabe, second-born child and sibling of a transplant survivor, is forever wondering whether his allotment of love measures up. Both of them want to know: Who do you love best? Who will you save first? Will you die for me? A *terrible* death? Underneath that, the bigger questions: Can you protect me? Will you find a way to keep me safe? Am I alone in this?

"Probably I would die for you," I said, "especially if you said *please*." They rolled their eyes. I should take their questions seriously. I should tell them the truth, that I'd do anything, anywhere, to save them. But then I'd have to admit the corollary truth: there are a host of things I can't do. No one can.

Brian and I should be in a state of dazed grace, amazed at our luck, seven days a week, every hour of the day. We aren't. If you sat us down, made us talk, scratched the surface, you would find it—the dumbstruck happiness. But we are also driving the kids to school, arguing over who gets enough time to write. Taking Gracie to acting class on Wednesday nights. Laundry, dinner, if we're lucky, a kiss in the mud room.

We're doing it all inefficiently and haphazardly, and with the full knowledge that it could have been otherwise.

We are doing this life, watching Gracie do hers, with the happiness that remains after you have leaned off the edge of the world into the black space beyond our atmosphere, breathed in the nothing—that thin, empty, sterile air that cannot nourish you—and then pulled back, restored to gravity, oxygen, old-growth trees, and the deep blue sea.

Gracie, for her part, takes her history in stride. Once, when she was eight, she said, "I was sick, but you wouldn't know anything if I didn't tell you. You would think I'm a normal kid. Unless you saw these." She lifted her shirt to show us the two starfish on her chest. Scars from where the "tubies" once entered her body, the sole outward mark of what she went through. She doesn't search for a swimsuit that covers them. She carries these blurry, blush pink stars embossed on her skin casually, as what they are: an affirmation of survival.

As relational as Gabe is, Gracie is quiet. She's private. She often seems to be listening to herself on some subterranean plane.

I hope what she hears are directions for happiness; the happiness blueprint.

But I don't think there is one. We find happiness, if we find it at all, on accident. We trip over it on our way somewhere else. It's woven out of the oddest circumstances. Sometimes we're engulfed by our senses: my God, what wine, what beautiful friends, and that smell of smoke, which sums up sexual giddiness, nostalgic longing, and primal well-being in one whiff. Other times it is a quiet happiness, a counterintuitive happiness.

The complicated joy of watching your children run away from you, through a gauntlet of parents on a Berkshire hilltop, assembled to say good-bye and invited to offer a benediction. The campers run through branching arms. "Laughter," says one parent; "sleep," calls another. "Belief in the bug's life," "birdsong," "river play," "friends," "the unplugged mind," "innocent romance."

"No tick bites," Brian whispers into my ear, "and no growing of any kind."

"Happiness," I shout, but too late.

Gracie and Gabriel, bearing their giant packs, their various scars, their own unshouted wishes, are past us already, cresting the hill. They can see what lies on the other side, and they don't look back.

AUTHOR'S NOTE

The truth is an impossible undertaking. However, I took many notes along the journey described in these pages: first in the form of a series of letters to my unborn child and later as a blog. I've tried not to ascribe language, especially to children, unless I'd recorded it verbatim. In certain cases, I've elected to use pseudonyms and/or change identifying details. But I have not created composites. When I've written about a child, I know precisely who they are, whether or not I felt free to name them. I know the name of every child we cared for in Durham. And of every child who died there. I remember you.

A final thought/wish: Shortly after Gracie's transplant, Brian's sister was diagnosed with leukemia and required a stem cell transplant to survive. Unfortunately, Brian was not a match for Melinda in the way Gabriel was for Gracie, but a kind-hearted young man living near Los Angeles was. This stranger saved Melinda's life; we can do that for one another. I urge anyone holding this book to register to become a bone marrow/stem cell donor. Registering is an easy, painless mouth swab, which might enable you to gift years of life without impairing your own health. Further information: **BeTheMatch.org**.

ACKNOWLEDGMENTS

Writing has the patina of a solitary art but anyone who has arrived at a finished manuscript knows it is the product of many minds, hands, eyes, and sensibilities. In this instance, I also owe thanks to the many people who helped us *live* the events described here, in order to write about them.

My mother, Jessica Flynn, and my brothers, Evan and Dylan Flynn, made a place for me back home when I needed one most.

A host of doctors and nurses helped Gracie survive her first five years of life. Their professionalism, medical ingenuity, and acts of compassion made the unbearable bearable. They include: Dr. Eric Scher and the staff of Marin General Hospital's Neonatal and Pediatric Units; Dr. Marion Koerper at UCSF Medical Center; Dr. Stacia Kenet and Dr. Lindy Woodard at Pediatric Alternatives; Dr. Marc Seigel at NYU; Dr. Blanche Alter at the NIH; Dr. Joel Brochstein at Hackensack Medical Center; Dr. Sam Lux at Boston Children's Hospital; and Dr. Joanne Kurtzberg and the entire team at Duke's Pediatric Blood and Marrow Transplant Program. In particular, many of the nurses who cared for Gracie offered our family incalculable kindness (see Bobbie Caraher). *Thank you* doesn't begin to express how we feel, but we are saying it every minute of every day.

We were carried through transplant, and beyond, by the many friends and family who formed a protective net. They include: Brian's mother, Tasha Morton; Brian's sister, Melinda Morton Illingworth, and her family; my father, Howard Harpham, and his wife, Louise Harpham; my stepmother, Mary Harpham (continuously whispering, *write about it*); my sister, Holly Rotlewicz, and stepsiblings Brian Evans, Debbie Evans, and Jason Evans, sunny boy, too soon gone; our two Greek columns of caring, the Manolis and Karsant families; Suzi Adams and David Kleiman; Mark Levinson and Melissa Brown; David and Leanne Kumin; Kristi Spessard and family; Howie and Kristen Parnes; Steve and Kathy Sears; Anne and Mae Woods, first friends of wellness; Virginia Veach and Leslie Gibson, who, respectively, led us in and led us out; and our beloved communities of Sarah Lawrence College, *Dissent* magazine, the Creative Arts Team, and World College West.

Rita Delfiner and the editorial staff of the *New York Post* made Gracie's plight clear to readers, inspiring many New Yorkers to donate to the medical care of a girl they'd never met. Children's Organ Transplant Association ably administered that fund.

Sometimes a heroic force in life doesn't appear on the page: Denise Rubinfeld put her post-college plans on hold to accompany our family to Durham and care for Gabriel with humor and love. At twenty-two, and without kids of her own, she taught me *a lot* about mothering. Nadia and Ne'dine Batts, twins and kind souls, also cared for Gabriel and Gracie in Durham. As does Amelia Martin, our satellite sister/daughter, who brings laughter and insight to our table.

We are so grateful for two rare, nurturing environments—the Early Childhood Center at Sarah Lawrence College and Blue Rock School of West Nyack—where Gracie and Gabriel learned to be ordinary again, in the best possible way.

The artistry of three teachers and path-lighters—Deborah Merola, Ruth Zaporah, and Deb Margolin—has had a profound effect on how I understand personhood, theater, words, story, and creative invention. Though they didn't read drafts of this manuscript, they helped write it.

Cassie Tunick's poetic imagination and her reliance on the unconscious to conjure our best selves have been inspiring and sustaining me since we were ten. And are, I hope, alive in these pages.

Cathleen Medwick kindly made room at *More* magazine for early versions of this material. Kim Larsen, Penny Wolfson, Kate Reynolds, and Barbara Feinberg formed a writing group whose liberating ethos was: *Write everything, you can take it out later.* In particular, Barbara's beautiful prose, devoted readership, and contagious habit of sitting down to write daily kept me in motion.

Kristy Davis touched this manuscript with a scythe of coherence that cut away the dead wood and gently demanded that I graft in truer feeling. It would not be this book without her.

Lauren Wein oh so generously read early pages and pointed me toward Sarah Burnes, the agent of any writer's dreams, fulfiller of mine. Sarah's irrational exuberance for the manuscript sent me back to work in an effort to make it more like the book in her mind. She's a fierce advocate, fair fighter, and the fairy godmother we all want in our corner.

At Holt, Caroline Zancan's genuine respect for the work that comes before her translates into a kind of physician's oath of editing, *First do no harm*. At the same time, she pushes for clarity, complexity, and originality. The many other magic-makers at Holt include Kerry Cullen, Maggie Richards, Ariel Cooper, Jason Liebman, Jessica Wiener, Gillian Blake, Molly Bloom, Meryl Levavi, Karen Horton, Tracy Locke, Vicki Haire, and, of course, Steve Rubin. Holt's hospitality at every turn has made it feel like home.

For their forbearance and generosity in allowing me to share the most difficult part of their lives, I am grateful beyond words to Jake Pedersen and his family and to Ramya and Deepak Bhaskaran.

And finally, my deepest gratitude goes to my family for their patience with my absence during the many stolen moments it takes to make *anything*, even a cake, definitely a book. Gracie and Gabriel, thank you for letting me try to capture you in words (doomed task if ever there was one). Brian Morton, my mate, infused this book with his faith that writing can bring humanity and humor and heart to a senseless world, in which we seek sense. Without him, there would be no story. With him, every story rings sweeter and more true.